Literary
New York

Literary
New York

A History and Guide

Susan Edmiston
and Linda D. Cirino

Illustrated with photographs
and maps

NEW JERSEY

UPPER

STATEN
ISLAND

LOWER

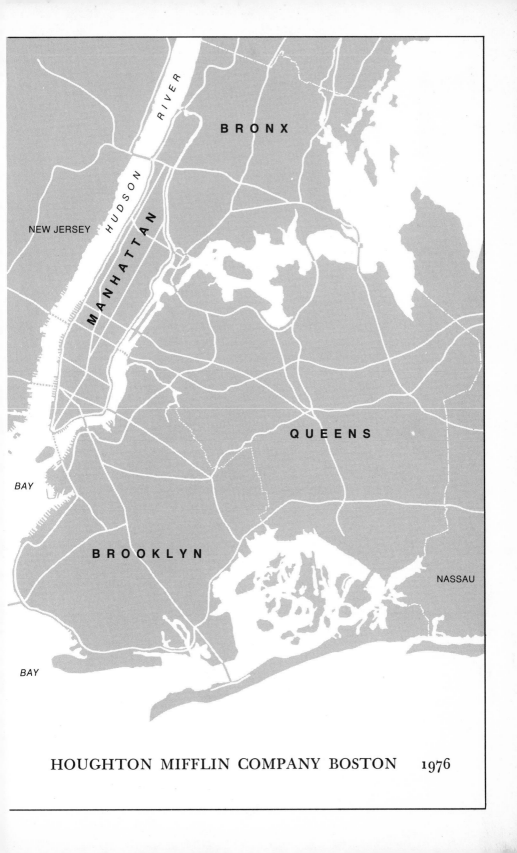

HUDSON RIVER

BRONX

NEW JERSEY

MANHATTAN

BAY

QUEENS

BROOKLYN

NASSAU

BAY

HOUGHTON MIFFLIN COMPANY BOSTON   1976

Maps by John V. Morris

Library of Congress Cataloging in Publication Data

Edmiston, Susan.
Literary New York.

Includes bibliographical references and index.
1. Literary landmarks — New York (City)   2. Authors,
American — Homes and haunts.   3. New York (City) —
Intellectual life.   I. Cirino, Linda D., joint author.
II. Title.
PS144.N4E3   974.7'1   75-44068
ISBN 0-395-24349-1
ISBN 0-395-24353-X pbk.

Printed in the United States of America

M   10   9   8   7   6   5   4   3   2   1

The authors are grateful for permission to reprint from the following:
An Autobiography by Van Wyck Brooks, copyright © 1954, 1957, 1961 by
Van Wyck Brooks; new edition copyright by Gladys Brooks. Published by E. P.
Dutton & Co., Inc. and reprinted with their permission. *The Beat Generation* by

Acknowledgments

THE AUTHORS would like to thank the National Endowment for the Humanities for the grant that enabled them to complete this book. Gratitude is due to Nancy Milford and Russell Lynes for their support of this project and to Lola Szladits for the continuing inspiration of her encouragement, friendship and example.

Many writers gave of themselves and their time in letters or interviews; among them were Louis Auchincloss, the late W. H. Auden, Luigi Barzini, the late Arna Bontemps, Vance Bourjaily, Paul Bowles, Susan Jenkins Brown, Curtis Cate, John Henrik Clarke, Wayne Cooper, Gregory Corso, Malcolm Cowley, James T. Farrell, Jack Gelber, Allen Ginsberg, E. Stanly Godbold, Jr., Rosa Guy, Elizabeth Hardwick, Michael Harrington, the late Hiram Haydn, Hettie Jones, Matthew Josephson, Alfred Kazin, Seymour Krim, Clay Lancaster, Julius Lester, Townsend Ludington, Dwight Macdonald, Mary McCarthy, Arthur Miller, Lewis Mumford, Larry Neal, Anaïs Nin, Ann Petry, William Phillips, Mary Pitlick, the late Ted Poston, Norman Rosten, Isidor Schneider, George S. Schuyler, Isaac Bashevis Singer, Patsy Southgate, William Styron, Ellen Tarry, Virgil Thomson, Louis Untermeyer, Dorothy Van Doren, James Sibley Watson, John Hall Wheelock, E. B. White, and Herman Wouk.

Additionally, for help and information, we are grateful to

Marjorie Pearson, James Dillon and Michael Gold of the Landmarks Preservation Commission of the City of New York; Elizabeth Kray of the Academy of American Poets; Jean Hutson and Ruth Ann Stewart of the Schomburg Collection of the New York Public Library; Andreas Brown of the Gotham Book Mart; Andrew Anspach of the Algonquin Hotel; Diana Haskell of the Newberry Library; Tony Zwicker of the National Arts Club; John Lindenbusch formerly of the Long Island Historical Society; Stanley Bard of the Chelsea Hotel; Edwin Fancher and Dan Wolf, founders of the *Village Voice*; Heyward Ehrlich and Hans Bergmann of the Melvilleans; Ann Small of Arno Press; Loring McMillen of the Staten Island Historical Society; the Reverend James Harold Flye; Joseph Slade; Mary Bowling of the Butler Library of Columbia University; Lee Roberts; Marjorie Content Toomer; Pearl M. Fisher; Mrs. Rudolph Fisher; Emerson Harper; Henry Lee Moon; Carl Cowl; Ron Hobbs; Alice Davis Tibbetts; Mrs. Ralph Ellison; Ann McGovern Scheiner and Robert B. Glynn. The New York Public Library provided the authors with work space in the Frederick Lewis Allen Room and the Wertheim Study, and was invaluable for research in general. The Leonia New Jersey Public Library generously provided access to quiet work space when needed. The facilities of the Hackensack New Jersey Public Library, and in particular the assistance of Mary Otchy in locating obscure volumes, were of significant help.

For special help in locating and providing photographs we would like to thank Alice Bonnell, formerly of the Columbiana Collection; the late Poppy Cannon; Louise Dahl-Wolfe; Peter Dzwonkoski, Yale University Library; Alfred A. Knopf; Charlotte La Rue of the Museum of the City of New York; Ruth Lester, Institute of Concerned Photography; Charles Lockwood; Pack Memorial Library, Asheville, North Carolina;

George Plimpton; Frances Steloff of the Gotham Book Mart; Neda M. Westlake, University of Pennsylvania Library; and Hortense Zera, American Academy of Arts and Letters.

The authors would like to thank Joyce Hartman for her patience and editorial guidance and copy editor Frances L. Apt for her dedication to detail and pursuit of perfection.

Susan Edmiston would like to thank Kathryn Paulsen and Alice K. Turner for editorial suggestions; Wendy Weil for patient and unstintingly generous help in both practical and personal matters; and Peter H. Edmiston, who trudged miles of neighborhood tours, spurred lagging inspiration with maps, books and other treasures, and, most important, shared faith and enthusiasm.

Linda Cirino feels immeasurable gratitude for the encouragement of friends and family, particularly the loyalty, tolerance and support of Antonio Cirino. Paul and Mark Cirino, though small, merit large gold medals for being remarkably respectful of the file cards and papers continually within their reach. Florence Grammerstorf deserves special personal thanks.

S. S. E.
L. D. C.

Preface

FOR THOSE OF US who live with books, what we read is as much a part of our personal history as the events we participate in. For each of us certain fictional scenes burn with a reality equal to the high points of our own experience. And the writers who created them have a special relation to us; they are sometime collaborators in our lives. Rediscovering their homes, the rooms where they gathered, the things they saw as they went from place to place, we learn something about the sources of their experience and, indirectly, ours. Such was the emotion that impelled us, two New Yorkers who love the city and its literature, to write this book.

We began with the simple motive of seeking out the houses of writers who had lived in New York and the places they wrote about. It soon became apparent that to present what we found in a readable way we should have to describe how writing developed in New York and suggest something of the city's character and style at various times, and so this book became a combined exploration in history, literature and biography. What influence the city had on the shaping of literature remains to be examined in greater depth. Over a drink at the Century Club Alfred Kazin told us, "I can't prove it but I'm sure New York is the single most important factor in American writing." He himself has written of the "aesthetic born of the extraordinary number of stimuli . . . in the modern city," exemplified in García Lorca's *The Poet in New York*, Hart Crane's *The Bridge* and Dos Passos's *Manhattan Transfer*. "The modern city," says Kazin, "has created new imperatives of literary form as well as of social thinking."

We leave it for others to delineate the esthetic impact of the city on literature. Our goal was more concrete. Exploring neighborhood by neighborhood, we have attempted to retrace the steps of the city's major writers, re-create the literary circles and currents in which they moved and pinpoint landmarks — writers' homes, haunts, gathering places and the settings of their work. We hope that others will discover, as we have, an additional dimension to the most mundane corners of the city; by association with the literary past a house, restaurant or street takes on new significance and evokes fresh emotions.

We have been hampered in our efforts by the ever changing nature of the physical city. Some buildings were demolished even as we wrote and others will have disappeared by the time this book reaches publication. By discovering and documenting those landmarks that still exist — some of them previously unknown — we hope to aid in their preservation. One other disclaimer: our reasons for including some writers and not others were sometimes complicated and arbitrary. In general, we followed the principle of emphasizing writers in proportion to their critical reputations. However, we also took into consideration how great a force the city was in their work and how much they were involved in the life of the city. Practical considerations intervened. Better biographical data exist on some past figures than on others, and some living writers preferred not to provide us with information. We also hesitated to write too extensively of those whose reputations are in the process of formation; as a general rule, we tried to include comprehensively all those who were established by the fifties. Ultimately, this book is a personal one — some writers, groups, incidents, situations and places simply aroused our interest and affections more than others.

New York has such a complex identity that it is not often characterized as a literary town. Yet the city saw the launching of a national literature with Washington Irving and James Fenimore Cooper; its coming of age with Edgar Allan Poe, Herman Melville and Walt Whitman; its exuberant development in the work of dozens of twentieth-century writers. In fact, except for the second half of the nineteenth century, when ascendancy passed to New England, New York has been and is the literary capital of America. This book, we hope, begins to bring coherence and perspective to the vast and varied history of the city's involvement in literature.

Susan Edmiston

Linda D. Cirino

New York, 1975

Contents

Illustrations

STREET MAPS ACCOMPANY EACH
NEIGHBORHOOD TOUR

Literary
New York

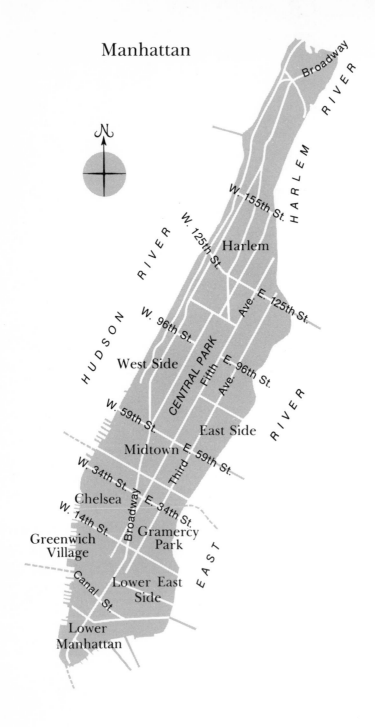

Manhattan

I. Lower Manhattan

NEW YORK made its appearance in literature before the first white settler stepped ashore. "After a hundred leagues," Giovanni da Verrazzano wrote in 1524, "we found a very agreeable place between two small but prominent hills; between them a very wide river, deep at its mouth, flowed out into the sea." Financed by France, Verrazzano had embarked in search of a western waterway to China. Instead, he was the first explorer to sight the island the Indians called *Manhatta*. The place between "the two small but prominent hills" was the Narrows; the very wide river, the Hudson. Verrazzano noted that the natives there "dressed in birds' feathers of various colors, and they came toward us joyfully, uttering loud cries of wonderment." Because of the tides, the mariner and his crew were forced to return to their ship, though they left the land "with much regret on account of its favorable conditions and beauty."

The territory that would become New York was not settled until over a hundred years later. In 1609 Henry Hudson visited and returned to Holland with a bundle of beaver skins as evidence of the new land's potential for the fur trade. Impressed by his reports, a group of businessmen organized the Dutch West India Company to establish commerce in the New World, and in 1624 sent out a shipload of settlers, who established themselves on Governor's Island. The following year the first permanent

settlement was started on Manhattan. In its earliest years the
fledgling city must have seemed a veritable Eden, magnificent
in its natural beauty and the wealth and variety of its wild
life. Rodman Gilder, in his history of the Battery, described
the island as it was to remain for at least a century: "Safe
from the fury of ocean gales, it was washed by a great river,
and by the salt waters of a noble bay and the strait now
called the East River. For food, the Indians were not limited to
the bountiful supplies of oysters, clams, terrapin, fish, and
giant lobsters that surrounded them. There were deer, par-
tridges, turkeys, and clouds of pigeons, swans, and ducks.
Maize and tobacco were readily cultivated near the fresh-water
ponds that clotted the island; and, in season, wild strawberries
and grapes could be had for the picking."

By the middle of the seventeenth century the settlement
of New Amsterdam was well established. It stretched from the
present Greenwich Street on the west to Water Street on the
east and was bounded by Wall Street on the north. (Landfill
operations during the eighteenth and nineteenth centuries
would broaden the island and add almost the whole of Battery
Park at its tip.) The Dutch brought the flavor of their home-
land with them, building their houses gable end to the street,
as in crowded Holland, although here they had no lack of
space. They scattered windmills about the landscape, and used
an inlet that ran up Broad Street as a canal. In this setting
New Amsterdam's first poet, Jacob Steendam, made his appearance. A clerk for the Dutch West India Company, he arrived in 1653. Thanks to the Castello Plan and Nicasius de
Sille's census of New Amsterdam's houses,* we know exactly

* The Castello Plan, so named because it was found in the collection of the
Villa Castello near Florence in 1911, is the only known plan of New Amsterdam
to have survived from the Dutch period. It depicts the town with all its buildings
as it was in 1660. It is presumed to have been discovered in Holland by Cosimo
de' Medici on a trip he made there in 1669. De Sille's census lists all the houses

where he lived. His house stood on the north side of Pearl Street between State and Whitehall, roughly opposite where Herman Melville would be born over 150 years later. The plan shows a fair-sized house with a stable in the rear, and a trim garden with fruit trees. Here, in 1659, Steendam wrote "The Complaint of New Amsterdam to Her Mother," which he sent to Holland for publication. He followed it in 1661 with "The Praise of New Amsterdam," which included these lines:

> See, two streams my gardens bind
> From the East and North they wind
> Rivers pouring to the sea,
> Rich in fish beyond degree,
> Milk and butter; fruits to eat
> No one can enumerate,
> Every vegetable known,
> Grain the best that e'er was grown.

A glance at a map of the time shows that the two streams literally did bind Steendam's gardens; he was located at almost the very tip of the island.

In 1664 the British took over New Amsterdam. During the early days of their rule the colony's literary output increased slightly; there was an occasional history, political satire or description of the city written to attract new settlers. But literature was hardly one of New York's more vital concerns. Unlike the other colonies it had been founded for purely commercial purposes, and commercial it was to remain. William Smith, author of one of the few histories, wrote in 1757 that for a long time his own father and James De Lancey "were the only

---

by block in New Amsterdam on July 10, 1660. By matching the plan and the list it is possible to see just who lived in the town and where.

The Castello Plan, showing all the buildings in New Amsterdam in 1660.

A diagrammatic version of the Castello Plan superimposed on modern lower Manhattan. Jacob Steendam lived in the second house from the top of "Pearle Straet" in Block G.

academics" in the province, and that, as late as 1745, there were
only thirteen more. "What a contrast," he exclaimed, "in everything respecting the cultivation of science, between this and
the colonies first settled by the English!"

.

New York's literary tradition began with its journalism. In 1725
William Bradford started the first newspaper, the *New York
Gazette,* in Hanover Square. The city narrowly lost having
Benjamin Franklin among its literary forefathers when Bradford turned down his request for a job. "I offer'd my services
to . . . old Mr. William Bradford . . ." Franklin wrote in
his *Autobiography.* "He could give me no employment, having
little to do, and help enough already; but says he, 'My son at
Philadelphia has lately lost his principal hand . . . If you go
thither, I believe he may employ you.' "

Bradford's paper was controlled by New York's Governor
William Cosby, whose financial corruption had aroused public
indignation. A party formed to oppose Cosby and decided to
publish a paper of its own, the *New-York Weekly Journal,* with
John Peter Zenger, then Bradford's apprentice, as editor.
The *Journal* used satirical means to attack the government.
As Edward Ellis records in *The Epic of New York City,* mock
advertisements represented the sheriff as "a monkey of the
larger sort, about 4 feet high," and the city recorder as "a large
spaniel, of about 5 feet 5 inches high," that "has lately strayed
from his kennel with his mouth full of fulsome panegyrics."

Issues of the paper were burned, and Zenger was accused
of libel and thrown into jail in the City Hall at the corner of
Wall and Nassau streets. He remained there nearly a year
before his trial in August 1735. Andrew Hamilton, first attorney general of Pennsylvania and America's most famous
lawyer, came forward for the defense. Through his efforts

Zenger was acquitted, and Hamilton's expertise was commemorated in the expression "Philadelphia lawyer."

Although the Zenger case established the crucial principle
of freedom of the press, it was not until several decades had
passed that the pragmatic needs of the Revolution would spur
the press to produce anything of great literary interest. Thomas
Paine's pamphlets and Philip Freneau's patriotic satires would
stir men to passion and action; later others would sit down
to thrash out in writing the principles under which the new nation would be governed. In addition to the largest Tory population of the colonies, New York had a strong faction of militant
revolutionaries — the combination made the city a center of de-
bate. As the Revolution approached, the flow of propaganda, in
handbills and newspapers, quickened.

Among those who arose on the side of the rebels was Philip
Freneau. Although his family home was in New Jersey,
Freneau had been born on New York's Frankfort Street and
had attended boarding school in the city. When he was a student at Princeton he had begun to write poetry, and with his
roommate, Hugh Henry Brackenridge, produced America's
first known work of fiction, a novel called *Father Bombo's Pilgrimage to Mecca in Arabia*. After several attempts at settling
on a career, Freneau came to New York in 1775 and gained a
reputation as a political satirist with such poems as "American
Liberty" and "Libera Nos Domine." At the end of the year
he left New York for St. Croix, where he sailed as a privateer
and turned to the more lyrical verse on which his literary
reputation rests. His life exemplifies the predicament of the
writer in a time when writing was not a profession; he had no
independent income and was plagued continually by the prob-
lem of how to earn a living. In a piece called "Advice to Authors," he pretended to be a Mr. Robert Slender, who supported
himself by weaving stockings "on a curious loom of his own

invention." He advised his readers that "all you have to do
. . . is to graft your authorship upon some other calling, or
support drooping genius by the assistance of some mechanical
employment, in the same manner as the helpless ivy takes hold
of the vigorous oak and cleaves to it for support — I mean to
say, in plain language, that you may make something by weaving garters, or mending old sails, when an Epic poem would
be your utter destruction." Freneau's advice came from his
own experience. After being taken prisoner by the British
in 1778 when piloting his privateer, he served in the New
Jersey Militia for several years. He then edited the *Freeman's
Journal* in Philadelphia and later returned to the sea as captain
of a cargo ship that plied the waters of the Atlantic seaboard.

Meanwhile, in 1787 and 1788, two New Yorkers, Alexander
Hamilton and John Jay, joined with James Madison (who
had been a classmate of Freneau's at Princeton) in writing
what was to become America's first literary classic, *The Federalist*.* This too was in the journalistic tradition; the eighty-
five essays that composed it were originally published in several of the city's newspapers. New York's ratification of the
Constitution hung in the balance and the writers attempted
to tip the scales in its favor. Generally regarded as one of the
highest achievements in political writing, *The Federalist* thoroughly explicated the principles of the new government. The
young and brilliant Hamilton, who wrote at least fifty-one of
the essays, lived at 58 Wall Street; Jay, who wrote five, lived
nearby at 133 Broadway; and Madison, visiting from Virginia,
stayed in a boarding house at 19 Maiden Lane.

---

* The men who figured in the early literary history of New York were members
of a very small educated elite. There were only twelve students in Freneau
and Madison's class at Princeton. Jay was one of six awarded degrees in 1764
at King's College, later called Columbia; twenty-one were awarded degrees in
1774, the year Hamilton entered King's. (Classes were suspended at King's
from 1776 to 1784 during the Revolution and Hamilton, therefore, never graduated.)

Two short years later these men shifted their political alignment. In 1890 Hamilton backed the formation of a newspaper called the *United States Gazette,* which advocated antidemocratic policies. Madison was alarmed and wrote to Jefferson that "a free newspaper, meant for general circulation, and edited by a man of genius of republican principles would be some antidote to the doctrines and discourses circulated in favor of Monarchy and Aristocracy." Freneau, in New York again as a newspaper editor, was the "man of genius" Madison had in mind. With the approval of Jefferson, Freneau was set up as editor of a paper in Philadelphia to rival Hamilton's. He was now a thorough-going democrat, often adding to the Robert Slender pseudonym the letters O.S.M., which stood for "One of the Swinish Multitude." By contrast, Hamilton and Jay lived an aristocratic life replete with pseudo-English formal dinners, receptions and dances.

For two years the *National Gazette,* the principal advocate of Jeffersonian democracy, battled the *United States Gazette.* As a result, the editor found himself despised by many of America's influential men. George Washington referred to him as "that rascal Freneau" and Washington Irving called him "a barking cur." What was perhaps more sad, he sacrificed the development of his poetry. After the financial failure of the *Gazette,* he spun out his days in unsuccessful newspaper ventures in New York and on his family farm in Mount Pleasant.

The career of Thomas Paine paralleled that of Freneau in several respects: as author of *Common Sense* and the *Crisis,* he used his pen in the service of the Revolution; as editor of the *Pennsylvania Magazine,* he earned his living as a journalist on the side of the democrats; and as a revolutionary who out-lived his time, he ended as the object of violent hatred. "He was regarded as worse than a common felon and outlaw," says literary historian Vernon Parrington, "because more dangerous."

John Wesley Jarvis's portrait of Thomas Paine.

Paine was in New York only at the end of his life. He had lived in America, mostly in Philadelphia, from 1774 to 1787, but then spent sixteen years in France and England. After returning to this country, he arrived in New York in 1803 and lived alternately in boarding houses in the city and on a farm in New Rochelle presented to him by the state in recognition of his services during the Revolution. But hostile neighbors made attempts on his life, and in 1806 he gave up the farm and went to live permanently in the city. He spent his happiest months living with John Wesley Jarvis, a prominent portrait painter, at 85 Church Street. Although Paine was in his seventies and Jarvis in his thirties, the two had much in common. Paine's biographer Alfred Aldridge writes, "Both were staunch Jeffersonians; both enjoyed a somewhat Bohemian manner of life, and both were avid talkers . . ." Jarvis and Paine often sat up late discussing religion, government and the rights of man. Paine spent six months with Jarvis and then stayed briefly at several more boarding houses. Finally in July 1808, by this time requiring almost constant attention to his failing health, he moved out in the country to Greenwich Village. He died there a year later.

.

At the end of the eighteenth century, there was not one full-time professional man of letters in all of America. Washington Irving would be the first when in 1809 his brilliant satire, *A History of New York, by Diedrich Knickerbocker,* delighted Americans and Europeans alike and established his career. Irving was born in 1783 at 131 William Street, but a few weeks later his family moved across to 128, a modest two-story house of wood and brick with a garden filled with flowers, apricots, greengage plums and nectarines. As a boy Irving loved plays and often attended the nearby Park Theatre. He would run home in time for prayers and then climb out his bedroom window and go back to catch the afterpiece.

After his father's death in 1802, Irving's mother moved the family to a house on the northwest corner of Ann and William streets (marked today by a plaque), and it was here that he began to write. His first efforts were the sketches dealing with the theater that he signed Jonathan Oldstyle. Then in 1807

Irving, his brother William and his brother-in-law James K. Paulding founded the popular periodical *Salmagundi*,* a series of pamphlets satirizing life in New York. The three authors, who wrote under pseudonyms in the custom of the day — Washington was Launcelot Langstaff, William was William Wizard and Paulding was Anthony Evergreen — met regularly at William's home at 17 State Street.

It was in *Salmagundi*'s pages that the city was first called Gotham, a usage that survives to this day. Richard Henry Dana, editor of the leading literary journal of the time, the *North American Review,* wrote that "it was exceedingly pleasant morning or after-dinner reading, never taking up too much of a gentleman's time from his business and pleasures nor so exalted and spiritualized as to seem mystical to his far reaching vision. It was an excellent thing in the rests between cotillions

* The word *salmagundi* referred to a hash made of minced veal, pickled herrings, anchovies and onions served with lemon juice and oil.

A view of William Street in Washington Irving's time.

and pauses between games at cards; and answered a most convenient purpose in as much as it furnished those who had none of their own with wit enough, for sixpence, to talk out the sitting of an evening party."

On October 27, 1809, the following item appeared in the *New York Evening Post:*

DISTRESSING

Left his lodgings some time since, and has not since been heard of, a small elderly gentleman, dressed in an old black coat and cocked hat, by the name of *Knickerbocker* . . .

This was the first move in the nation's earliest literary hoax. In answer, the *Post* printed a letter to the editor saying that a man fitting Knickerbocker's description had been seen by passengers on the Albany stage, resting by the side of the road above King's Bridge. He was carrying a small bundle tied in a red bandanna and appeared "fatigued and exhausted." Ten days later, the landlord of the Independent Columbian Hotel in Mulberry Street published a notice saying that "a very curious kind of a written book" had been found in the room of one Diedrich Knickerbocker and would have to be disposed of to satisfy the landlord for his unpaid boarding and lodging. Then on November 28 came the finale: an advertisement for the soon to be published *A History of New York,* "found in the chamber of Dr. Diedrich Knickerbocker, the old gentleman whose sudden and mysterious disappearance has been noticed."

The book, amusing even today, was a satirical history of New York "from the Beginning of the World to the End of the Dutch Dynasty." Although descendants of the old Dutch families charged that Irving had defamed them, his book was an

A detail from the Ratzer Map, 1767, shows the prerevolutionary city below Reade Street on the west and Delancey's Square on the east. The "Road to Greenwich" (far left) and the "Road to Bloomingdale" (top center) went to the villages that bore those names. (Edgar Allan Poe lived in Bloomingdale Village in the mid-nineteenth century.) The *"Bowry* Lane" led to the farm of Peter Stuyvesant, marked at the right center of the island. Branching off from the lane is the "Road to King's bridge" where Diedrich Knickerbocker was seen carrying a knapsack on his way out of the city. Other sites of interest are Abraham Mortier's estate (center left), later occupied by Vice President John Adams and Aaron Burr at different times;

immediate and resounding success. It was the first work by an American to be known abroad; Charles Dickens wore out a copy, and Samuel Taylor Coleridge read it at one sitting. By the end of 1810, it had brought Irving $2000, the largest amount earned by any writer to that day. The name Irving gave his quaint hero, Knickerbocker, rapidly came to characterize New Yorkers of Dutch descent, and today refers to all New Yorkers.

After the publication of the *History,* Irving fell back into the desultory life he had known before. He had studied law in a casual way for seven or eight years, was admitted to the bar in 1806 and even was listed in the 1808 city directory as "Washington Irving, attorney, 3 Wall Street." But there is no record that he ever had a client. In the absence of any more compelling interest, he became an inactive partner in his brothers' hardware business at 135 Pearl Street. He wrote little, though he managed to revise the *History* in 1811 while sharing rooms with Henry Brevoort in Mrs. Ryckman's boarding house at 16 Broadway. He alternated between periods of society, during which he was the undisputed literary lion of New York, and solitude. In 1815 he went to Europe, where he was to remain, reigning over the American literary scene in absentia, for the next seventeen years.

.

In the years following the Revolution, New York City had played a role in the early development of the novel. In 1791 *Charlotte Temple, A Tale of Truth* by Susanna Rowson, a New

Alexander Hamilton died at William Bayard's home (upper left) after dueling with Burr in Hoboken across the river. To the northeast of the Bayard residence is the estate Captain Thomas Clarke called "Chelsea," a name that survives in the neighborhood today. Other points of interest are Kip's Bay and Turtle Bay and the numerous holdings of the Delanceys, the most prominent patroons of the New York area and the family from which James Fenimore Cooper's wife, Susan, was descended.

Englander of British birth, was first published. The book, set in New York, was eventually to run through 200 editions and remain the nation's best seller until it was supplanted by *Uncle Tom's Cabin* half a century later. It was said to have been based on the true story of Charlotte Stanley. The daughter of an English clergyman, she was persuaded to elope to this country in 1774 by John Montresor, who was already married. Montresor and his wife lived on Montresor's Island, now known as Randall's Island. Charlotte died, abandoned by Montresor, after bearing his child, and was buried in Trinity churchyard. In 1793, the story goes, Susanna Rowson, who was Montresor's cousin, visited the grave while it still bore the name "Charlotte Stanley." Today, a dark slab on the north side of the church near Broadway bears the inscription "Charlotte Temple."

Although Charles Brockden Brown, the Gothic novelist, was born in Philadelphia and spent most of his life there, the years in which he tried writing were spent in New York. In 1798 he came to stay with William Dunlap, playwright, theatrical historian and manager of the Park Theatre, at 15 Park Row. The yellow fever epidemic that year provided material for his novels, particularly *Arthur Mervyn*. Around 1803 Brown became discouraged and returned to Philadelphia to publish a magazine.

Despite the efforts of Rowson and Brown, it was not until James Fenimore Cooper wrote *The Spy* in 1821 that the novel came to be firmly established in America. Six years younger than Irving, Cooper was a gentleman farmer in Scarsdale when he threw down one of the popular novels of the day and told his wife that he could write a better one. Since the name of the book Cooper vowed to surpass is unknown, we cannot judge whether his *Precaution,* published in 1820, was in fact better; we do know that it was not very good. The experience, however, made a novelist of Cooper. With hardly a pause he started on *The Spy,* inspired by a story told to him by the old Federalist John Jay, who had retired to nearby Bedford. After its publication Cooper moved his family to New York to become a literary man.

In her "Small Family Memories," Cooper's daughter Susan recalled the house they took as being "one of two recently built by the Patroon, on Broadway just above Prince Street. It was then almost 'out-of-town.' Directly opposite to us was a modest two-story house occupied by John Jacob Astor." Their house was replaced, even in Susan Cooper's time, by Niblo's Garden, an outdoor theater. The following spring the Coopers moved to a narrow three-story brick house with marble steps and oak doors at 3 Beach Street. Here Cooper wrote *The Pilot,* America's first sea novel, also undertaken as a self-imposed challenge. Cooper, who had been in the navy, maintained at a dinner party that the current best seller, Sir Walter Scott's *The Pirate,* was too error-ridden to have been written by a real sailor. On the way home he outlined a plot.

In 1825 the Coopers decided to move again. The Beach Street house was "out of repair," as Susan Cooper delicately put it. "The number of rats was really alarming; I remember distinctly their running over the bed in which I slept." On May 1, the day on which New Yorkers traditionally moved, the Coopers went to 345 Greenwich Street, "at that time a quiet dignified part of the town." They summered in Bayside or Hallett's Cove, now known as Astoria, and Cooper traveled to New York by sloop almost daily.

During this period of his life, Cooper was a highly sociable man. William Cullen Bryant compared his character to "the bark of the cinnamon, a rough and astringent rind without and an intense sweetness within. Those who penetrated below the surface found a genial temper, warm affects, and a heart with ample place for his friends . . ." Seeking out company, Cooper began to meet his friends in the Den, a small room in the bookstore on New Street belonging to his publisher, Charles Wiley. And so began New York's first literary club. Originally called the Cooper Club or the Lunch, the group was known as the Bread and Cheese when it was organized on a more formal basis. Bread signified a vote for a new member and cheese one against. The original members were Charles Wiley; William Dunlap; Henry Brevoort; the Shakespearean scholar Gulian Verplanck; the city's leading poet, Fitz-Greene Halleck; and James Kent, whose *Commentaries* were the definitive interpretation of the law. Irving, abroad in Europe, was named an honorary member. Bryant and Samuel F. B. Morse, one of the foremost painters of the day and later inventor of the telegraph, joined in 1825. The club's membership represented the literary elite of the city and embraced the most prominent writers of the Knickerbocker period.

In 1825, the entire Cooper family began studying French in preparation for going abroad the following year. Cooper's stature can be measured by the fact that, when he left, the Bread and Cheese gave him a farewell dinner, attended by Governor DeWitt Clinton, at the City Hotel. While abroad, Cooper started to write critically of America and when he returned in 1833 he found his reputation totally changed. Four days after his arrival he attended a banquet for an old friend. Many of the people he knew did not speak to him and those who did were cold and constrained. He found it impossible to sit out the dinner, and later thought it wise to decline an invitation to the obligatory City Hotel banquet honoring his return.

Disapproval soon became public as well as personal and Cooper found himself frequently vilified in the press. Rather than ignoring the attacks, he charged the publishers with libel and pleaded his own cases against them in court. These suits, which he often won, were a major contribution to the redefinition of the libel laws, establishing the illegality of public attack without supporting evidence.

Cooper's work after his return, notably *Home as Found,* criticized life in New York, with its social hypocrisies and fancy-dress balls. Among those who fell under his disapproval was the man he once had made an honorary member of his club. He now found Irving, intent on making money and gaining social esteem, the epitome of the bourgeois culture he detested. The two first titans of American literature were, therefore, never to meet during the two years they both lived in the city. Irving, who had returned from Europe in 1832, was at 3 Bridge Street with his brother Ebenezer or at John Jacob Astor's "Astoria," until he moved to Tarrytown in 1836. By this time the fashionable residential district had progressed up Broadway to Greenwich Village and Cooper and his family had taken a house on Bleecker Street. He continued to spend his winters in New York although he considered Otsego Hall in Cooperstown his home. The two men met only once, years later, in 1850, at the offices of their publisher, Putnam. They chatted pleasantly for an hour.

With Cooper and Irving retired to the country, William Cullen Bryant took the center of New York's literary stage. Having written "Thanatopsis" at seventeen, he was already known for his poetry when he arrived in New York in 1825 at the age of thirty-one. Like Irving, he had studied law, a popular profession for young men of indefinite inclination or limited means. (At the time medicine was financially unrewarding, and the ministry required a college degree.) But he found the profession uncongenial — he wrote of "the disagreeable, disgusting drudgery of the law" — and came to New York to try to earn a living as editor of the *New York Review and Athenaeum.* In 1826 he augmented his income by becoming assistant to William Coleman, editor of the *New York*

Evening Post. The magazine eventually folded and Bryant went to work on the *Evening Post* full-time. In 1829, Coleman died and Bryant became editor.

The *Evening Post* had been founded in 1801 by Alexander Hamilton and his followers, who hoped to produce a Federalist editor the equal of the great democrats, Paine and Freneau. By the time Bryant took over, however, the paper was primarily commercial. It consisted of a single sheet folded to make four pages; of these, all but page two were devoted to advertising, legal notices and other information of commercial interest.

Bryant gave the paper, which had collaborated in Irving's hoax, an increased literary flavor by printing news of writers and frequent book announcements. These were not real reviews, which were not to be found in the New York press until the days of Edgar Allan Poe and Margaret Fuller; Bryant usually did not have time to read the books. His real strength as an editor (he had only one assistant much of the time and no news staff until much later) was as a writer of eloquent, morally impeccable editorials on the issues of the day. He took controversial positions, in favor of free speech and labor unions and against slavery, that often lost the newspaper circulation and advertising. The greatest peril of his profession, he wrote in 1851, "is the strong temptation . . . it sets before men, to betray the cause of truth to public opinion, and to fall in with what are supposed to be the views held by a contemporaneous majority, which are sometimes perfectly right and sometimes grossly wrong."

As an editor Bryant combined great efficiency with great disorder. His desk was piled high with papers except for a small clear space in the middle where he worked. Like "paper-sparing Pope," he did all his writing on the backs of old letters and manuscripts. John Bigelow, an early biographer, explained his motive: "He believed that everybody in the world was made the poorer by everything that is wasted, and no one so much as he who wastes, for he experiences a waste of character as well as of property."

In personal relations, Bryant was remote with all but a very few close friends. Richard Henry Dana, who was one of his intimates, once wrote encouraging him to make the acquaintance of Poe. Bryant replied, "I do not know that I ever got acquainted with anybody, of set purpose, in my life. The three things most irksome to me in my transactions with the world are to owe money, to ask a favor, and to seek an acquaintance. The few excellent friends I have I acquired I scarcely know how — certainly by no assiduity of my own." Bryant knew Cooper but is said to have been somewhat intimidated by him. Bryant's son-in-law, Parke Godwin, described them as appearing little fitted for friendship: "Cooper, burly, brusque, and boisterous, like a bluff sailor, always bringing a breeze of a quarrel with him; Mr. Bryant, shy, modest, and delicate as a woman."

In his early years in New York, Bryant moved from boarding house to boarding house. When he first arrived he lived with a French family named Evrard on Chambers Street, where his wife and daughter joined him later in the year. Next they moved into rooms at Mrs. Meigs's at 88 Canal Street and in 1830 were on Broome Street between Hudson and Varick. Wherever Bryant lived, he followed the same regime. He rose at five-thirty and did an hour's exercises, which included chinning himself from the door frame and jumping back and forth over his bed, aided by a vaulting pole. Then, after a small breakfast, he walked to his office in lower Manhattan.

•

The great writers of the Knickerbocker period — Cooper, Irving and Bryant — made the first strides toward an American literature; they gave the country a sense of self-realization. "As Audubon 'discovered' the American birds and Catlin discovered the Indians," wrote Van Wyck Brooks, "these writers discovered, for Americans, their woods and fields, their scenery, their flowers, their rivers and prairies and mountains." But although Cooper was to survive until 1851, Irving until '59, and Bryant until 1878, their time in literature was over much sooner. By 1835, the reality of the city was clearly antithetical to their earlier vision. The grid street plan, devised for New York in 1811, probably the single most destructive influence on the city's physical character, had begun to be implemented. "The face of the island was originally diversified into hill and valley, ledge and swamp; and the more ancient parts of the city still present very nearly the same uneven surface as in the olden time," wrote Asa Greene in an 1837 guidebook to New York. "But the levelling genius of our city government has reduced to an almost entire flat the more new and recently built parts of the town. They have said emphatically, 'Stoop down ye hills! ye valleys rise!' "

With the decline of the natural and physical side of New York, in literature and in fact, came a simultaneous growth of the commercial. New York was the publishing capital of the nation. The book trade had evolved to the point where the reader, or editor, had made his appearance. Asa Greene noted, "As certain Kings and great men . . . used, in former times to keep a taster, whose business it was to see that the food was not poisoned: so do Harper & Brothers employ a reader. This course . . . not only insures the purity of the moral, and the briskness of the intellectual atmosphere, as far as the press of Harper & Brothers is concerned; but also provides effectually against the assertion that their books 'are never read.' "

Newspapers had entered a great surge of development. In

September of 1833 Benjamin H. Day began publishing the *Sun*, the first penny newspaper to survive. Until then New Yorkers had regarded a newspaper as a luxury; a year's subscription to the *Evening Post* cost eight dollars, or ten days' wages for a working man. The *Sun* did no more reporting than Bryant's *Post*, but it served the common man by bringing the newspaper within the range of his purse and printing a great many help wanted ads.

In 1835 James Gordon Bennett founded the *Herald* in a cellar at 10 Wall Street, and with it a new journalism. Bennett was the first editor to go in search of news. He started work at 5:00 A.M., and made the rounds of business offices collecting stock tables and gossip every afternoon. To be sure to get the European newspapers first, he kept a clipper ship off Montauk and ran a special train the length of Long Island. Bennett also gave the city a kind of news — the violent, vulgar and sensational — it had never known before. In 1840 he announced his own engagement with these headlines: TO THE READERS OF THE HERALD — DECLARATION OF LOVE — CAUGHT AT LAST — GOING TO BE MARRIED — NEW MOVEMENT IN CIVILIZATION.

Greatest of the newspapermen to come up in the thirties was Horace Greeley, whose *Tribune* was the first paper to be nationally distributed on a wide scale. With 250,000 readers, many of them in the frontier states, the *Tribune* was said to be second only to the Bible in influence in the emerging West. Greeley's aim was to educate his readers morally, politically and culturally. He published some of the leading writers of the day, including Poe, Dickens, and Karl Marx, then in London, who wrote a column on European politics and economics.

In the 1830s and 1840s many of the city's newspapers, magazines and book publishers gathered on Nassau Street, earning it the name "newspaper row." Going north from Fulton Street were, at various times during the forties, the *Herald* at the

Printing House Square, showing the *Times*, *Tribune* and *World*
buildings in 1864.

corner of Fulton, the *Sun* at 91 Nassau, the *Literary World*
at 109, the *Aurora and Union* at 111, the *New York Times* at
118, the *Broadway Journal* at the corner of Beekman, the
Knickerbocker at 139, the *Mirror* at 148 and the *Tribune* at 160.

Among the men on their staffs was Walt Whitman, who
moved to Manhattan in 1841 to work for the *Aurora*. He lived
in a series of boarding houses, among them a Mrs. Chipman's at
12 Centre Street. While staying there, he went home for lunch
every day and then took a walk down Broadway to the Battery
before returning to the office. His description of the trip back
uptown re-creates the city of 1842: "Coming up Broadway, from
the Bowling Green, an observer will notice, on each side, tall,
quiet looking houses, with no great aspect of life or business.
These are mostly boarding houses . . . After passing Trinity
Church, however, the crowd thickens, and the ground stories of

the buildings are principally occupied as shops." Farther on one passed what Whitman described as "that very respectable city, the Astor House," and "that most villainous specimen of architecture," the Park Theatre. "By and by, you arrive at an open space . . . In all probability your ears will be greeted with the discordant notes of the newsboys, who generally muster here in great force."

Whitman delighted in the variety of the city's people, particularly the omnibus drivers, whom he called "a strange, natural, quick-eyed and wondrous race." He often rode next to them on their rounds. Although he later lived mostly in Brooklyn, he sometimes visited the city several times a day and called himself "Manhattanese." He describes the city in several poems, including "Mannahatta":

My city's fit and noble name resumed,
Choice aboriginal name, with marvellous beauty, meaning,
*A rocky founded island — shores where ever gayly dash the coming,
      going, hurrying sea waves.*

In 1849 Whitman began frequenting Fowler and Wells's Phrenological Cabinet at 131 Nassau Street. Lorenzo Fowler charted the bumps on his head: "Leading traits of character appear to be Friendship, Sympathy, Sublimity, and Self-Esteem, and markedly among his combinations the dangerous faults of Indolence, a tendency to the pleasure of voluptuousness and alimentiveness and a certain reckless swing of animal will, too unmindful, probably, of the conviction of others." When some booksellers refused to handle the first edition of *Leaves of Grass,* which Whitman published himself, Fowler and Wells sold it in their bookstore at 308 Broadway. The phrenologists published the second edition.

•

In the 1840s New York's literati yearned for the emergence of
the genius who, breaking with the English tradition represented
by the Knickerbockers, would write in a way that was completely and characteristically American. Although they were
unable to recognize it at the time, they got just what they
wanted. Into New York came two great, incontrovertibly
American originals — Herman Melville and Edgar Allan Poe.

Poe had first visited the city in 1831 when, expelled from
West Point, he prepared his third book of poetry in Elam Bliss's
bookstore at 111 Broadway. Later, while editing *Graham's
Magazine* in Philadelphia, he used a New York event as the
basis of "The Mystery of Marie Roget." After reading newspaper accounts of the murder of Mary Cecilia Rogers, who lived
at 114 Liberty Street, he made the victim's name French and
transferred the setting to Paris so that the story could serve as a
sequel to "The Murders in the Rue Morgue." In 1844 Poe
moved permanently to New York. Although he is often remembered in romantic terms — eccentric, undisciplined, ill and ad-
dicted to drugs and alcohol — he had a sound reputation as one
of the country's most astute and successful critics and editors.
Under his direction, the *Southern Literary Messenger* had become famous for the authority of its reviews, and he had made
Graham's the foremost monthly in the country. During the
three years of his editorship, its circulation rose from fifty-five
hundred to forty thousand.

On arriving in the city, Poe became editor and part owner of
the *Broadway Journal,* at the southwest corner of Beekman and
Nassau streets. He published "Art-Music and Heart Music" by
Walt Whitman, who described Poe as "very kindly and human,
but subdued, perhaps a little jaded." The Poes lived at 130
Greenwich Street in 1844 and in the back room on the third
floor of a tenement at 195 East Broadway the following year.
In the few years Poe had left to live, his distaste for the city and

concern for the health of his wife drove him first to the suburbs in Greenwich Village and later to the outlying countryside — the Brennan Farm near Broadway and 84th Street, the Miller Farm in Turtle Bay and finally the cottage in Fordham.

Poe's attitude toward New York was perhaps best expressed in a series of letters about the city he wrote for the *Columbia Spy* in Pottsville, Pennsylvania. He appreciated the natural setting while deploring the changes made in the name of progress. In 1844 he wrote:

> I have been roaming far and wide over this island of Manna-hatta. Some portions of its interior have a certain air of rocky sterility which may impress some imaginations as simply *dreary* — to me it conveys the sublime . . . On the eastern or "sound" face of Mannahatta are some of the most picturesque sites for villas to be found within the limits of Christendom. These localities, however, are neglected — unimproved. The only mansions upon them (principally wooden) are suffered to remain unrepaired, and present a melancholy spectacle of decrepitude. In fact, these magnificent places are doomed. The spirit of Improvement has withered them with its acrid breath. Streets are already "mapped" through them, and they are no longer suburban residences but "town-lots." In some 30 years every noble cliff will be a pier, and the whole island will be densely desecrated by buildings of brick, with portentous *façades* of brown-stone . . .

Unlike Poe, Melville was a native New Yorker — in some ways the quintessential New Yorker. He was born in 1819 at 6 Pearl Street (a plaque marks the site) with an ancestry that perfectly reflected the mixture of nationalities peculiar to New York — British, Dutch and a dash of French. His mother, Maria Gansevoort, came from a family of prominent Dutch patroons. His father, like Irving's, was a Scot, and the Melvilles had married among the French Huguenots. The elder Melville was an importer of French goods, and when his business failed the family moved to Albany. Herman taught school and in the early forties made the sea voyages that would form the background of most of his books.

Melville first entered the New York literary world in 1845 when he was arranging for an American edition of his first book, *Typee.* (Irving had helped him find a publisher in England.) He made frequent visits in connection with his books before moving to the city after his marriage in 1847. The residential district had shifted gradually uptown and the Melvilles settled down in Greenwich Village. They lived there until 1850, when Melville went to Pittsfield to write *Moby-Dick.* In June 1851 he wrote to Hawthorne, "In a week or so, I go to New York, to bury myself in a third-story room, and work & slave on my 'Whale' while it is driving thro' the press."

When *Moby-Dick* was finally published, the reaction was not what Melville had expected. Instead of recognizing it as the great American novel they had been waiting for, the New York literati responded with mixed, lukewarm reviews. Exhausted by bringing forth what Melville scholar Henry Murray called "that wild Everest of art," and bitterly disillusioned at its reception, Melville poured out his fevered emotions in *Pierre,* the book that would irrevocably damage his literary reputation. Intertwined with a theme that encompasses incest, Oedipus and the mysteries of the unconscious is the story of a young man who comes to New York and tries to earn his living as a writer in the shivering cold of a "third-story room." Not only is Pierre's masterpiece, like Melville's, ungratefully received; it is rudely condemned. In a satiric chapter entitled "Young America in Literature," Melville vented his scorn on the New York literary world.

Pierre contains many autobiographical strands and it seems likely that its third-story room is based on the one in which

Melville finished *Moby-Dick*. The fictional room is located in a building in the courtyard of one "Church of the Apostles." Murray speculates that this was modeled on the South Baptist Church at 82 Nassau Street. Melville then would have been living behind it on Dutch Street. Another scholar, Hans Bergmann, notes that the agreement between Melville and his publisher provided for the printing of *Moby-Dick* from "plates in the possession of R. Craighead." Craighead's shop was on Fulton Street between Nassau and Dutch. If Melville in fact had been involved in overseeing the stereotyping of the book, as the words "drive the book through the press" might suggest, a room on Dutch Street would have been a most convenient place to stay.

After *Pierre,* which was universally condemned as *Moby-Dick* was not, Melville might well have sunk into obscurity had it not been for C. F. Briggs, editor of the literary magazine, *Putnam's.* Over the next several years he would publish Melville's "The Encantadas," "Israel Potter" and "Bartleby the Scrivener," which re-creates the Wall Street law offices of the 1850s.

·

With the decline of Melville's reputation came the decline of New York as the nation's literary capital. The second phase of American literature had already begun in New England, where it found more hospitable soil. Unlike New York, which was cosmopolitan, commercial, anti-intellectual and fragmented by dispute, New England boasted a homogeneous people, passionately interested in learning, united in a coherent intellectual and literary movement — transcendentalism.

Later Lower Manhattan would have its literary visitors. When Henry James revisited New York in 1904, the area had already acquired the totally modern character it has today.

James observed "the multitudinous sky-scrapers standing up to the view, from the water, like extravagant pins in a cushion already overplanted." On Wall Street "the new landmarks [were] crushing the old quite as violent children stamp on snails and caterpillars." And "the special sky-scraper that over-hangs poor old Trinity to the north" was "a south face as high and wide as the mountain-wall that drops the Alpine avalanche, from time to time, upon the village, and the village spire, at its foot . . ."

In the 1920s Thomas Wolfe came to observe the activity of Washington Market and the desperation of the homeless men who spent cold nights in the public latrine opposite City Hall. E. E. Cummings visited the Aquarium, then at the Battery, and took John Dos Passos to eat at a Syrian restaurant on Washington Street. There was even an occasional resident. In 1911, after shipping out as a seaman, Eugene O'Neill came to live in a flophouse over a saloon called Jimmy the Priest's, near the waterfront at 252 Fulton Street. " 'Jimmy the Priest's' certainly was a hell hole," O'Neill said. "It was awful. One couldn't go any lower . . . The house was almost coming down and the principal housewreckers were vermin." The old red brick build-ing has been torn down but the saloon and the men O'Neill met there are depicted in his play *Anna Christie* and his story "Tomorrow." More recently, the poet and anthologist Oscar Williams and his wife, the poet Gene Derwood, lived on the top floor of an old warehouse building, now a parking lot, at 35 Water Street. But for the most part, when writers came back to the city, the city had moved uptown.

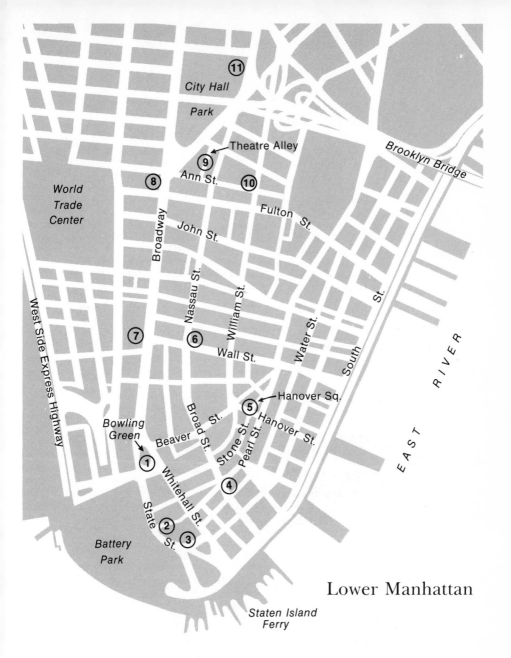

Lower Manhattan

Lower Manhattan Tour

Virtually no literary landmarks remain in Lower Manhattan.
As the financial capital of the world, its real estate value is so

high that it has been rebuilt many times. Then, too, much of the
early city was destroyed by fires. One fire in 1776 devastated a
fourth of the area, and a second, in 1778, burned an additional
sixty dwellings and numerous stores. A few buildings and
several plaques, however, help to re-create the times of literature's beginnings in New York.

In 1771 an iron fence was erected around Bowling Green (1)
to prevent it from becoming a "receptacle of all the filth and
dirt of the neighborhood." The fence stands today, with the
exception of decorative crowns or iron balls, said to have been
used as ammunition during the Revolution. In the mid-
nineteenth century there was a fountain on the green, which
Edgar Allan Poe said looked like a "small country jail in a hard

Bowling Green Fountain, described by Poe as looking like "a small
country jail in a hard thunder shower."

thunder shower." Herman Melville's birthplace at 6 Pearl Street (2) is marked by a plaque. Washington Irving's brother William lived around the corner at 17 State Street and Washington, William and James K. Paulding met there regularly around 1807 to work on *Salmagundi*. The last survivor from that time is the James Watson house at 7 State Street (3). The easterly portion of the Watson house, two windows wide, was built in 1793; the rest, with its curved porch and Ionic columns, was added in 1806. This house was the subject of H. C. Bunner's *The Story of a New York House*, a historical novel written in 1912.

Fraunces Tavern at the corner of Pearl and Broad streets (4) is a reconstruction based on typical buildings of the mid-eighteenth century rather than on the actual structure that once stood there. Originally built in 1719 as a private home, it was converted into a tavern in 1762 and was later run by the celebrated West Indian innkeeper, Samuel Fraunces, who was George Washington's steward. (A more faithful survivor of the Revolutionary period is the three-story Edward Mooney house at 18 Bowery.)

A plaque on the Cotton Exchange on the northwest corner of the intersection of Stone, Hanover and William streets (5) marks the site of the city's first newspaper, William Bradford's *Gazette*. The structure that was the U.S. Customs House and Subtreasury Building at Wall and Nassau streets (6) has been renamed the Federal Hall National Memorial, in recognition of the fact that it stands on the site of the original Federal Hall, which formerly was the New York City Hall. There John Peter Zenger was imprisoned until his trial in August 1735.

Trinity Church at Wall Street and Broadway (7) has been rebuilt twice since the fires of the 1770s but its churchyard remains. Here can be seen the graves of William Bradford and Alexander Hamilton, and the tombstone bearing the inscription

"Charlotte Temple," marking the spot where the heroine of Susanna Rowson's novel is said to be buried. Six blocks north at Broadway and Fulton Street (8) is St. Paul's Chapel, Manhattan's only surviving pre-Revolutionary building. One block north and one block east is Theatre Alley (9), which Washington Irving probably took to get from his home to the Park Theatre on Park Row. A plaque on the northwest corner of Ann and William streets (10) marks the site of Irving's childhood home. A statue of Horace Greeley (11), which stood in front of the *Tribune* building before it was torn down, is now located in City Hall Park opposite the City Court Building.

II. Greenwich Village

No OTHER NEIGHBORHOOD in New York, perhaps in the world, has been the birthplace of more literature than Greenwich Village. Several distinct phases of literary activity correspond to stages in the Village's evolution as a community. In the 1800s, when writing was apt to be a more patrician than bohemian endeavor, the elegant residential community around Washington Square was home, meeting place and subject for New York's literary figures. After the turn of the century, when the area had entered a decline, the young, most often poor, artists and writers discovered in the rundown but still charming neighborhood cheap rents and a congenial setting. The bohemians, whose rediscovery of the neighborhood raised real estate values, were eventually replaced by middle-class academics and those writers who were sufficiently established to have respectable incomes.

The Nineteenth-Century Village: Washington Square

It has a kind of established repose which is not of frequent occurrence in other quarters of the long, shrill city; it has a riper, richer, more honorable look than any of the upper ramifications of the great longitudinal thoroughfare — the look

of having had something of a social history. It was here, as
you might have been informed on good authority, that you
had come into a world which appeared to offer a variety of
sources of interest; it was here that your grandmother lived
in venerable solitude, and dispensed a hospitality which com-
mended itself alike to the infant imagination and the infant
palate; it was here that you took your first walks abroad,
following the nursery-maid with unequal step, and sniffing
up the strange odour of the ailanthus-trees which at that
time formed the principal umbrage of the Square, and diffused
an aroma that you were not yet critical enough to dislike as it
deserved . . .

Henry James, in his description, was looking back from the
vantage point of 1881 to the 1840s, when Washington Square
was at its peak. The country village of estates and small wooden
houses where Thomas Paine had lived in 1808 had grown to
become the city's prime suburb. New York's residential center
had moved uptown in response to two forces. With each attack
of smallpox, cholera or yellow fever (there were major epidem-
ics in 1819, 1822 and 1823) the population of the city fled the
downtown area for the open country to the north. Most of the
necessary shops and businesses were hurriedly transplanted and,
as each panic subsided, a few more remained permanently behind. Simultaneously, the expansion of the business section
pressed the residential district northward. Fashionable New
York zigzagged up the island from Lower Manhattan, east to St.
John's Park, back over to Broadway and up toward Bond Street
and Astor Place.

The movements of a number of literary families in the 1820s
and 1830s reflect this pattern of migration. In 1824 the Melvilles — Herman was still a boy — moved from Cortlandt Street
to 33 Bleecker and in 1828 to 675 Broadway. William Cullen
Bryant's peregrinations traced a similar route; in 1831 he
abandoned the St. John's Park area for 4th Street and Broad-

Thomas Paine's home at 309 Bleecker Street.

way. James Fenimore Cooper, who had lived near St. John's Park on Beach Street, took a house on Bleecker Street between Laurens (now La Guardia Place) and Thompson when he returned from Europe in 1833. This house, which had been selected for the Coopers by their friend Samuel F. B. Morse, was "too magnificent for our simple French tastes," wrote Mrs. Cooper. Nevertheless the family settled in with French furni-

ture, four Swiss servants and a French tiger cat named Coque-
licot. The Coopers later moved to St. Mark's Place (see Chapter
III, The Lower East Side) .

One of the most elegant residential developments to result
from the northward surge was Washington Square. The park,
originally an execution ground and potter's field, was formally
dedicated in 1828, and the houses built on the south side of the
Square that year made the area fashionable. In the spring of
1831 several prominent New Yorkers agreed to construct an
even more distinguished row on the north side. The houses,
many of which remain today, had elegant architectural features.
Inside there were Italian carved marble mantels and gilt-bronze
chandeliers. Walks laid in alternating black and white marble
squares led up to the white marble steps. Behind, there were
gardens with flower borders and white grape-covered trellises.

In the 1840s, when Henry James was just opening his eyes to
the world, literary gatherings were taking place regularly around
Washington Square. The most scholarly were held at Evert
Duyckinck's house at 20 Clinton Place. Duyckinck was then an
editor for the publishers Wiley and Putnam and for a critical
magazine called the *Literary World*. He was said to know the
field of English and American literature as "seamen know the
sea," and, as author of the *Cyclopaedia of American Literature,*
he chronicled the development of the nation's writing. He was
a thoughtful and generous friend, bringing writers into congenial company, midwiving their works into being and lending
them money and books from the eighteen thousand-volume
library that lined the rooms of his house.

Among those who gathered regularly in Duyckinck's basement study was Melville, who lived at 103 Fourth Avenue from
1847 to 1850 while writing *Mardi, Redburn* and *White-Jacket.*
It was here that Melville began his literary education — meeting
Irving and Bryant, reading voraciously in Duyckinck's library

and engaging in the spirited conversation that would be reflected in *Mardi*. In 1851, after moving to Pittsfield, Melville was writing nostalgically to Duyckinck:

> "I suppose the Knights of the Round Table still assemble over their cigars and punch, and I know that once every week the 'Literary World' revolves upon its axis. I should like to hear again the old tinkle of glasses in your basement, and may do so, before many months."

More social evenings were held by Anne Charlotte Lynch, a poet and teacher of English composition sometimes credited with having had the first salon in America. Miss Lynch lived first at 116 Waverly Place, where she entertained in a large double parlor with fires burning at either end. Her guests included Bryant, Melville, Margaret Fuller, Fitz-Greene Halleck, Bayard Taylor, Catharine Sedgwick and, most notably, Edgar Allan Poe, who is said to have read "The Raven" there.

Poe lived nearby at 18 Amity Street in 1844 and 85 Amity in 1845 while editing the *Broadway Journal*. Earlier, when he had come to the city penniless in 1837, he had lived in the older section of the Village, first in a red brick house on the corner of Sixth Avenue and Waverly Place and later in a frame house with a high-pitched roof and shuttered windows at $113\frac{1}{2}$ Carmine Street.

In 1843 the man who was to set Washington Square in the public mind was born at 21 Washington Place. Henry James, revisiting the site of his birth when he came home in 1904 from a long residence in England, was shocked to find that the house had been "suppressed," as he called it, because of the construction of a new building by New York University. The interloper, which had taken the place of the old Gothic university building as well as the house where James was born, was "a high square, impersonal structure" that so blocked his view of the past that he felt he had been "amputated of half his history." In the convoluted prose that had become characteristic of him, James noted:

> The grey and more or less "hallowed" University building — wasn't it somehow, with a desperate bravery, both castellated and gabled? — has vanished from the earth, and vanished with it the two or three adjacent houses, of which the birthplace was one. This was the snub . . . that, whereas the inner sense had positively erected there for its private contemplation a commemorative mural tablet, the very wall that should have borne this inscription had been smashed as for demonstration that tablets, in New York, are unthinkable . . . Where, in fact, is the point of inserting a mural tablet, at any legible height, in a building certain to be destroyed to make room for a sky-scraper?

Today there is a tablet commemorating James, but he would doubtless consider it ironic that it is in the wrong place — on the NYU Brown Building half a block from his birthplace.

James lived at the Washington Place house only six months before his parents took him to Europe. His family did not return to New York until 1847, when they stopped briefly at 11 Fifth Avenue and then moved to 57 West 14th Street, the house from which most of the author's childhood memories date. Here he met Thackeray and remembered the occasional presence of "the great and urbane" Emerson, in addition to lesser literary figures: Parke Godwin, Charles Dana, Rufus Griswold and N. P. Willis. Here James's brother, William, told him Poe's stories, "The Gold-Bug" and "The Pit and the Pendulum," and recited "The Raven," "Lenore" and " 'Annabel*lee*.' " From this house he went to school, first in Waverly Place, where his teacher was "a stout red-faced lady with grey hair and a large apron, the latter convenience somehow suggesting . . . that she viewed her little pupils as so many slices cut from the

Henry James's grandmother's home, third house from the right,
19 Washington Square North.

loaf of life and on which she was to dab the butter of arithmetic
and spelling, accompanied by way of jam with a light applica-
tion of the practice of prize-giving." Later, when he went to
school on East 23rd Street, he took great pleasure in the walk
home past the "country-place," a big brown house on the northeast corner of 18th Street "in 'grounds' peopled with animal
life . . . two or three elegant little cows of refined form and
colour, two or three nibbling fawns and a larger company, above
all, of peacocks and guineafowl . . ."

During these years James also spent many hours at 19 Washington Square North in the "maternal parlours" of his grandmother Elizabeth Walsh. Here he absorbed the atmosphere he
would later re-create in *Washington Square.* James transformed
an anecdote told to him by the English actress Fanny Kemble
into a study of the interplay of wills between Dr. John Sloper and
his daughter, Catherine, and set it in the scene of his boyhood.

"The ideal of quiet and genteel retirement, in 1835," James wrote in the opening pages, "was found in Washington Square, where the Doctor built himself a handsome, modern, wide-fronted house, with a big balcony before the drawing-room windows, and a flight of marble steps ascending to a portal which was also faced with white marble. This structure, and so many of its neighbours, which it exactly resembled, were supposed . . . to embody the last results of architectural science, and they remain to this day very solid and honourable dwellings."

In later years when James revisited New York, he was to write that, after experiencing the congestion of uptown, getting back to Washington Square "was as if the wine of life had been poured for you, in advance, into some pleasant old punch-bowl . . . To come and go where East 11th Street, where West 10th opened their kind short arms was at least to keep clear of the awful hug of the serpent." Coming back to America in 1904 after an absence of twenty years, he found some points of reference in the midst of change. One was the home of Mary Cadwalader Jones at 21 East 11th Street, still very much as it must have been in James's time. Minnie Jones, as she was known, was a friend of James's from his youth and had been married to Edith Wharton's brother, though the two writers did not meet until 1888. Her house, where Brooks and Henry Adams, Theodore Roosevelt, Augustus Saint-Gaudens and John Singer Sargent often came to Sunday lunch, was known as something of a salon. On James's visit, he was given rooms on the first floor, where he stayed whenever his travels that year brought him back to New York.

Edith Wharton, like Henry James, is linked to Washington Square, although the two knew somewhat different sides of it. As Edith Wharton — Edith Jones before her marriage — was to become painfully aware, the writers and thinkers who found their way so frequently to the Jameses' house would have been out of place in the drawing rooms she frequented as a young woman. Years later she ruefully remarked, "I was a failure in Boston . . . because they thought I was too fashionable to be intelligent, and a failure in New York because they were afraid I was too intelligent to be fashionable." As Louis Auchincloss has observed: "The Jameses were more like the English Arnolds or Darwins, a deeply congenial family of inherited means and large ideas whose generations were united by a love of the arts and sciences. Young Henry was encouraged from the beginning to become a writer. Not so Edith Jones." Wharton belonged to a much more fashionable set.

She was able, however, to use the values and mores of her world as material for her art, and she described the concrete details of life in fashionable New York with incomparable vividness. The stories in *Old New York* trace society's uptown progress. In "False Dawn," subtitled "The 'Forties," the Raycie family has a town house in Canal Street and a country house on the Sound, as the upper portion of the East River was then called. By the 1850s, the period in which "The Old Maid" takes place, society has progressed several miles uptown. Delia Lovell, whose parents' house is in Mercer Street, marries James Ralston and goes to live in Gramercy Park. By "New Year's Day (the 'Seventies)" the residential area has reached 31st Street.

Edith Wharton's family's geography closely parallels that of her stories. Her grandparents and aunt lived in Mercer Street and when her parents were married they set up a house in Gramercy Park, "then just within the built-on limits of New York." By the time Edith was born in 1862 they were living on 23rd Street. Despite the northward movement of younger generations, the older patriarchs stayed in Washington Square and so, in a sense, old New York society remained grounded there. (Their

Edith Wharton: "too fashionable to be intelligent
. . . too intelligent to be fashionable."

tenacity in holding on to their houses was one of the factors
that enabled the Old Row on the north side of the Square to
remain uninterruptedly aristocratic; some of the houses were
kept by the original families until 1935 and 1936.) Thus the
spirit of Washington Square and its passing dominates Wharton's greatest novel, *The Age of Innocence,* even though it is

set in the 1870s. It is the values of the venerable old family homes in University Place and lower Fifth Avenue — " 'purest 1830,' with a grim harmony of cabbage-rose-garlanded carpets, rosewood consoles, round-arched fireplaces with black marble mantels and immense glazed book-cases of mahogany" — that are the central concern of the book. Although Wharton was to live in Washington Square only a short time (when she returned from Europe in 1882 after her father's death), the fashionable society it symbolized was her artistic territory.

•

In the second half of the nineteenth century, when New England dominated the national literary scene, only a few writers were connected with the Village. In the sixties a tavern named Pfaff's at 653 Broadway became a center for those associated with the *Saturday Press,* New York's liveliest and most important literary publication. The *Press* printed Whitman's poetry, then considered unpublishable elsewhere, and introduced Mark Twain to readers with "The Jumping Frog of Calaveras County," later the title story in his first book. William Dean Howells had also appeared in the *Press*'s pages, and when he came to New York looking for a job he stopped by Pfaff's to meet Whitman. The group associated with the magazine was considered bohemian because, as Howells wrote, it was violently opposed to "all existing forms of respectability." Emerson was introduced to the Pfaff's crowd by Whitman and found them "noisy and rowdy firemen."

A few other writers were scattered here and there. Melville, his literary career virtually over, had returned from Massachusetts in 1866 and was working as a customs inspector on the piers near Gansevoort Street. In 1870 Bret Harte came east and stayed at his sister's home at 16 Fifth Avenue. Around 1875 he took an apartment at 713 Broadway.

Mark Twain at the billiard table, where he spent
many hours while living at 21 Fifth Avenue.

In 1900, at the height of his popularity, Mark Twain came to live in New York and chose the still fashionable precincts of Washington Square. The Clemens family spent the winter in a furnished house at 14 West 10th Street, which suddenly became one of the most "conspicuous" residences in New York. Clemens's daughter Clara recalled: "One could never begin to describe in words the atmosphere of adulation that swept across the threshold. Every day was like some great festive occasion. One felt that a large party was going on and that by and by the guests would be leaving. But there was no leaving. More and more came." The following year Clemens moved his family to Riverdale, where his wife became seriously ill. After her death in 1904 he again returned to the Village, this time to a house at 21 Fifth Avenue designed by James Renwick, Jr., the architect of St. Patrick's Cathedral and Grace Church.

Clemens spent most of his days lying in a huge Italian carved bed — pillows placed at the foot so that he could enjoy the ornate headboard — receiving visitors, dictating and smoking eternally. Each evening he had his secretary play for him on the Aeolian Orchestrelle, an immense player organ that performed sixty selections of classical music. During this time he worked on *The Mysterious Stranger* and *2,000 Years Among the Microbes*. In 1906 Clemens accepted Albert Bigelow Paine's suggestion that the latter become his biographer. Paine moved in, acting as companion and editor as well as the stimulus for Clemens's intensified autobiographical dictations.

William Dean Howells, who was living in New York at this time, recalled Clemens's residence on Fifth Avenue as the period of "his efflorescence in white serge." Howells noted in *My Mark Twain:* "Until he imagined the suit of white serge, he wore always a suit of black serge, truly deplorable in the cut of the sagging frock ... But the white serge was an inspiration which few men would have had the courage to act upon." Clemens loved to walk up and down Fifth Avenue, glorying in the recognition of the crowds. When John Dos Passos was just a boy, his father introduced him to Clemens on Fifth Avenue one day. "But all I remember," Dos Passos wrote, "was his flowing hair and white suit, which seemed incongruous on such a cold day, and the fact that his name wasn't really Mark Twain at all."

Clemens's last two years at the Fifth Avenue house were primarily played out at a billiard table he had received for Christmas in 1906. The table displaced his bed, which was moved into the study, and Clemens enlisted Paine in long sessions, often lasting into the early morning hours. In 1908 Clemens moved to Redding, Connecticut, where he died in April of 1910. His body was placed on view at the Brick Presbyterian Church, then on Fifth Avenue and 37th Street. Van Wyck Brooks, who had never seen him alive, was one of the viewers and remembered Clemens "with his white hair spread loose, dressed for the last time in his white flannels."

The Birth of Bohemia

Mark Twain was the last in the gentlemanly tradition of Washington Square. By the turn of the century Greenwich Village, as a symbol of the artists' bohemia, had begun to take shape. In the early 1900s it would become what Max Eastman, editor of the *Masses,* called "a self-conscious entity, an American Bohemia or Gipsy-minded Latin Quarter." For most of the nineteenth century the neighborhood, known as the "American Ward" for its lack of immigrants, had remained undisturbed by the classic progression of city development from residential area to business district to slum. But in the 1890s tenements began to creep toward the center of the Village. The area south of Washington Square had been predominantly Negro during the

nineteenth century* but in the 1890s and 1900s the Negroes
were supplanted by Italians as the old houses were replaced with
six- and seven-story stacks of railroad flats. Simultaneously, tenements spread from the waterfront through the old West Village.

The pattern of migration of young artists, writers and political rebels followed the decline in real estate values; they settled
in the western and southern sections of Greenwich Village.
One of the most desirable locations was the south side of
Washington Square, where the once elegant brick homes, affected by the pressure of the tenements at their backs, had been
converted into rooming houses. (The houses on the north side,
buffered by the park, remained private homes.) In the prewar
period the center of Village literary life was Washington Square
South and MacDougal Street.

"Of all the ambitions of the Great Unpublished, the one that
is strongest, the most abiding, is the ambition to get to New
York," Frank Norris wrote in *Blix*. "For these, New York is the
point de départ, the pedestal, the niche, the indispensable vantage ground." Writers came to New York, which had become
the country's publishing center, to find publishers for their
work; editors and publishers looked to the West for talent to
staff their newspapers and magazines. Norris was a case in point.
S. S. McClure had discovered his work in a San Francisco literary
magazine and asked him to come to New York to write for
McClure's Magazine. Norris arrived in 1898, first living on 33rd
Street and later settling in the Village. He took a small front
bedroom at 61 Washington Square,† where his San Francisco

---

* In 1865 one fourth of the city's black population concentrated in the area
around Bleecker, Sullivan, Thompson and MacDougal streets, which was
known as "Little Africa." The first Negro newspaper in the country, *Freedom
Journal,* was published here in 1827, and the first Negro theater, the African
Grove, opened on Mercer Street in 1821. Whites were segregated into the back
seats because, according to a handbill, they "do not know how to conduct
themselves at entertainments for ladies and gentlemen of color."

† Sixty-one Washington Square was known as Mme. Katharine Branchard's

friend Gelett Burgess had stayed, and ate his meals at the Judson Hotel at 63 Washington Square.

Edwin Arlington Robinson had moved to New York from Maine in 1899. After several years in Chelsea, he took a room in the Judson Hotel in 1906. President Roosevelt had gotten him a sinecure in the U.S. Customs House and he slept late each day, appearing at his office in the afternoon, if at all. When Roosevelt left the White House in 1909, Robinson found himself out of a job. Fortunately, he almost immediately acquired another patron, Mrs. Clara Potter Davidge, who built a studio for him behind her house at 121 Washington Place. He moved there in December 1909 and stayed off and on for several years. From 1913 to 1922 he lived in other parts of the city. Then, temporarily lacking a place to stay, he knocked at the door of his friends James and Laura Fraser at 28 West 8th Street (Fraser, a sculptor, designed the buffalo nickel); they not only gave him a room for the night but asked him to stay permanently in the skylighted studio on the top floor of their house. Here Robinson wrote his most popular work, *Tristram*.

Next to arrive, also brought by McClure, who had discovered her teaching school in Pittsburgh, was Willa Cather. In 1906 she took a studio at 60 Washington Square, where Edith Lewis, who was to be her lifetime friend, also had a room. "In 1906," Lewis wrote in her biography, *Willa Cather Living,* "Washington Square was one of the most charming places in New York. On the north side the long row of houses of rose-red brick, residences of aristocratic old New York families, gave it an aura of gentility and dignity. On the south side, writers and artists

---

"House of Genius" because, in addition to Norris, Stephen Crane, Theodore Dreiser, O. Henry, Eugene O'Neill, John Reed, Lincoln Steffens, Willa Cather, John Dos Passos and Allan Seeger were said to have lived there. There is no evidence, however, that any of these writers did, with the exception of Seeger and Norris. Cather, Reed, O'Neill, Steffens and Dos Passos lived on the Square, but at different addresses.

lived. But it was a very sedate Bohemia; most of the artists were poor and hard-working." During her first years in the city, Cather became managing editor of *McClure's,* but eventually she left to devote all her time to writing. Years later she drew on her days in Washington Square for her story "Coming, Aphrodite!" which deals with the relationship between a painter who has a big room on the top floor of an old house on the Square and a young woman who comes to live in the rooms next to his. Cather was here for two years before moving to the six-story apartment house at 82 Washington Place and finally to her long-time Village residence at 5 Bank Street in 1913.

In 1911, John Reed, a young Harvard graduate, came to live in an apartment at 42 Washington Square South with several classmates. Handsome and high-spirited, Reed rapidly became a central Village figure. He plunged zestfully into his new life, which he described in a poem called "Forty-Two Washington Square":

> But nobody questions your morals,
> And nobody asks for the rent —
> There's no one to pry if we're tight, you and I,
> Or demand how our evenings are spent.
> The furniture's ancient but plenty,
> The linen is spotless and fair,
> O life is a joy to a broth of a boy
> At Forty-two Washington Square!

Reed dedicated this bit of doggerel to Lincoln Steffens, who had found him a job on the *American Magazine.* Steffens had been a friend of Reed's father, who had asked him to keep an eye on his son, an occupation from which the veteran muckraker derived much pleasure. In 1912, after his wife died, Steffens went to live at 42 Washington Square in the room below Jack Reed's. "I used to go early to bed and to sleep," he wrote, "but I liked it when Jack, a big, growing, happy being, would slam into my room and wake me up to tell me about the 'most wonderful thing in the world' that he had seen, been, or done that night. Girls, plays, bums, I.W.W.'s, strikers — each experience was vivid in him . . ."

One night in 1913, in a Village apartment, John Reed heard the I.W.W. leader Bill Haywood describe the plight of silk weavers striking for an eight-hour day in Paterson, New Jersey. One of them had been killed by the police but the press had refused to cover the strike. Mabel Dodge, who had a brief but memorable salon in 1913 at 23 Fifth Avenue, was present and suggested, "Why don't you hire a great hall and re-enact the strike over here?" John Reed sprang up and said, "I'll do it!" And he did. The strike — killing, funeral, graveside speeches by Haywood and Elizabeth Gurley Flynn — was re-enacted by a thousand people on the stage of Madison Square Garden. Thus began the radicalization of John Reed and his affair with Mabel Dodge. The affair was relatively short-lived but the radicalization was to last until his early death in Moscow in 1920.

Mabel Dodge had come to New York after a sojourn in Florence and made the acquaintance of a number of talented New Yorkers, including Jo Davidson, Carl Van Vechten, Lincoln Steffens, Hutchins Hapgood and Walter Lippmann. Soon they were visiting frequently and bringing others. The salon that developed was very much a collaboration between Mabel Dodge and her friends. She credited Steffens with the idea that she set aside a particular evening for her callers, and Lippmann with the suggestion that each evening be organized around a theme. She provided the setting; her apartment was decorated with white paper-covered walls and windows draped with white linen. In the front room a white bearskin rug lay before a white marble fireplace, and a large porcelain chandelier covered with colorful birds and flowers hung from the ceiling. Against the white background, she placed gray French chairs and chaises

John Reed, left, before leaving to cover the First World War, with
Fannie Hurst and Boardman Robinson in Washington Square Park.

upholstered in light gray blues and pale yellows. On her "evenings," according to Steffens,

> she sat quietly in a great armchair and rarely said a word: her
> guests did the talking, and with such a variety of guests, her
> success was amazing . . . Her secret, I think, was to start the
> talk going with a living theme. She would seize a time when
> there was an I.W.W. strike to invite, say, Bill Haywood es-
> pecially. He would sit or stand near her and strike out, in the
> hot, harsh spirit of his organization, some challenging idea,
> answer brutally a few questions, and — that evening every-
> body talked I.W.W. Emma Goldman said something about
> anarchism one evening when the anarchists were in the news,
> and that night we discussed anarchism. It was there and thus
> that some of us first heard of psychoanalysis and the new
> psychology of Freud and Jung . . .

The affair between Mabel Dodge and John Reed dissolved
toward the end of 1913, and with it the salon. Reed's story,
"War in Paterson," which only the *Masses* would publish, led
the *Metropolitan* to send him to Mexico to cover the uprising of
Pancho Villa, and the dispatches he sent back established him,
at the age of twenty-seven, as the country's leading war cor-
respondent. Next he went to Europe to cover the beginning of
the First World War. His interviews with French soldiers convinced him that the war was a clash between "traders," not a
struggle for democracy and liberty. Each of the dispatches he
sent the *Masses* ended with the words "This is not our war." On
a trip home to Oregon in 1915, Reed met a young woman named
Louise Bryant and brought her to live with him at Washington
Square.

·

As the new Villagers arrived in the area around Washington
Square South, the stage was set for the development of several
institutions that would influence American culture. Two strains

WHEN LIFE IS VERY STRENUOUS AND SPIRITS ARE WAY DOWN,
YOU'D BETTER GO TO POLLY'S IN LITTLE GREENWICH TOWN
FOR THERE THE CLANS ARE GATHERED - ITS THERE YOU'L FIND 'EM ALL
THE ARTISTS AND THE WRITERS RANGED ALONG THE WALL,
MISS POLLY TAKES THE MONEY AND MIKE SAYS HE JUST CAN'T
WAIT ANY FASTER ON THE FOLKS IN POLLY'S RES-TAU-RANT
J.T.B.

GREENWICH VILLAGE - NEW YORK

JESSIE TARBOX BEALS

Polly's Restaurant at 137 MacDougal Street, downstairs from the
Liberal Club and next door to the Washington Square Book Shop.

— the political and the artistic — were present from the beginning. The Liberal Club was organized in the early teens as "A
Meeting Place for Those Interested in New Ideas," in rooms on
the second floor of a house at 137 MacDougal Street — two large
parlors and a sunroom with high ceilings, fireplaces, mahogany
doors and cubist and futurist art on the walls. Conveniently
located downstairs was Polly's, a restaurant run by Paula Holliday with Hippolyte Havel as cook and waiter. Havel was an
anarchist who was fond of calling the patrons "Bourgeois pigs!"
The Liberal Club, with Polly's, was important not for anything
it did, but because it provided a gathering place for the exchange
of ideas. Among those who frequented it were Theodore
Dreiser, Upton Sinclair, Vachel Lindsay, Lincoln Steffens, Sin-

clair Lewis, Sherwood Anderson, Louis Untermeyer and Max Eastman.

Next to develop was the *Masses,* a magazine organized in 1911 by an anarchist named Piet Vlag. Vlag apparently conceived the endeavor as an artists' and writers' cooperative, but he quickly tired of his role as amateur editor and publisher and left the magazine, without funds, in the hands of its contributors, a group that included the painter John Sloan and his wife, Dolly, Louis Untermeyer and the artist Art Young. They in turn decided that Max Eastman, a young man from Elmira, New York, who was teaching philosophy at Columbia, would be the ideal editor and fund-raiser. They sent him a note in Connecticut, where he was spending the summer, saying, "You are elected editor of the *Masses.* No pay."

Under Eastman, the *Masses* became an invigorating mixture of politics, art, literature and humor. The magazine generally defended all causes on the left but was open to a wide range of socialist opinion rather than committed to one point of view, a policy that eventually led to serious disagreement among the contributors. In literature and criticism it published the early work of Untermeyer, Carl Sandburg, Harry Kemp, Randolph Bourne and William Rose Benét. The text was broken by political drawings and cartoons, and several professional humorists were prominent among the contributors. The artists were represented by Sloan, Young and Glenn O. Coleman, and the political thinkers by Reed, Eastman and a young poet named Floyd Dell. Dell, who later became managing editor, listed the magazine's causes as "Fun, Truth, Beauty, Realism, Peace, Feminism, and Revolution."

The *Masses* quickly became a focus of Village intellectual life, both at its offices at 91 Greenwich Avenue and at the monthly meetings held in the roomy studios of Sloan or Young, where contributors met to vote on material that had been submitted for publication. "We had a custom," said Eastman "of inviting our friends to these meetings — a good part of New York's intelligentsia turned up at one time or another — and we always urged them to join the voting." The crowd included everyone from John Reed to Hippolyte Havel, who would protest that voting was bourgeois. "Voting! . . . Poetry is something from the soul! You can't vote on poetry!" The crowd's fund-raising costume balls, held at Webster Hall on 11th Street near Third Avenue, became a Village tradition.

The playful atmosphere around the *Masses* darkened as the country became increasingly involved in the First World War and the magazine became a spearhead for the resistance to it. In the summer of 1917 the *Masses* lost its mailing privileges, which deprived it of its subscription income; simultaneously its large contributors withdrew their financial support. In November the Department of Justice charged Eastman, Reed, Dell and several others with "conspiracy against the government" and "interfering with enlistment," and the magazine closed its offices.

Two trials were held, one in April and one in October of 1918. Both resulted in hung juries. John Reed, who had been covering the Russian revolution, returned to stand trial with the others. He and Louise Bryant took an apartment in Patchin Place and he wrote the articles that comprised *Ten Days That Shook the World* in an upstairs room at Polly Holliday's new restaurant at 147 West 4th Street.

In order to publish Reed's articles, Eastman started a new magazine, the *Liberator,* at 138 West 13th Street. He continued to print art and writing by those connected with the *Masses* and added the work of Edna St. Vincent Millay, William Carlos Williams, Elinor Wylie, E. E. Cummings, John Dos Passos and Ernest Hemingway. Where the *Masses* had been fascinated by the "Russian experiment" as only one facet of its interest in socialism, the *Liberator* became more fully committed to the

Communist line. In 1922 Eastman resigned because of political disagreements, and left the magazine in the hands of Michael Gold. It merged in 1924 with two smaller magazines and became a Communist party organ.

·

Many of those involved in the Liberal Club and the *Masses* were also involved in the formation of the Provincetown Players, which, through its connection with Eugene O'Neill, was to be responsible for changing playwrighting in America. "Before O'Neill, the United States had theater," wrote one magazine. "After O'Neill, it had drama."

Eugene O'Neill had arrived in the Village in 1915 and lived in a room he called "the garbage flat" at 38 Washington Square. He wrote six or seven hours a day and spent his evenings at the Golden Swan, a saloon at the corner of Sixth Avenue and 4th Street, popularly known as the Hell Hole. The saloon had a mixed crowd — thugs, writers, artists, coachmen and streetwalkers — and a proprietor named Tom Wallace, who, it was said, had never ventured outside in twenty years. Here O'Neill met Hippolyte Havel and another anarchist named Terry Karlin. Years later the playwright used the Hell Hole and the people he knew there in *The Iceman Cometh*. Harry Hope, the fictional saloon's owner, is modeled on Wallace; Larry Slade is based on Karlin; and Hugo Kalmar bears a strong resemblance to Havel. The philosophy of the play, perhaps learned in his Hell Hole days, is, in O'Neill's words, "that there is always one dream left, one final dream, no matter how low you have fallen, down there at the bottom of the bottle. I know because I saw it."

In the summer of 1916 O'Neill went off to Provincetown with Terry Karlin. The previous year a group of Villagers vacationing there had started a summer theater led by a Chicagoan named George Cram "Jig" Cook. Cook met Karlin one day

The Provincetown Playhouse, 133 MacDougal Street, around 1920.

and asked him if he had any plays. He said he hadn't but that
O'Neill had a trunkful. The production that season of O'Neill's
Bound East for Cardiff was such a success that it inspired John
Reed to broach the idea of continuing the theater during the
winter. A constitution was drawn up, Jig Cook was elected
president and the Provincetown Players was born. Back in the
Village, Cook opened the theater on the parlor floor of a house
at 139 MacDougal Street, next door to Polly's first restaurant
and the Liberal Club. The following year the players moved to
larger quarters nearby at 133 MacDougal, where they were to
remain for ten years. During the summer O'Neill had fallen in
love with Louise Bryant and in the fall he took a room at 42

Washington Square to be near her. (Jack Reed was then ill in the Johns Hopkins Hospital in Baltimore.) The affair formed the basis for *Strange Interlude*.

The actors and writers in the Provincetown Players gathered in a number of homes, restaurants and taverns. In addition to the Cooks' on Milligan Place, they met at the home of James and Susan Light (he was an actor, director and stage manager of the Provincetown) at 86 Greenwich Avenue, called Maison Clemenceau because the French statesman had once lived there. The Lights had a seven-room apartment and at various times rented rooms to Matthew Josephson, Djuna Barnes and Kenneth Burke. Other meeting places included Polly's; the Hell Hole; a speakeasy called the Black Knight, across the street from the playhouse and Luke O'Connor's, better known as the Working Girls' Home, at the corner of Christopher and Greenwich. (John Masefield had worked there as a janitor in 1895.) A series of tearooms, primarily operated for tourists, began to flourish during Prohibition but the only one frequented by authentic Villagers was Romany Marie's, on the southeast corner of Thompson and Washington Square South. (In 1929 Romany Marie moved to a spot on the site of 40 West 8th Street and Buckminster Fuller decorated her new restaurant. In return, she said he could eat one meal a day there for the rest of his life.) The only tearoom or saloon to survive from this era is the Jumble Shop, at 176 MacDougal Street, in recent years renamed Shakespeare's.

When the Villagers were feeling flush, they patronized two other establishments that were to play host to literary New Yorkers for several decades. Special occasions were celebrated at the Brevoort Hotel, on the northeast corner of Fifth Avenue and 8th Street, diagonally across from the site of Henry Brevoort's home, where Washington Irving had often visited. There was a basement café, reminiscent of those in Paris, divided into small rooms with mirrored partitions and marble-topped tables. Steffens, O'Neill, Edna St. Vincent Millay, Isadora Duncan, Dreiser, Lippmann, Reed, Dodge and Eastman could often be found here in the early days. John Dos Passos wrote to a friend about sitting at the table next to Emma Goldman's in 1917: "It was wonderful," he said. "She's a Bronxy fattish little old woman who looks like a rather good cook. She has a charmingly munchy fashion of eating sandwiches and pats her myrmidons on the head and kisses them in a motherly fashion."

The Lafayette Hotel, on the southeast corner of University Place and 9th Street, also had a European-style café with marble tables and newspapers on racks. Villagers came here for more informal occasions to drink and talk. Although, according to Matthew Josephson, the drinks were bad and cost twice as much as anyplace else and the waiters were surly, the Lafayette was the unrivaled meeting place of high bohemia during the twenties.

As new people arrived in the Village, they in turn created their own institutions, particularly a spate of "little magazines" that explored new ground in poetry and fiction. Next door to Polly's and the Liberal Club was Albert and Charles Boni's Washington Square Book Shop, which would serve as a seedbed for American publishing with the founding of Boni and Liveright and the Modern Library. In 1913 the Bonis agreed to finance a publication edited by Alfred Kreymborg, soon to become a perennial founder of little magazines. The magazine was called *Glebe,* an Old English word meaning "soil" or "field." Each issue was to be devoted to one person's work — "one-man shows on an intimate scale" said Kreymborg. After six issues Kreymborg resigned when the Bonis pressured him to include translations of European work. Undaunted, he started another magazine called *Others.* The contributors began gathering every Sunday at Kreymborg's home in Grantwood, New Jersey, but in the fall of 1915 he moved to Bank Street and the meetings

continued there. Among the regulars were Maxwell Bodenheim, William Carlos Williams, Wallace Stevens and Marianne
Moore.

In 1917 the *Little Review*, which had begun publication in
Chicago, joined *Others* in New York. The editor was a volatile
and inventive original named Margaret Anderson, who had
camped out on the shore of Lake Michigan when she had no
house, lived in an apartment furnished only with a grand piano
when she had no furniture and kept the *Little Review* going by
ingenuity when it had no financial support. She arrived in New
York with Jane Heap, the assistant editor, who always spelled
her name lower case, and found a basement studio at 31 West
14th Street to use as an office. She and Jane lived at 24 West
16th Street in the house that had once belonged to William
Cullen Bryant. "We bought gold Chinese paper at a Japanese
paper shop, in long oblong strips," she wrote. "Papering the
walls with these required Chinese patience, as they were disposed to tear under the most delicate touch. The woodwork
was pale cream, the floor dark plum, the furniture old mahogany. The feature of the room was a large divan hung from the
ceiling by heavy black chains. It was covered with dull-toned
blue and on it were four silk cushions — emerald green, ma-
genta, royal purple, tilleul . . . Here the poets, writers, painters came to see us . . ." Among those who came was Hart
Crane, who was living in a room on the top floor of the same
house, and Djuna Barnes, whose *A Night Among the Horses*
had been published in the magazine.

While in Chicago, the *Little Review* was devoted primarily to
criticism, but in New York it turned to experimental fiction and
poetry. The printing of Joyce's *Ulysses* in installments from
1918 through 1920 — its first publication anywhere — was possibly the magazine's most significant achievement. The editors
were convicted of obscenity and fined $100.

The last important Village magazine of the prewar period was *Seven Arts*. The magazine owed its existence, at least indirectly, to the burgeoning influence of psychoanalysis; the editor, James Oppenheim, and the patron, Mrs. A. K. Rankine, were both patients of an analyst who suggested it as a therapeutic project. With Waldo Frank and Van Wyck Brooks as associate editors, the magazine published Sherwood Anderson's *Winesburg* stories, Eugene O'Neill's first short story, "Tomorrow," and the work of many other fine writers, including D. H. Lawrence, S. N. Behrman, Robert Frost, Carl Sandburg, Amy Lowell, Stephen Vincent Benét and John Dos Passos. The magazine lasted only a year; Oppenheim's violent opposition to America's participation in the war caused the sponsor to withdraw her support.

·

In addition to providing a community for poets, editors, dramatists and political intellectuals, the prewar Village was home to two major twentieth-century novelists. Although Willa Cather and Theodore Dreiser were not recluses, they spent their working time in solitude and were not involved in the communal activities that occupied many of the early Villagers. In 1913 Cather had moved from Washington Place to 5 Bank Street, where she would write six novels, including *My Antonia*. The apartment, which she took with Edith Lewis, was seven high-ceilinged rooms on the second floor of a large brick house. (In later years, she also rented the apartment above, keeping it empty so that she would not be disturbed by noise.) The front three rooms were used as one huge living room. "At auction rooms on University Place," Edith Lewis recalls in her biography of Cather, "we bought mahogany chests and a round mahogany dining-room table for a few dollars. Among our possessions were a number of large oriental rugs; and we got some comfortable chairs." In the living room there were low open bookshelves and, over the mantel, a "large etching by Couture of George Sand — not because she [Cather] particularly admired George Sand, but because she liked the etching."

Visitors remember that there was always the scent of flowers at 5 Bank Street: in winter, the smell of orange blossoms, camellias, violets, freesias; in spring, jonquils, narcissuses, lilacs and dogwood. Each day Cather followed the same routine. Early in the morning she did the shopping at nearby Jefferson Market, hunting for red raspberries or perfect leaf lettuce, to be served with a dressing of olive oil, wine vinegar and tarragon. Then she went home to do her stint of work before the French maid came in to fix lunch.

In 1917 Cather began a Bank Street tradition of Fridays at home. People dropped in for tea but seldom were they the people involved in the *Masses,* the Provincetown Players or any of the little magazines. Cather was more allied to the older set associated with *McClure's,* and even refused to see the Provincetown's productions of O'Neill's plays. Nevertheless the Friday afternoons were popular, "so popular, in fact," writes Edith Lewis, "that eventually she had to give them up; instead of half-a-dozen or so of her friends dropping in for tea, it became at last too much of a responsibility." Among the literary people who visited were the D. H. Lawrences, who came in 1924 after having spent the summer in Ceylon. Edith Lewis remembers Lawrence imitating "the sounds the leopards made, when they leaped on the roof of the bungalow at night, hunting for mice in the thatch." In 1927, 5 Bank Street was demolished when the Seventh Avenue subway was built. Willa Cather and Edith Lewis moved to the Grosvenor Hotel at 35 Fifth Avenue, where they lived for five years before going uptown to 570 Park Avenue.

While Cather was pioneering the literature of the mid-

Willa Cather in the early 1930s.

western prairie, Dreiser was breaking other ground. He had first come to live in New York in 1895, when he stayed at the Mills Hotel (now the Greenwich Hotel) on Bleecker Street, paying twenty-five cents a night for a bed. By 1897 he was earning enough from writing popular magazine stories to move to the Salmagundi Club at 14 West 12th Street and then to his own apartment at 232 West 15th. Dreiser had grown up in rural Indiana, and the city—first Chicago, then St. Louis and Pittsburgh and finally New York — had a tremendous impact on him. With *Sister Carrie,* published in 1900, he created the "city novel," announcing the themes — alienation, the breakdown of tradition, the impact of mechanization, materialism, the conflict between the artist and society — that would occupy twentieth-century novelists from Dos Passos and Wolfe to the social realists of the forties. The city would be seen as a powerful force, sometimes as protagonist, as in Dos Passos's *Manhattan Transfer,* but usually as a disillusioning and destructive antagonist. And New York, in which all the qualities of urban life were writ large, was the ultimate city. Here even a world traveler as sophisticated as Howells felt the impact of the city anew, and Dreiser observed that not even Chicago had prepared him for Manhattan. "The thing that interested me . . . about New York," he wrote in *Color of a Great City,* ". . . was the sharp, and at the same time immense, contrast it showed between the dull and the shrewd, the strong and the weak, the rich and the poor, the wise and the ignorant."

But Dreiser did more than introduce a new subject. As Dos Passos was to remark, "the ponderous battering ram of his novels opened the way through the genteel reticences of American fiction." Not that the struggle was easy: *Sister Carrie* had been accepted for publication at Doubleday, Page and Company by Frank Norris and other editors there while Frank N. Doubleday and his wife were abroad. When they read the galleys, the Doubledays were horrified by Dreiser's realism and tried to get out of publishing the book. Dreiser forced them to proceed, only to find that critics branded the book immoral, bookstores refused to handle it and his friends slighted him on the street.

Dreiser was to have similar problems with *The "Genius,"* a book he finished while living at 165 West 10th Street. The autobiographically inspired novel tells the story of Eugene Witla, a painter who comes from Chicago to live in the area around Washington Square. Dreiser hired Floyd Dell to help him edit the book. Dell took large chunks of manuscript home and penciled out what he thought could be eliminated, only to find Dreiser, "with a large eraser, rescuing from oblivion such pages, paragraphs and sentences as he felt could not be spared." Again it was what Dreiser chose unflinchingly to include — his hero's infidelities and multiple sexual alliances — that got him into trouble. After the book was published in 1915, John S. Sumner, the head of the Society for the Suppression of Vice who later brought charges against the *Little Review* for its publication of *Ulysses,* threatened to arrest any bookdealer who dared to sell *The "Genius."* Despite the efforts of Mencken and other writers, the publisher withdrew the novel for ten years.

During his years in the Village, Dreiser kept to himself and spent little time in neighborhood haunts, with the occasional exception of Polly Holliday's. His few friends, among them Hutchins Hapgood and Waldo Frank, knew that he worked from nine to four and was not to be disturbed. In 1915 Dreiser and Kirah Markham, an actress he was living with at the time, announced that they would be "at home" on Sunday evenings between November and March. Friends, including Mencken when he was in town, came to listen to phonograph records and play the Ouija board. Once, at a special party in his honor, Edgar Lee Masters read from *Spoon River.*

In 1922, after three years in Los Angeles, Dreiser came back to the Village and rented the parlor floor at 16 St. Luke's Place.

Theodore Dreiser at 16 St. Luke's Place. The desk at rear was
made from his brother's piano.

This, like his other apartments, was furnished simply, except for
the desk he had made from his brother's piano. Sherwood
Anderson lived two doors away, at 12 St. Luke's Place. He
wrote:

> I decided I would go and call upon Dreiser . . . I went up the
> stairs and there was his name, on a little white card, and there
> was a bell to punch. My fingers trembled above the bell but
> I did not ring it. I turned and hurried away. "But how do I
> know he will want to see me?" I asked myself. To me he was

and has always remained a great man, one of the few really great ones of America. "He may be at work on a book," I said to myself. On several occasions I climbed the several steps to his door, my finger hovered over the bell but I did not ring it. And then, one morning, I did . . . And then the door opened and there he was . . .

"I am Sherwood Anderson. I thought I would come to see you."

"Oh, hello," he said. He shut the door in my face.

So there I was on the Dreiser's doorstep, facing the blank door. I was shocked. Then I was furious.

"The beast," I said. "The son of a bitch" . . .

I went along a street, muttering this against the Dreiser. I went into a saloon and had drinks. I got half drunk. And then later in the day, I went home to my apartment and there was a note from him. The man had simply been embarrassed, as I was, when we stood facing each other . . ."

In September 1923, Dreiser moved to 118 West 11th Street, one of the houses in Rhinelander Gardens, a once elegant row with a New Orleans-style ironwork balcony. Here he wrote *An American Tragedy*. Its great success enabled him to move uptown to 200 West 57th Street, his last New York address.

The Lost Generation

Around 1916 and 1917 a new younger crop of men and women, members of what Gertrude Stein was to characterize as the Lost Generation, began arriving in the Village. In the vanguard were Hart Crane, Edmund Wilson, Matthew Josephson and E. E. Cummings. Wilson and Cummings left in April 1917 for the war in France. When they returned, many others came with them. "After college and the war," Malcolm Cowley wrote in *Exile's Return*, "most of us drifted to Manhattan, to the crooked streets south of Fourteenth, where you could

rent a furnished hall-bedroom for two or three dollars weekly
or the top floor of a rickety house for 30 dollars a month . . .
We came because living was cheap, because friends of ours had
come already . . . because it seemed that New York was the
only city where a young writer could be published." Around
1919 and '20 the ranks were swelled by Cowley, Mark Van
Doren and William Slater Brown. But in 1921 many of the
writers, disillusioned with the situation of the artist in America,
exiled themselves to Europe. The Village chapter of this
group (the more famous exiles — Hemingway, Pound, Eliot,
Stein — were not associated with the Village) included Cowley,
Cummings, Josephson and Dos Passos. Their "exile" was
short-lived, however — they found European artists and intellectuals more defeated and demoralized than those at home —
and all of them were back in the Village by 1923.

Village literary life in the twenties was dominated by critics
and poets. Many of the Lost Generation's Greenwich Village
branch were to become "literary men," perhaps producing
a play, a few short stories, some poetry or even a novel, but
ultimately establishing their reputations as critics or editors.

Among the poets were Marianne Moore, Edna St. Vincent
Millay, Hart Crane and E. E. Cummings. Moore, one of the
central members of the *Others* crowd, had moved to the Village
from New Jersey in 1918. She and her mother took a ground-
floor apartment at 14 St. Luke's Place, across the street from
the Hudson Park branch of the New York Public Library,
where she worked from 1921 to 1925. Moore is most familiar
to us with her gray hair and three-cornered hat, but William
Carlos Williams described how she looked as a young woman:
"Marianne had two cords, cables rather, of red hair coiled
around her rather small cranium . . . and was straight up
and down like the two-by-fours of a building under construction." Alfred Kreymborg said that she was "an astonishing per-

son with Titian hair, a brilliant complexion and a mellifluous flow of polysyllables which held every man in awe." She was famous for knowing about everything, but Kreymborg once proposed to Williams that he could stump her. He took her to a Cubs and Giants game at the Polo Grounds (before her interest in baseball was known) and was stupefied to find that she knew all about Christy Mathewson.

Moore was the first of the *Others* group to be published in the *Dial*, the most important cultural magazine of the twenties. At first her poems were rejected. Then, she recalled, "Lola Ridge had a party . . . and much to my disgust, we were induced to read something we had written. And Scofield Thayer said of my piece, 'Would you send that to us at the *Dial?*'

" 'I did send it,' I said.

"And he said, 'Well, send it again.' "

In 1924 Marianne Moore received the Dial Award and in 1925 she became editor of the magazine.

Edna St. Vincent Millay had been known around the Village since 1912, when her poem "Renascence" was published in an anthology of the best poetry of that year. In 1917, after four years at Vassar, Millay arrived in person, intending to support herself by working as an actress. After a brief and discouraging experience with the Theatre Guild, she got a part in Floyd Dell's "The Angel Intrudes" at the Provincetown Playhouse. Dell helped her and her sister Norma find an unheated room with a fireplace at 139 Waverly Place. "She lived in that gay poverty," he wrote, "which is traditional of the village, and one may find vivid reminiscences of that life in her poetry." In the spring of 1918 Millay and her sister moved to a charming brick house at 25 Charlton Street, where another sister and her mother joined them. For the next several years she was active in the Provincetown Players, acting in and directing her own *Aria da Capo* and *The Princess Marries the Page*.

During these years Millay acquired a legendary reputation in the Village. To begin with, she and her sisters were extremely beautiful. "One cannot really write about Edna Millay," Edmund Wilson commented, "without bringing to the foreground of the picture her intoxicating effect on people . . . She was one of those women whose features are not perfect and who in their moments of dimness may not seem even pretty, but who, excited by the blood or the spirit, become almost supernaturally beautiful. She was small, but her figure was full, though she did not appear plump. She had a lovely and very long throat that gave her the look of a muse, and her reading of her poetry was thrilling." She apparently rejected the double standard, as did many other women of her day, and reserved to herself the right to take lovers on her own terms. Finally, her poetry, as Wilson wrote, "was her real overmastering passion," to which she subordinated everything, including the men in her life.

It was through Wilson, who fell in love with Millay upon meeting her in 1920, that she gained her immense popularity. He was then working at *Vanity Fair* and brought her to the attention of his editor, Frank Crowninshield. The magazine began publishing a great deal of her poetry as well as satirical dialogues and sketches that she wrote under the pen name Nancy Boyd. During the same year, her volume *Figs and Thistles* appeared. The "First Fig," which begins, "My candle burns at both ends," became the motto of a generation.

In 1921 Millay went to Paris on assignment for *Vanity Fair*. She returned in 1923, the year she won a Pulitzer Prize, and married Eugen Boissevain. They lived for a short time at $75\frac{1}{2}$ Bedford Street before moving to Steepletop, the farm in Austerlitz, New York, where she spent the rest of her life.

One of the youngest members of the Lost Generation and yet the one longest connected with the Village was Hart

Crane, who arrived from Cleveland in 1916 and took a room at 139 East 15th Street. His first poem, "C 33" (the number of Oscar Wilde's cell in Reading Gaol), had been published the previous year, when Crane was only fifteen years old, in a precursor of the Village literary magazines called *Bruno's Bohemia*. In 1917 Crane was living in the Village proper, first in a six-dollars-a-week room at 54 West 10th Street, then at 25 East 11th Street. Both structures, in Crane's day cheap rooming houses, have been restored to their former elegance. Crane moved several times every year and never had a permanent address until he went to Brooklyn Heights in 1925. In 1919 he took a room on the top floor of the building where Margaret Anderson lived. Despite the fact that she was "never a great fan of his poetry," the *Little Review* did more than any other magazine to establish his reputation.

Late in 1919 Crane went home to Cleveland for four years. When he returned, he sublet a room he particularly liked in an old house at 45 Grove Street. There was a good writing table and no "inquisitive landlady always looking through the keyhole." When the original tenant returned, Crane moved to 15 Van Nest Place.

E. E. Cummings was in the Village briefly in 1917, living at 21 East 15th Street and working at P. F. Collier, a mail order book company. When the war began he joined the ambulance service in France. There he met William Slater Brown, who was later imprisoned because his letters did not pass the censor. Cummings refused to abandon him and was imprisoned also, an experience he described in *The Enormous Room*. (Brown is the "B" of the novel.) When they were released in January 1918, they shared an apartment at 11 Christopher Street until Cummings was drafted and stationed in Massachusetts for the remainder of the war. Then they took a top-floor studio at 9 West 14th Street. Cummings accompanied the Lost Generation to Europe in 1921 and when he returned in 1923 found a studio on the top floor of 4 Patchin Place.

According to John Dos Passos, Cummings was the "hub" of a group of literary friends from Harvard that included Dr. James Sibley Watson, Scofield Thayer and Stewart Mitchell of the *Dial* and Dos Passos when he was in town. Cummings was briefly married to Thayer's former wife, Elaine Orr, whom Dos Passos described as "the poet's dream." Dos Passos and Cummings sometimes lunched at a Syrian restaurant on Washington Street and then wandered through the Washington Market stalls or walked to the Aquarium at the Battery. After an afternoon of work they would meet for tea at Elaine's apartment at 3 Washington Square North. Usually other friends would appear and they would all go to their "Italian speakeasy of the moment — as I remember they were all named Maria's — for supper." Dos Passos continued: "After a couple of brandies on top of the wine Cummings would deliver himself of geysers of talk. I've never heard anything that remotely approached it. It was comical ironical learned brilliantlycolored intricatelycadenced damnably poetic and sometimes just naughty. It was as if he were spouting pages of prose and verse from an unwritten volume. Then suddenly he would go off to Patchin Place to put some of it down before the fountain ceased to flow."

Cummings and his third wife, Marion Morehouse, gradually acquired most of the house at 4 Patchin Place except for the third-floor front room, which was occupied by a couple he called "radioactive" because they played the radio a lot. Cummings described the house:

"4" signifies a delapidated [sic] house perhaps 100 years young, perhaps younger. If asked "why" I live here,I'd answer "because" here's friendly,unscientific,private,human. Actually I live here in 2 places:away up & away down. The larger(ground-

E. E. Cummings outside 4 Patchin Place.

floor)"apartment" is really Marion's;but she shares it with me &
we both share it with the socalled world—& sometimes entertain
(more often are entertained by)our few friends. The smaller(top-
floor)"studio" is where I go to be alone & do my work

Other poets visited at Patchin Place. Allen Tate brought
T. S. Eliot; Ezra Pound came in 1939 when he made his first
visit to the United States in twenty-five years; and Dylan
Thomas, drinking in a bar on Christopher Street in 1950, pre-
vailed upon John Malcolm Brinnin to take him to meet Cummings.

.

Among those who would distinguish themselves primarily as
critics was Edmund Wilson, who first came to the Village after
graduating from Princeton in 1916. He got a job as reporter
for the *New York Evening Sun* and took an apartment on 8th
Street between Fifth and Sixth avenues with three friends from
Yale. The four roommates kept a Chinese servant and often
had people in for dinner. From 1917 to 1919 Wilson was
away serving in the army. When he returned he found an
apartment at 114 West 16th Street and a job as managing editor of *Vanity Fair.* In 1920 he met Edna Millay and, although
his relationship with her lasted only a year, allusions to her
appear in the writing he did during the next two decades.
Characters based on Millay appear in two plays, *The Crime in
the Whistler Room* and *This Room and This Gin and These
Sandwiches,* and in Wilson's novel *I Thought of Daisy,* where
she is represented as a poet named Rita. Rita leaves the Village, ending her affairs, among them one with the narrator.
In anger he rejects his love for her and turns to Daisy, a
chorus girl who exemplifies the popular culture.
    Around 1921 Wilson, now managing editor of the *New Re-
public,* moved to 3 Washington Square North. In 1923 he

married the actress Mary Blair and at the end of the year, with their new baby, they moved a few doors away to 1 University Place. At this time Wilson seemed to many a very serious, even pompous, young man, dressed in what Fitzgerald called his "inevitable brown get-up." At the same time, the critic had a witty, whimsical side. He and Elinor Wylie often played practical jokes on people. At other times his wife was his co-conspirator. Burton Rascoe reported in *A Bookman's Daybook:*

> About nine o'clock tonight a taxi drove up and there came trooping up the stairs Mary Blair, Wilson's wife, dressed in pajamas, house slippers and raincoat; Tallulah Bankhead in bathing suit and cutaway coat; and Edmund Wilson, Jr., in a brown dressing gown and top hat. They gave us forthwith a superb vaudeville performance. Tallulah imitated . . . Sarah Bernhardt. Mary recited "The Little Tin Soldier Is Covered With Dust" . . . and Bunny [Wilson] performed some feats of legerdemain and conjuring. It was all refreshing and amusing and I pondered the happy circumstances which allows [sic] so serious and studious a young man as Bunny to forget himself in a riot of giddy nonsense and absurdity. True enough, he did spoil it to a slight extent by becoming grave later on and reciting Anatole France's forlorn and pessimistic comment on the life of Racine . . .

John Dos Passos recalled the first time he met Wilson: "There appeared a slight sandyheaded young man with a handsome clear profile. He wore a formal dark business suit. The moment we had been introduced, while we were waiting for the elevator, Bunny gave an accent to the occasion by turning, with a perfectly straight face, a neat somersault."

Another of the critics, Malcolm Cowley, was living after the war at 16 Dominick Street in what he called the most battered and primitive lodging to be found in New York. According to

Matthew Josephson, Cowley's wife, Peggy Johns (she had previously been married to the poet Orrick Johns), often held all-night poker games. Cowley worked through it all in a corner, where he kept his typewriter, books and papers neatly arranged on a table. The Cowleys moved in a circle that included Hart Crane, William Slater Brown, Susan and James Light, Kenneth Burke, Allen Tate and Matthew Josephson. The group gathered often at the Lights's apartment at 30 Jones Street. Here Crane met Emil Opffer, a young ship's steward, who gave the poet a room in his Brooklyn Heights home. (Susan Light later married William Slater Brown, and Crane later became engaged to Peggy Johns Cowley.) They ate frequently at John Squarcialupi's restaurant, a speakeasy located first at 30 Perry Street and later on Waverly Place. It was there Tate had been introduced to the group one night when Hart Crane appeared, "accompanied by a wispy, blond young man with an enormous cranium and diminutive and delicate features." Tate, who had been a member of the "Fugitives" at Nashville's Vanderbilt University, came to New York in 1924 in search of the avant-garde. By the following year he was "disenchanted with the avant-garde and disgusted by the filth and confusion of the city" and moved to upstate New York. In 1927 he was back, living in a basement apartment at 27 Bank Street, where he worked as janitor in lieu of rent while writing his biography of Stonewall Jackson.

Cowley recalled the evenings at Squarcialupi's: "We were all writing poems then and, sitting after dinner around the long table in the back room, we used to read them . . . Kenneth Burke would wipe his spectacles with a napkin and give an affirmative 'mhmmm.' — 'That's good enough to read again,' Allen Tate might say; 'I'd like to catch the rhyme scheme.' John Squarcialupi would stand in the kitchen doorway listening, with a bottle of red wine in each hand . . .

We were all about 26, a good age, and looked no older; we were interested only in writing and in keeping alive while we wrote, and we had the feeling of being invulnerable . . ."

Susan Light Brown remembers that Cowley's job was to compute everyone's share of the check and that Crane often played popular songs by ear on the upright piano, "a foot on the loud pedal, accentuating the pronounced rhythms, shaking his head with its bristly, brush-cut stand of hair in time to the music." Cowley, Burke, the Lights and Mary Blair Wilson had all gone to Peabody High School in Pittsburgh and sometimes they would sing the school song, accompanied by Crane on the piano.

The group was involved with several literary magazines. While in Europe, Josephson, unofficially aided by Cowley, had been editor of *Secession*. Gorham Munson had started the magazine but after several issues returned to New York, where, assisted by Kenneth Burke, he tried to control its content. He and Josephson fell out, whereupon Josephson was fired. When Josephson and Cowley returned to New York in 1923, they went to work for *Broom*, an international magazine of the arts started by Alfred Kreymborg and Harold Loeb. (Loeb, proprietor of the Sunrise Turn Bookshop at 51 East 44th Street, was the model for Robert Cohn in Hemingway's *The Sun Also Rises*.) *Broom* had been publishing in Europe but moved to an office at 3 East 9th Street with Josephson as editor, Cowley as coeditor and William Slater Brown as associate editor.

Foremost among the little magazines of the twenties was the *Dial*. As Marianne Moore noted, it had gone through several metamorphoses. It was founded in 1840 in Cambridge, Massachusetts, as an organ for the transcendentalists, with Margaret Fuller and later Ralph Waldo Emerson as editor, but was discontinued after four years. In 1880 it was revived in Chicago and published until 1916 as "a sedate, critical fort-

nightly review." In 1917 it moved to New York under new
ownership and became a fortnightly with a socially analytical
and humanitarian emphasis. During this period Conrad
Aiken, Randolph Bourne, Van Wyck Brooks and Scofield
Thayer were associated with it. In 1920 it sold out to Scofield
Thayer and Dr. J. Sibley Watson, Jr., who made it a non-
political monthly of arts and letters. It was in this incarnation that the *Dial* gained its greatest distinction. Its aim was
to present "the best of European and American art, experimental and conventional," and it fulfilled this intention with
greater taste and knowledgeability than any other literary
magazine of its day. Three quarters of its pages were devoted
to criticism of the arts; the remaining fourth was given to
stories, poems and reproductions of paintings and sculpture.

Although the *Dial* drew criticism from all quarters, it was
simply the best there was. William Carlos Williams attacked
it over the reproduction of a Chagall in 1921: "If there is a
loonier pack of nitwits in the world than you fellows who are
making *The Dial,* they are not advertising it to the world as you
are. This is the brazenest kind of prostitution, because it is
colossal affectation. The Greenwich Village brand of moral
and spiritual and artistic degeneracy. You are not discovering
new worlds, but only helping to ruin the beauty in this." But
Williams changed his mind. He accepted the Dial Award in
1926; "an epoch making event for me, it put me on my feet."
T. S. Eliot wrote that the *Dial* competed in dullness with the
Atlantic Monthly and that "there is far too much in it, and it is
all second rate and exceedingly solemn," yet chose it for the
first publication of *The Waste Land.* Although Cowley attacked it, his ultimate assessment was that "it was the best magazine of the arts that we have had in this country."

The *Dial*'s offices were in a brick house at 152 West 13th
Street. Marianne Moore, who edited it from 1925 until it

closed in 1929, wrote: "I think of the compacted pl
of those days . . . and the three story brick build
carpeted stairs, fireplace and white mantelpiece rooms,
office in the first storey front parlour, and of the plain g\   ͜ar
block letters, The Dial, on the windows to the right of the
brown stone steps leading to the front door . . . There was
for us of the staff a constant atmosphere of excited triumph —
interiorly, whatever the impression outside; and from Editor
or Publisher a natural firework of little parenthetic wit too
good to print — implying that efflatus [sic] is not chary of sur-
plus."

.

During the twenties two major novelists, John Dos Passos and
Thomas Wolfe, were closely associated with the Village. Dos
Passos was in the city only intermittently because, as he noted,
"at the slightest excuse, and particularly upon the occasion of
the publication of a book, I bolted for foreign parts. It was
during these years that I lost track of the number of times I
crossed the Atlantic . . . Young women I met at cocktail
parties liked to tell me I was running away from myself."

His sporadic residence in New York notwithstanding, he
managed to absorb enough of the city to make it the subject of
his second book, *Manhattan Transfer*. The novel draws its detail, like the Syrian restaurant on Washington Street, directly
from his own experience. The character most like Dos Passos,
a journalist named Jimmy Herf, lives first in a "small square
bleak room on the south side of Washington Square" and later
at 190 West 12th Street. Dos Passos himself had a room on the
Square in 1922, in the studio building behind 3 Washington
Square, which he rented from Elaine Cummings.

Thomas Wolfe arrived from Harvard late in 1923 to write
plays and teach at New York University. (His classes were

held in the Brown Building.)   He drew an unflattering picture
of the college, his students and his colleagues in *Of Time and
the River.*   During this period, he lived in Room 2220 at the
Hotel Albert (the Hotel Leopold in the novel) on University
Place.   He was totally unknown and uninvolved in the Village literary scene.

In 1925 Wolfe met Aline Bernstein, the stage designer, who
was to become his mistress and exert a strong influence on his
artistic life.   She rented a loft for thirty-five dollars a month at
13 East 8th Street.   The address had once been an elegant one;
in 1888 Richard Watson Gilder, editor of the *Century Magazine,* had made the house, with its high front stoop and climbing wisteria, a gathering place for artists and writers.   In Wolfe's
time it had changed radically.   "I am living in a dilapidated
old building over a pressing club down in Eighth Street," he
wrote his mother.   "I have no bath, but cold water, toilet, and
a huge room with skylights — the whole floor, formerly a sweatshop, I believe."   Aline Bernstein used the room as her studio
and Wolfe lived there, getting his mail and his baths at the
Harvard Club.   It was here that Wolfe began *Look Homeward,
Angel.*   He later described the house, transposed to Waverly
Place, in *The Web and the Rock,* the autobiographical novel
dealing with this period of his life.   It had, he said, "the sag
and lean of an old house, the worn modeling of time from
which all sharp new edges and all solid holds have been
worn away."

Wolfe next moved to 263 West 11th Street, where he and Aline
Bernstein split the $135-a-month rent.   She used the front
room as a studio and place to receive clients and he wrote in
the one in the rear.   He again described his home to his
mother: "It is a magnificent place in an old New York
house . . . I have a garden behind, and a quiet old New
York street — one of the few remaining — in front.   It is

one of the old parts of town, 8 minutes from the University."
A similar house — this time transposed to 12th Street — appears in the opening pages of *You Can't Go Home Again*.
Wolfe wrote:

> He loved this old house on Twelfth Street, its red brick walls,
> its rooms of noble height and spaciousness, its old dark woods
> and floors that creaked; and in the magic of the moment it
> seemed to be enriched and given a profound and lonely
> dignity by all the human beings it had sheltered in its ninety
> years. The house became like a living presence. Every object seemed to have an animate vitality of its own — walls, rooms,
> chairs, tables, even a half-wet bath towel hanging from the
> shower ring above the tub, a coat thrown down upon a chair,
> and his papers, manuscripts, and books scattered about the room
> in wild confusion.

After a trip to Europe, his fourth since 1924, Wolfe moved
to a second-floor rear room at 27 West 15th Street in December
1928. (The house, haphazardly remodeled, is still there.) In
1930 he again left for Europe and when he returned in March
of 1931 he moved to Brooklyn Heights to elude Aline Bernstein and escape from the public he had acquired with the publication of *Look Homeward, Angel* in 1929.

All his subsequent books were set in New York, which he
used as much more than a background. The city is a force
against whose values and meanings the hero, always a newcomer, is tested. Speaking of the thirties, Wolfe later wrote:
"The life of the great city fascinated me as it had always done,
but also aroused all the old feelings of naked homelessness, rootlessness, and loneliness which I have always felt there. It was,
and has always remained for me, at least, the most homesick
city in the world; the place where I have felt mostly an alien
and a stranger."

"About the year 1924," Malcolm Cowley has noted, "there began a great exodus toward Connecticut, the Catskills, northern New Jersey and Bucks County, Pennsylvania." Some left because they preferred the country; others simply because the rents were too high. The decline in Village real estate values had been reversed; the progress of the tenements had stopped and there was now a residential backflow to the Village. Young professionals and members of the middle class came back; old houses were restored; rooming houses were reconverted to apartments and single residences; apartment houses were built. The rents were driven up and the artists and writers were driven out. In 1927 the *Christian Science Monitor* ran a headline: GREENWICH VILLAGE TOO COSTLY NOW FOR ARTISTS TO LIVE THERE: VALUES INCREASE SO THAT ONLY THOSE WHO CAN WRITE FLUENTLY IN CHECK BOOKS CAN AFFORD IT: ONE ROOM AND BATH COST $65. Some few writers remained and some who had already made their reputations or had secure jobs within the literary establishment chose this time to return.

Among them were William Rose Benét, a former editor of the *Century* who was associated with the *Literary Review* (the progenitor of the *Saturday Review of Literature*) from its inception in 1920, and his wife, Elinor Wylie. Wylie had originally arrived in the Village from Washington, D.C., in 1921, preceded by her reputation. She had married at twenty, but left her husband and child five years later for Horace Wylie, who was also married. They lived abroad for five years as "Mr. and Mrs. Waring." When they returned, Horace Wylie got a divorce — Elinor's husband had killed himself — and in 1916 they were married. In Washington Elinor was not forgiven and had few friends. However, as Carl Van Doren wrote, "What in Washington had seemed shocking, in New York seemed dramatic. Almost nobody knew exactly what her story was, but everybody knew she had a story and thought of her as some kind of heroine." Doubtless her great beauty helped. Louis Untermeyer said she looked like Nefertiti: "the same imperious brows; the high cheekbones and the scooped-out cheeks; the proud and narrow nose; the small taut mouth; the carved and resolute chin; the long smooth column of the throat." Carl Van Doren said she was like "iced chalk," a description she liked. "White faced . . . she had no color but in her lustrous eyes and her bronze hair."

In 1921, after Harcourt, Brace and Howe decided to publish a book of her poetry, Elinor began coming to New York for a few days every two weeks. The following year she left Wylie, whom she divorced two years later, and found a large high-ceilinged room on the entrance floor of 1 University Place, "then still one of the great old houses facing the Square." Like Margaret Anderson, Wylie had the ability to create a great deal of style out of very little. "That one room," her sister Nancy Hoyt remembered, "looked like a mixture of Horace Walpole, Lady Mary Wortley Montague and Miss Austen . . . In the dusk of early spring the lamps and candles glowed under the high ceiling of a drawing room which would have been suitable as one of a lady's 20 rooms but seemed slightly ridiculous and almost unbelievable as the only dwelling place of a human being." Elinor was able to conceal all the practicalities — cooking utensils, dressing table accoutrements and such — in the bathroom. To this apartment came Benét, Wilson, Dos Passos (the young woman who prepares endless cups of coffee in her bathroom-kitchen in his *Most Likely to Succeed* may have been inspired by Wylie) , John Peale Bishop and others. They often went to Marta's, at 75 Washington Place. During this period Elinor was employed by *Vanity Fair* as poetry editor at fifty dollars a week.

In 1923 Elinor married William Rose Benét, who had been at Yale with her brother. They first lived near Sheridan Square in "a tiny, cheerful apartment on a short, sunny rather messy side street," but soon moved to 142 East 18th Street. After a winter there, they bought a house in New Canaan, Connecticut. By 1926, however, they were back in the Village at 36 West 9th Street. Both names, BENÉT and WYLIE, were on the bell. The apartment took up the whole second floor of the house. "The front room was the formal sitting-room and dining-room, with a little study off it crowded with Bill's books and pictures. White shelves of books, gay and leather bound . . . lined the walls. There were high windows onto 9th Street." The living room was furnished with the blue velveteen sofa, the Wedgwood lamp, the eighteenth-century Sheffield silver mirror and the beautifully shaped chairs Elinor had had at 1 University Place. There was a kitchen and a double bedroom and a room where Elinor worked on "an enormous deal table unpainted and unvarnished." She used greenish blue pencils and typed on blue bond paper with a bluish green typewriter ribbon.

In August 1928, shortly before Elinor Wylie's untimely death in December at the age of forty-three, the Benéts' old friend Sinclair Lewis came to live a block away at 37 West 10th Street with his new wife, the journalist Dorothy Thompson. (Lewis had, in 1910, lived briefly at 10 Van Nest Place, now 69 Charles Street, in the same row of houses Hart Crane later inhabited.) Dorothy Thompson used the second floor as a studio. Lewis was at this time America's most famous writer and Dorothy must have expected, as Vincent Sheean has written, that life "in the largest of American cities, on an income which even for the United States was really large, would have some elements of variety, glitter, change and excitement. Not at all." Lewis did not like to go out to the theater or to other people's homes, refused to make plans in advance, yet would invite any number of guests to his own home on the spur of the moment. "Red's hospitality was incorrigible," wrote Sheean. "He always asked everybody to come and never wanted anybody to go. If he felt the need of solitude, or even of sleep, he would abandon the company and retire for an hour, almost always with the solemn injunction that nobody was to go away . . . Dorothy was also extremely hospitable but she did have the habits of civilization; she could tell lunch from dinner; if she asked you for cocktails she did not expect you to stay all night; and furthermore she always recognized that other people had other things to do, which Red treated as a chimerical notion." Thus began the dissolution of the Lewis marriage. They were at 10th Street only a year.

Toward the end of the decade, what Allen Churchill has called "the most exclusive — not to say respectable — literary group in the Village" gathered around Bleecker and West 11th streets. Mark Van Doren bought a house at 393 Bleecker and with his neighbors on Perry and West 11th "demolished back fences and outbuildings at one stroke, paved the space thus opened up, planted the edges of it with shrubs and trees, and there was Bleecker Gardens." Although the Van Dorens moved to Connecticut in 1959, the families on Bleecker between 11th and Perry still contribute to a common fund for the maintenance of the Gardens. Van Doren had first lived in the Village in 1920, when he and Joseph Wood Krutch took an apartment at 43 Barrow Street. Krutch lived in the back room, which was heated by a gas radiator, and Van Doren had the front room, with a potbellied stove that burned hard coal. During this period Van Doren, who was to win a Pulitzer Prize for poetry in 1939, was literary editor of the *Nation* and taught English at Columbia. His brother, Carl, who was also teaching at Columbia and who had preceded Mark as literary editor of the *Nation,* was literary editor of the *Century Magazine* from 1922 to 1925 and of the Literary Guild from 1926 to 1934. "What first made me want to live in Greenwich Village," he wrote in *Three Worlds,* "was the houses I looked down on as I passed over them in the elevated on the way between my flat near Columbia and my office at the *Nation* in Vesey Street: picturesque, small, weathered houses excitingly unlike the piled-up tiers of flats on Morningside . . . The Canbys [Henry Seidel Canby had founded the *Literary Review*] had a house in Charlton Street, which architecturally belonged in the American wing of the Metropolitan Museum and which stood on ground which Aaron Burr had once leased from Trinity." Carl Van Doren took this house, 47 Charlton Street, in 1922, and five years later moved to a house at 123 West 11th Street.

Among Mark Van Doren's close friends was James Thurber, who was living in the same building as E. B. White on West 13th Street. Thurber had a furnished room and White had an apartment with three other Cornell alumni. Later in the year, Thurber moved to a basement apartment on Horatio Street near the Ninth Avenue El. "I used to walk quickly past the house in W. 13th Street between 6th and 7th where F. P. A. [Franklin P. Adams] lived, and the block seemed to tremble under my feet," White wrote in *Here Is New York.*

Perhaps drawn partly by his distinguished colleagues, Lionel Trilling, then an instructor at Columbia, moved downtown in 1929. "I signalized my solidarity with the intellectual life by taking an apartment in Greenwich Village," he wrote.

> I was under no illusion that the Village was any longer in its great days — I knew that in the matter of residential prefer-ence I was a mere epigone. So much so, indeed, that my apart-ment was not in a brownstone house or in a more-or-less reconditioned tenement, but in a brand-new, yellow-brick, jerry-built six-story apartment building, exactly like the apartment buildings that were going up all over the Bronx and Brooklyn. Still, the Village was the Village, there seemed no other place in New York where a right-thinking person might live . . .

What is more, my address was Bank Street, which, of all the famous streets of the Village, seemed to me at the time to have had the most distinguished literary past . . .

After the Twenties

As Lionel Trilling noted, by 1929 the great days of the Village were over. A period of relative inactivity followed, a literary hibernation from which the area would not emerge until after the Second World War. By the thirties most of the major figures had gone: Dreiser and Cather, now successful, lived uptown; Crane, Wolfe and Marianne Moore had moved to Brooklyn; Djuna Barnes and Margaret Anderson had gone to Europe. There remained only a few of those who had made the late teens and twenties a vital literary period. Cummings stayed in the Village until his death in 1962; the Mark Van Dorens remained until 1959; their friend Joseph Wood Krutch lived at 144 West 12th Street and then 11 West 11th until he moved to Arizona in 1958.

Sherwood Anderson was living on his farm, Ripshin, in Trout-dale, Virginia, but when he came into New York during the thirties he stayed at the home of his good friend Mary Emmett at 54 Washington Mews. She was the widow of Burton Emmett, who had been Anderson's patron. Anderson found himself unable to work in Mary's house. "There is too much ringing of phones," he wrote. "And besides, Mary is too rich. There are too many rare books and art objects about. There is something of the monk in me. I like bare walls." So Anderson went to a neighborhood hotel, where he got a room at half price because the proprietor had read his books. He came to work one morning and found the chambermaid reading his manuscript.

The proprietor and chambermaid were both Jewish and Anderson took their interest in writing to be a racial characteristic. "Is it not an amazing race?" he wrote.

James Agee in his apartment at 172 Bleecker Street during the 1940s.

Other writers came for brief periods. Sara Teasdale moved to 1 Fifth Avenue in 1932, and in the midst of a depression committed suicide there in 1933 by taking all the barbiturates she had been prescribed to help her sleep. Nathanael West lived at the Brevoort during the winter of 1935 and the spring of 1936 while James T. Farrell was also in residence. Farrell came to West's room to read him parts of the *Studs Lonigan* trilogy, which he was finishing at the time.

One of the few new arrivals was James Agee, who moved into a basement apartment at 38 Perry Street in 1932. Agee had just been at Harvard, where he had worked on a parody of *Time* magazine that had landed him a job with *Fortune,* another Time-Life publication. He wrote his Tennessee friend Reverend James H. Flye that he was living in two large rooms in "a nice and unusually old house" that had "a broad and sheltered back porch, and a large yard with pool, large trees, incipient grass, flower beds and ivy." Later Agee moved to 121 Leroy Street. Then, during the summer of 1936, he and the photographer Walker Evans went south to do a study of tenant farmers. *Fortune* considered the article too liberal for its readers so Agee decided to turn it into the book that would be called *Let Us Now Praise Famous Men.* He retired to New Jersey to work on it, returning to the city late in 1939 to take a job at *Time.* His main address during this period was 172 Bleecker Street, where four flights up (or 172 steps, according to Father Flye) he had a floor-through apartment, which he occupied from 1941 to 1951. He also kept a studio at 33 Cornelia Street, where he did his writing. He was reviewing the same movies, often differently, for both *Time* and the *Nation.*

Agee was a familiar Village figure. A heavy but solitary drinker, he could often be seen at the San Remo, which became the hub of Village literary life in the late forties and fifties. After suffering a heart attack in 1951 he abandoned the Bleecker

Street walkup and bought a house at 17 King Street, where he lived until his death in 1955.

As the clouds of war gathered, some of the expatriates began returning home. Djuna Barnes came back to 5 Patchin Place. The publication of her extraordinary novel, *Nightwood,* in Paris in 1936 had made her reputation legendary. T. S. Eliot called it "so good a novel that only sensibilities trained in poetry can wholly appreciate it." But in New York she lived the life of a recluse.

Anaïs Nin, who had grown up on the West Side but spent the thirties in Europe, returned in January 1940. After living at several temporary addresses, she found an apartment at 215 West 13th Street for sixty dollars a month. It was a skylight studio on the top floor — one room, a kitchen and bathroom — with a terrace overlooking the backyard. "I bought the simplest of unpainted furniture, beds and large tables," she wrote in her *Diary.* "The tenants left a brown wall-to-wall carpet, and I covered this with American Indian serapes." In 1942, intending to publish her own work, Nin bought a press and rented an attic studio at 144 MacDougal Street for thirty-five dollars a month. Her first project was her novel, *Winter of Artifice;* she set the type herself and the book was published in May 1942. Next came a book of drawings by Max Ernst and, in January 1944, *Under a Glass Bell,* a collection of Nin's stories that drew the praise of Edmund Wilson. In 1944 the press moved to "more businesslike quarters," an office in a small green two-story house at 17 East 13th Street.

Several others arrived before the postwar period blossomed. Tennessee Williams came to New York in 1939 after winning a Rockefeller Fellowship and took a course in play-writing at the New School. At the end of 1941 he shared an apartment with an abstract painter in the warehouse district of the West Village and worked, waiting on tables and reciting poetry, in the Beggar's Bar. In 1942, when he was eighteen, James Baldwin left Harlem for Greenwich Village. His first apartment was twenty-five dollars a month and had two toilets and a roof garden. Baldwin also worked as a waiter to earn his living; he found a job in a basement restaurant on Sullivan Street called the Calypso. Richard Wright, whom Baldwin had already sought out in Brooklyn, was a frequent patron. The restaurant was run by a West Indian woman who, Wright said, "would tolerate no ill manners from bigots." In November 1945, Wright and his family moved to a four-room apartment on the third floor of 82 Washington Place, the same building in which Willa Cather had lived thirty-five years earlier. Later Wright bought a brownstone, replaced now by an apartment building, at 13 Charles Street.

Baldwin was a familiar figure around the Village until he went to Paris in 1948. "By the time I was 24," he told his biographer, Fern Eckman, "— since I was not stupid, I realized there was no point in my staying in the country at all. If I'd been born in Mississippi, I might have come to New York. But, being born in New York, there's no place that you can go. You have to go *out. Out* of the country."

The major literary institution of the late thirties and forties was the *Partisan Review,* which had its offices slightly east of the Village at 45 Astor Place. It had begun in 1934 as a publication of the New York City John Reed Club — one of many established throughout the country by the Communist party as forums for the discussion of Marxist-Leninist doctrine as it applied to art and literature. The earlier Village hero, Reed, was considered the exemplary radical intellectual for having immersed his life and art in revolutionary journalism. Founding editors of *PR* were Philip Rahv and William Phillips, and the first issue featured an excerpt from James T. Farrell's *Studs Lonigan.* In 1937 the magazine announced its independence

from any organized political group, and Dwight Macdonald
and F. W. Dupee joined its staff. Mary McCarthy met the editors at Farrell's apartment when she was living at 18 Gay Street
after separating from her first husband, and became *PR*'s
drama critic. "It was a period of intense happiness," she recalled. ". . . I moved into a one-room apartment on a crooked
street in Greenwich Village and exulted in being poor and
alone." The crowd associated with *PR* often met at Farrell's, at Macdonald's on East 10th Street, or in the forties at
Phillip's on West 11th Street or Rahv's on West 10th. William Barrett, who joined the staff in 1945, wrote of Phillip's
apartment:

> For some of us it was a kind of home away from home, and no
> doubt we abused his amiability and patience. Nevertheless, his
> apartment continued during the late 40's as a center for what-
> ever currents were alive at the time. "Salon" is too stuffy a
> word for it. It was always informal, sometimes rowdy in argu-
> ment, but open in its ideas and attitudes. All kinds of people
> flowed through it, and visiting foreigners — like Camus and
> Merleau-Ponty — entered easily into the general verbal melee . . .
>   By contrast an evening at the Rahv's was a much more
> sedate, careful, and measured affair; and one had sometimes,
> depending on the guests, to tread warily. The late Isaac Rosen-
> feld, who was a sometime guest until Philip decided he was no
> longer a "winner," once described a typical evening very well:
> "It was like throwing darts."

Such excitement surrounded the magazine that it overflowed
into the streets. "There was a ceaseless flow of dialogue," Elizabeth Hardwick recalled. "Harold Rosenberg, Meyer Schapiro,
William Phillips, Lionel Abel, Philip Rahv — you could always see these people in the Village, talking on the streets."
Simone de Beauvoir, who visited New York in 1947, took away
another impression. She described a party given for her by

Dwight Macdonald: "I found myself surrounded by the staff of a review which called itself Left-wing and *avant-garde* and whose aggressiveness surprised me . . . To like the American literature we admired at home was to insult the intelligentsia of the U.S.A. They treasured Faulkner, but they tore to pieces Hemingway, Dos Passos, Caldwell, and, above all, Steinbeck, their *bête noire*. I was bewildered; I did not know their review at all well."

After World War II a period of renewed literary activity began in the Village. In a number of ways, this period was similar to the one that had followed the First World War. Again there was an influx of young writers, many of them veterans studying on the G.I. Bill. Again there was an interest in psychoanalysis — this time focused on Wilhelm Reich rather than on Sigmund Freud. Again there was a social life centered on bars — this time the San Remo, Minetta's, Louis' and later the White Horse.

For a time in the late forties many writers frequented the San Remo, an Italian restaurant at the corner of Bleecker and MacDougal streets. Baldwin had often been there earlier, Agee was still a habitué, as was Maxwell Bodenheim, a relic from the earlier bohemian period. The socialist writer Michael Harrington, who went there every night after arriving from Chicago in 1949, remembered that there were "bad, yellowed paintings over the bar and the Entr'Acte from Wolf-Ferrari's *Jewels of the Madonna* on the jukebox." The regular crowd included seamen on the beach, "heterosexuals on the make; homosexuals who preferred erotic integration to the exclusively gay bars then on Eighth Street; Communists, Socialists and Trotskyists; potheads . . . and innovators of the future . . ." In the last category were William Burroughs, Allen Ginsberg, Gregory Corso and Jack Kerouac. Although Ginsberg and Kerouac lived on the Lower East Side, or the East

William Burroughs
outside the San Remo in
the early 1950s.

Village, as it came to be known, they still came to the San Remo
to do their drinking. Corso had been born in 1930 at 190
Bleecker, across the street from the San Remo, when "all it was
was an Italian neighborhood with people running around taking
bets." In 1950 he met Ginsberg in a Lesbian bar on West 4th
Street called the Pony Stable and so began his career as a poet.
Ginsberg told him, "I want you to meet a Chinaman — a Wise
One," and took him to see Mark Van Doren on Bleecker Street.

The San Remo reigned as the social center of the Village, its overflow pouring into Minetta's up the street, until about 1950, when it was the subject of what *Village Voice* publisher Ed Fancher called "an incredible social phenomenon." The Remo's tough bartenders would occasionally beat up the Village crowd and after one incident everybody left and moved to a bar called Louis' near Sheridan Square. "Before the incident, there would be four hundred people in the Remo; after that there were five." Though the San Remo regained some of is clientele, "it was never quite the same again," said Fancher.

Among those who frequented the Remo and Louis' was William Styron, who came to New York in 1947 to work as a junior editor at McGraw-Hill. He took "a horrible single room ($11 a week) at a fleabag elegantly known as the University Residence Club on West 11th Street between 5th and 6th Avenues." He "was very lonely, had a bout of hepatitis, and did not know any girls." His take-home pay after taxes was thirty-four dollars a week.

In the fall, after being fired from McGraw-Hill (reportedly for flying a paper airplane into a superior's office), Styron enrolled in the first writing class given by a Bobbs-Merrill editor named Hiram Haydn at the New School. After reading the first twenty pages of *Lie Down in Darkness,* Haydn told Styron it was a waste of time for him to stay in the class and took an option on the novel for his company. The start of the novel, as Dorothy Parker later remarked, "took your heart and flung it over there." Styron found the rest of the book did not come as easily, however, and went home to North Carolina for a year. In 1949 he was back, living in Rockland County, where he finished the first half of the novel that fall and the following spring. He then commuted between a brownstone apartment at 314 West 88th Street and the home of a young woman with whom he was "keeping company," who lived in a five-floor walkup on the east side of 6th Avenue below Prince Street. The last 15 or 20 pages of the novel were written there.

Styron's precocious achievement — he started *Lie Down in Darkness* when he was twenty-three and finished it when he was just twenty-six — doubtless helped Hiram Haydn's class acquire its legendary reputation. The class was limited to twelve students each year, who, throughout the twelve years Haydn taught it, included Mario Puzo, Bel Kaufman and three Prix de Rome winners.

After finishing his book, Styron went into the Marines, returning in time for its publication in 1951. That fall and winter he had "a tiny but rather nice (my first nice) apartment at 45 Greenwich Avenue." He was a Village celebrity and young women, impressed by the understanding of their sex evinced in his novel, would ring his doorbell.

Another late forties arrival was Edward Albee, who left home at the age of twenty for an apartment on lower Fifth Avenue. Albee, the adopted son of the heirs to the Keith-Albee vaudeville chain, was the beneficiary of a $100,000 trust fund set up by his grandmother. For the next ten years he supplemented his income with a succession of odd jobs as record salesman, waiter, copy boy, counterman and Western Union messenger, and lived in a series of inexpensive apartments in the Village, Chelsea and Little Italy. His evenings were spent in literary and philosophical discussions in MacDougal Street coffee houses or Village bars. Nine years after leaving home, Albee wrote *The Zoo Story* "on a wobbly table" in the kitchen of the apartment where he was living at the time — 238 West 4th Street. "I did a draft, made pencil revisions, and typed a second script, and that's the way I've been doing my plays since," he recalled in an interview. "I finished *The Zoo Story* in three weeks." The play, set in a crumbling apartment house on Columbus Avenue inhabited by a black homosexual, a Puerto Rican and a woman who cries all day behind a locked door, was presented at the Provincetown Playhouse on January 14, 1960. It is fitting that O'Neill's successor as the major innovative force in American theater should have had his first play produced by O'Neill's playhouse. In 1961 Albee moved to a six-room, ground-floor apartment on West 12th Street. Here he wrote his greatest commercial success, *Who's Afraid of Virginia Woolf?* In a *Paris Review* interview, Albee recalled the genesis of the title:

> There was a saloon — it's changed its name now — on Tenth Street, between Greenwich Avenue and Waverly Place . . . and they had a big mirror on the downstairs bar in this saloon where people used to scrawl graffiti. At one point back in about . . . 1954 I think it was — long before any of us started doing much of anything — I was in there having a beer one night, and I saw "Who's Afraid of Virginia Woolf?" scrawled in soap, I suppose, on this mirror. When I started to write the play it cropped up in my mind again. And of course, Who's afraid of Virginia Woolf means who's afraid of the big *bad* wolf . . . who's afraid of living life without false illusions.

Albee became a member, with Richard Barr and Clinton Wilder, of a group called Theater 1964, which produced plays, including the works of Beckett and Pinter, at the Cherry Lane Theater. He reinvested part of the profits from *Who's Afraid of Virginia Woolf?* to found a playwrights' school, called the New Playwrights Unit Workshop, that supported the work of LeRoi Jones and others.

In the fifties, the White Horse Tavern at Hudson and 11th streets succeeded the San Remo as the favorite Village literary hangout. Norman Mailer, who was living in the East Village in 1951, became the center of a group that gathered there. Dan Wolf, who founded the *Village Voice* in 1955 with Mailer and Ed Fancher, suggested that Mailer make it a Sunday afternoon tradition to go to the White Horse. "Norman found that if

you invited people to your house it was not that easy to get rid
of them," Wolf recalled. The White Horse was the perfect
alternative. "It had a pleasant atmosphere; it was in the right
setting — the 'real' Village; it was an old bar and had a quiet
neighborhood quality." Wolf went only once but Mailer went
regularly and a group of young writers gathered around him.
Some time later Dylan Thomas began telling people he drank
there, and as Michael Harrington recalled, "every English
major in the Northeast corridor began to make a pilgrimage to
the White Horse." Thomas died in the Village in 1953 at St.
Vincent's Hospital on Seventh Avenue and 12th Street.

For more than ten years Harrington himself went to the
White Horse every night when he was in New York. "As the
people of Königsberg were said to set their clocks by Immanuel
Kant's walks, you would see me, punctually dissolute, appear
on week nights at midnight and on weekends at one o'clock."
When the White Horse closed early, the regulars would go
across the street to a bar called the Ideal, which was nicknamed
the Ordeal because of confrontations there between bohemia
and square America.

Another group, which gathered at the home of Vance Bourjaily at 49 Grove Street, included Merle Miller, Louis Auchincloss, Gore Vidal, Hortense Calisher, William Styron and
Calder Willingham. At one party, Bourjaily recalled, James
Jones met Montgomery Clift and "they decided then and there
that he should play Pruitt [in *From Here to Eternity*]."

Since the fifties the Village has lost most of its literary residents. There are a few exceptions: Djuna Barnes still lives in
Patchin Place, Anaïs Nin spends part of the year in Washington
Square Village and Michael Harrington now owns a house on
Perry Street. In the sixties Edward Albee owned a carriage
house at 50 West 10th Street and Marianne Moore returned
from Brooklyn and lived at 35 West 9th Street until her death
in 1971. In the seventies Westbeth, a special housing project

Dylan Thomas at the White Horse Tavern,
where he held court in the early 1950s.

for artists in all fields, provides reasonably priced housing for
young writers. But in general the Village has become too expensive for those just starting out and does not offer the large
apartments required by those with families. For the most part,
writers have had to turn to other parts of the city to find living
space.

The Village has such a great concentration of literary landmarks that only buildings still standing or sites marked by

plaques are noted in the tours. Other sites of former buildings are omitted. Tour 1 covers the area east of Sixth Avenue and Tour 2 the area west of Sixth.

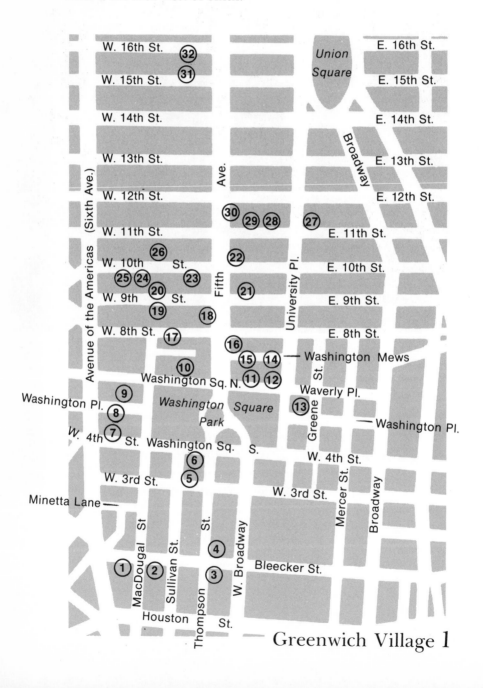

Greenwich Village 1

Greenwich Village Tour 1

The Beat poet Gregory Corso was born in the tenement building at 190 Bleecker Street (1) in 1930. During the fifties he was one of the writers who frequented the San Remo across the street on the northwest corner of Bleecker and MacDougal. The bar has been replaced by a Chinese restaurant. James Agee, an earlier habitué of the San Remo, had a floor-through apartment on the top floor of the red brick building at 172 Bleecker Street (2) from 1941 to 1951. The Mills Hotel, now the Greenwich Hotel, at Thompson and Bleecker streets (3) was Theodore Dreiser's first address when he came to New York in 1895. Dreiser paid twenty-five cents a night for a bed. Across the street at 145 Bleecker Street (4) is the house James Fenimore Cooper occupied in 1833. When Cooper lived here this block of Bleecker Street was named Carroll Place; he lived at number 4. Mrs. Cooper considered the house, now badly run-down, "too magnificent for our simple French tastes." Edgar Allan Poe lived at 85 West 3rd Street (5) when it was 85 Amity Place. The two lower stories have been remodeled.

The Judson, now called Judson Hall, at 51 Washington Square South (6) was a hotel when Edwin Arlington Robinson stayed here in 1906. Polly Holliday had her second restaurant at 147 West 4th Street (7). John Reed wrote the articles that comprise *Ten Days That Shook the World* in an upstairs room here. Today the restaurant is Bertolotti's. The six-story apartment house at 82 Washington Place (8) was home to Willa Cather from 1908 to 1913 and to Richard Wright in 1945. The building, of Beaux Arts inspiration, dates from 1903. Marta's Restaurant, still operating at 75 Washington Place (9), was a favorite eating place for Elinor Wylie, William Rose Benét, John Dos Passos and others around 1921.

Henry James's grandmother lived at 19 Washington Square

Part of James Fenimore Cooper's block on Bleecker Street
as it looked in the 1890s.

North (today it would be number 18 if it were standing), and
the other houses on the block (10) suggest what hers was like.
James spent many childhood hours here and drew the setting
for *Washington Square* from that experience. Edith Wharton
lived on the other side of Fifth Avenue at 7 Washington Square
North (11) in 1882, after her father died and she and her
mother returned from Europe. This, known as the "Old Row,"
is considered by the Landmarks Commission to be the "most
important and imposing block of early 19th-century houses in

the city." In the twenties, 3 Washington Square North (12), the only building in the Old Row to have been remodeled, was the home at various times of Elaine Orr, who later married E. E. Cummings, and Edmund Wilson. Although Henry James was born at 21 Washington Place east of Greene Street, a plaque commemorating his birthplace has been placed on New York University's Brown Building (13) between Greene Street and Washington Square East. The charming buildings in Washington Mews were once the stables for the houses in the Old Row. An exception is the studio building located behind 3 Washington Square North or between 14 and 15 Washington Mews (14). John Dos Passos rented a room here from Elaine Orr Cummings in 1922. Painters who had studios here included Edward Hopper, William Glackens and Rockwell Kent. Sherwood Anderson often stayed with his friend and patron Mary Emmett at 54 Washington Mews (15). Sara Teasdale took an apartment at 1 Fifth Avenue (16) in 1932; she committed suicide there the following year.

Edwin Arlington Robinson lived with his friends the Frasers in the brick house at 28 West 8th Street (17) during the twenties. Robinson had the skylighted studio at the top of the house. In 1870 Bret Harte came east and stayed at his sister's home at 16 Fifth Avenue (18). A plaque at that address marks his residence there. In 1926 Elinor Wylie and William Rose Benét were living in the attractive brick house at 36 West 9th Street (19), where they had the entire parlor floor. Marianne Moore lived across the street in apartment 7B at 35 West 9th Street (20). Her living room furnishings have been reassembled in a remarkably similar room at the Rosenbach Foundation in Philadelphia. The offices of *Broom* were in the basement at 3 East 9th Street (21), a brick house that belonged to Marjorie Content, the former wife of Harold Loeb, who was the model for Robert Cohn in *The Sun Also Rises*. She later married Jean

Toomer, whose *Cane* was regarded as the best work of the Harlem Renaissance of the twenties.

A plaque on the northeast corner of Fifth Avenue and 10th Street (22) commemorates the residence of Willa Cather in the Grosvenor Hotel, which once stood at 35 Fifth Avenue. Mark Twain lived nearby in the handsome house at 14 West 10th Street (23) in 1900. Edward Albee occupied the carriage house at 50 West 10th Street (24) during the sixties and Hart Crane lived at 54 West 10th (25), a five-story brick house, in 1917. Sinclair Lewis and Dorothy Thompson lived across the street in the house at 37 West 10th Street (26) after their marriage in 1928.

The Albert Hotel at University Place and 11th Street (27) was Thomas Wolfe's first address when he came to New York from Harvard to write plays and teach at New York University. He lived in Room 2220. Hart Crane was at 25 East 11th Street (28) in 1917. Then a cheap rooming house, the building has been remodeled and is one of a row of five lovely houses dating from 1845. Mary Cadwalader Jones, Henry James's hostess in New York on his trips back from England, lived at 21 East 11th (29). The sister-in-law of Edith Wharton, she entertained many writers and painters. The Salmagundi Club, formed in 1871 for "the promotion of social intercourse among artists," was named for Washington Irving's satirical magazine. The club, at 47 Fifth Avenue (30), now occupies the last of the brownstone mansions that once lined Fifth Avenue.

Thomas Wolfe lived in a second-floor rear room in the five-story house, now renovated, at 27 West 15th Street (31) in 1928. The historic house around the block at 24 West 16th Street (32) was home to three literary people. William Cullen Bryant lived here from 1867 to 1878; Margaret Anderson, the editor of the *Little Review,* had a floor here in 1917; and Hart Crane had a room on the top floor in the same period.

Greenwich Village Tour 2

At the southwest corner of the Village lies the Charlton-King-Vandam Historic District. The land was once the site of the

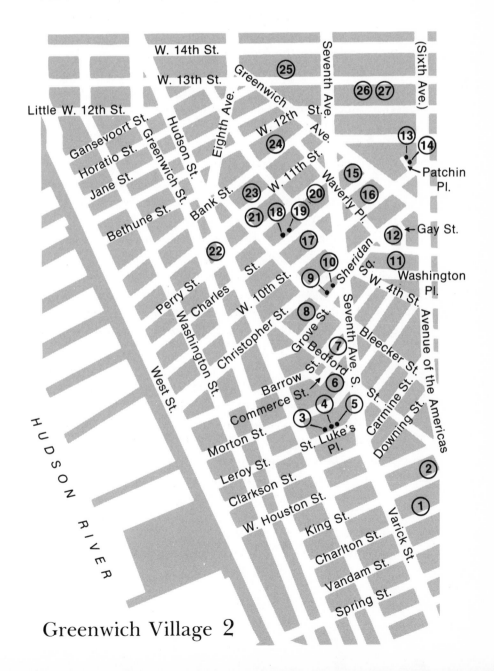

Greenwich Village 2

great mansion known as Richmond Hill. George Washington used the house as his headquarters in 1776; John Adams occupied it when he was Vice-President (it was cheaper than living in town) ; and in 1794 Aaron Burr bought it and made it the center of brilliant social gatherings, which at various times included such men as Talleyrand, Jefferson and Madison. John Jacob Astor bought the land in 1817, leveled it and divided it into lots. Two literary people have occupied the houses that were built during the 1820s. In 1918 Edna St. Vincent Millay and her mother and two sisters lived in the three-and-a-half-story brick house at 25 Charlton Street (1) . In 1951 James Agee bought the old house, now rundown, at 17 King Street (2) and lived there until his death in 1955.

The lovely Italianate houses on St. Luke's Place, one of the city's most pleasant blocks, were built between 1852 and 1854. In 1922 three important writers were living there simultaneously. Marianne Moore and her mother had the basement apartment at 14 St. Luke's Place (4) from 1918 to 1929. The poet worked part-time in the Hudson Park branch of the New York Public Library across the street before becoming editor of the *Dial*. Theodore Dreiser had the parlor floor at 16 St. Luke's Place (5) in 1922 and 1923. And Sherwood Anderson lived at 12 St. Luke's Place (3) in 1922.

The tiny house, only nine and a half feet wide, at 75$\frac{1}{2}$ Bedford Street (6) is known as the "Edna St. Vincent Millay house" although the poet lived there only briefly after her marriage to Eugen Boissevain. In 1920 Joseph Wood Krutch and Mark Van Doren shared an apartment in the old three-story brick house at 43 Barrow Street (7). Late in 1919 Hart Crane sublet a room he particularly liked in the house at 45 Grove Street (8). Described by the Landmarks Commission as "undoubtedly one of the finest and largest Federal residences in Greenwich Village," the house was originally surrounded by spacious grounds and had its own hothouse and stables. It was built in 1830 but remodeled in 1870, when its basement and parlor floor were converted into stores and triangular neo-Grecian pediments were added over its windows and doorways.

Across Bleecker Street at 49 Grove is the orange brick apartment building where Vance Bourjaily lived in the fifties (9). Writers who gathered at his home included Merle Miller, Louis Auchincloss, Gore Vidal, William Styron and James Jones. Close by is the plaque marking the place where Thomas Paine died. In 1808 he had moved from Lower Manhattan to a house on Herring Street (now Bleecker). During his last months he was totally confined to his bed and begged his old friend Madame Bonneville to take care of him. She rented a house only seventy-eight yards away. Paine was carried there in an armchair and died a month later in the back room, which was on the site of the present 59 Grove Street (10).

In 1909 Mrs. Clara Potter Davidge built a studio, one large room with a sleeping loft, for Edwin Arlington Robinson behind her house at 121 Washington Place (11). The poet lived there on and off for several years. When he was in residence, breakfast was brought to him each morning. Gay Street (12), the picturesque block portrayed by Ruth McKenney in the popular comedy *My Sister Eileen,* was also the street where Mary McCarthy "exulted in being poor and alone" after separating from her first husband. Ruth McKenney, whose sister Eileen married Nathanael West in 1940, lived at 14 Gay Street and Mary McCarthy lived at number 18. Another charming alley, Patchin Place, was the long-time home of two members of the Lost Generation. E. E. Cummings lived at number 4 (13) from 1923 until his death in 1962. Djuna Barnes has lived in a one-room apartment at 5 Patchin Place (14) since the early forties.

In 1951, after the publication of *Lie Down in Darkness,* William Styron had his first "nice" apartment at 45 Greenwich Avenue (15) in a five-story brick apartment building. Edward

Albee wrote *The Zoo Story* in an apartment in the tenement
building at 238 West 4th Street (17). He saw the words
"Who's Afraid of Virginia Woolf?" scrawled in soap on the
mirror over the downstairs bar in a saloon on Tenth Street between Greenwich Avenue and Waverly Place. The saloon is
now the Ninth Circle (16).

Charles Street between Bleecker and West 4th streets was
called Van Nest Place when Sinclair Lewis and Hart Crane
lived in the same row of four-story brick houses there. Lewis
was at 10 Van Nest, now 69 Charles Street (19), in 1910 and
Crane was at 15 Van Nest, now 79 (18), in 1920.

When James Agee arrived from Harvard in 1932, he took a
basement apartment at 38 Perry Street (20), a charming three-
and-a-half-story brick house. Mark Van Doren had been living
since 1929 in "Bleecker Gardens," an informally organized
group of fifteen houses with a common garden around Bleecker,
Perry and West 11th streets. The Van Dorens were at 393
Bleecker (21). In the fifties, the White Horse Tavern at 567
Hudson Street (22) became a literary hangout when first Norman Mailer and later Dylan Thomas held court there. Farther
east, Thomas Wolfe lived in what he described as "a magnificent place" at 263 West 11th Street (23). The tall four-story
red brick house makes its appearance, transposed to Twelfth
Street, in the pages of *You Can't Go Home Again*.

Allen Tate lived in the basement apartment at 27 Bank Street
(24) in 1927 when he was writing his biography of Stonewall
Jackson. He served as janitor of the four-story brick house in
lieu of rent. Anaïs Nin took a skylight studio on the top floor
of 215 West 13th Street (25) in 1940 after returning to New
York from Europe. The *Dial* magazine had its offices in the
house at 152 West 13th Street (26) and the *Liberator* was a few
doors away in the four-story brick house at 138 West 13th (27).

III. The Lower East Side

The Immigrants' City

In 1890 a Danish immigrant named Jacob Riis drew the attention of America to the section of New York then known as the "East Side." Riis was a reporter for the *New York Sun* and his classic work of journalism, *How the Other Half Lives,* described trenchantly the city's immigrant neighborhoods. Each morning at 2:00 A.M. Riis walked through them from his office on Mulberry Street near Houston on his way home to Brooklyn. First came the Italian section, culminating in "the Bend," where Mulberry Street "crooks like an elbow." Here, in what Riis called the "foul core of New York's slums," was a vast marketplace with two rows of hucksters' and peddlers' booths against a background of tenements. East of Mulberry were the streets of Chinatown, their opium dens jammed "with these hapless victims of a passion which, once acquired, demands the sacrifice of every instinct of decency to its insatiate desire." A little farther on, roughly where Pearl Street intersects Park Row today, was Five Points, historically one of the worst slums in the world. Charles Dickens had visited it in 1842 and written, "all that is loathsome, drooping, and decayed is here . . ." And across the Bowery to the east was the Jewish district, according to Riis "picketed from end to end with the outposts of Israel . . . Hebrew faces, Hebrew signs, and incessant chatter in . . . Hebrew."

Jacob A. Riis's photograph of Mulberry Bend, "the foul
core of New York's slums," about 1888.

   Like all New York's old neighborhoods, the East Side had
once been fashionable. On his walk Riis would have passed
the Mulberry Street house that had once belonged to Stephen
Van Rensselaer, member of one of New York's wealthiest
Dutch families. Still farther on, close to Five Points, he would
have come to the former home of Edward Mooney, a wholesale
meat merchant. And perhaps he occasionally would have
passed the house at 1 Cherry Street where George Washington
had lived during the brief year when New York was the nation's
capital. Riis himself remarked the changes that were particu-

larly apparent in the President's old neighborhood: "We stand upon the domain of the tenement. In the shadow of the great stone abutments, the old Knickerbocker houses linger like ghosts of a departed day. Down the winding slope of Cherry Street — proud and fashionable Cherry Hill that was — their broad steps, sloping roofs, and dormer windows are easily made out; all the more easily for the contrast with the ugly barracks that elbow them right and left . . ."

The changes Riis documented had begun as early as the 1840s, when Walt Whitman, then a young Manhattan newspaperman, described the area as "the region of Jews, jewelry, and second-hand clothing." Chatham Square was filled with dray carts, coaches and cabs. "On the right loom up small hills of furniture, of every quality," wrote Whitman, "with here and there an auctioneer, standing on a table or barreltop, and crying out to the crowd around him, the merits of the articles and the bids made for them." (During the same decade the ever impoverished Edgar Allan Poe had lived for a short time in a tenement at 195 East Broadway.) The area east of the Bowery had been the home of Irish and German immigrants, among them many German Jews, since the 1840s. But between 1880 and 1910 successive waves of immigrants from Eastern Europe, spurred by pogroms in Russia and Poland, swelled the neighborhood and gave it what was to be its most enduring ethnic quality. Riis was writing at the peak of the immigration. In all, one third of Eastern European Jews came to America, and in 1892 75 per cent of them were to be found on the Lower East Side. By 1900 the area bounded by Cherry Street, the East River, the Bowery and 10th Street was called "the great ghetto" and was known throughout Europe. (There were three other New York ghettos: Brownsville and Williamsburg in Brooklyn and an area between 98th and 116th streets east of Central Park.) In 1886 the words of Emma

Lazarus, herself a New York Jew whose father had been a founder of the aristocratic Knickerbocker Club, were inscribed on the Statue of Liberty, welcoming "the huddled masses yearning to breathe free." But on the Lower East Side the tenements were packed tightly together, with light and air available only to the apartments at the end of the row. In between the streets were crevices several feet wide with names like Blind Man's Alley, Penitentiary Row and Jews' Alley, where the most indigent lived in squalid conditions.

Jacob Riis, who himself had slept in Bowery doorways when he first arrived in 1870, was already known as a pioneering journalist when *How the Other Half Lives* was published. As a reporter, he found the deeper story behind the daily spate of crimes to lie in the social conditions that produced it. Lincoln Steffens, who studied Riis's methods when he first became a newspaperman, credited him with "the wiping out of whole blocks of rookeries, the making of small parks, and the regulation of the tenements." He said that Riis "not only got the news; he cared about the news."

Among those who were profoundly influenced by Riis's book was a young writer named Stephen Crane. Crane, who was to write *The Red Badge of Courage* before he had ever seen war, composed the first version of *Maggie: A Girl of the Streets* before he had ever experienced life on the Bowery. The first draft was written while he was a student at Syracuse University. The following summer Crane began frequenting the Lower East Side, staying in hotels or returning home at night to New Jersey. His experiences filled out the next three revisions of the book.

Crane later remarked that "it was on the Bowery that I got my artistic education." It was not that the Bowery showed him things he had never seen before, but that it taught him a new way of seeing. In one inscription of *Maggie*, Crane wrote, "It is inevitable that you be greatly shocked by this book, but continue, please, with all possible courage to the end. For it tries to show that environment is a tremendous thing in the world and frequently shapes lives regardless." *Maggie* is the story of a young woman in love with a Bowery bartender who offers her relief from the harshness of her life. When Maggie is seduced by her lover, her hypocritical family, condemning the victim rather than the seducer, throws her out of the house. Her lover abandons her and she is driven to prostitution and, finally, suicide. The story is set against the slum background, which Crane described vividly:

> Eventually they entered a dark region where, from a careening building, a dozen gruesome doorways gave up loads of babies to the street and the gutter . . . A wind of early autumn raised yellow dust from cobbles and swirled it against a hundred windows. Long streamers of garments fluttered from fireescapes. On all unhandy places there were buckets, brooms, rags, and bottles. In the street infants played or fought with other infants or sat stupidly in the way of vehicles. Formidable women, with uncombed hair and disordered dress, gossiped while leaning on railings or screamed in frantic quarrels. Withered persons, in curious postures of submission to something, sat smoking pipes in obscure corners. A thousand odors of cooking food came forth to the street. The building quivered and creaked from the weight of humanity stamping about in its bowels.

In Crane's day the Bowery, which he called "the only interesting street in New York," had a total of eighty-two bars along its fourteen-block length, an average of six per block. Today the bars are still there and the Bowery remains New York's skid row, but the upper floors of many of the tenement buildings have been converted into artists' lofts.

Crane's characters were Irish, but by the time his book was

published in 1893 the area behind the Bowery to the east had become the center of a separate Yiddish culture, which was developing its own distinctive journalism, literature and politics. For many decades the central figure in this community was to be Abraham Cahan, who arrived from Vilna, Poland, as a young man in 1882. He got a job stripping tobacco and after learning English began teaching it to other immigrants at the local YMHA. He moved to a different address in the East Broadway area every few years but considered "the best years of my life in America" the ones he spent at 213 Clinton Street, a two-story private house where he had a slant-roofed attic room. In 1892 Cahan went to work on the *Arbeiter Zeitung,* a Yiddish labor weekly. William Dean Howells, who had written in passing about the Lower East Side in *A Hazard of New Fortunes,* sought out Cahan there to ask for information on labor unions for his book *A Traveler from Altruria.* Howells encouraged Cahan to write about the life he knew on the Lower East Side. Cahan took his advice and in 1894 finished *Yekl,* a novel about the problems between a "greenhorn," as a new immigrant was called, and her already Americanized husband. Through Howells's influence the book was published by D. Appleton in 1896. Despite good reviews, including praise from Howells, it sold poorly, and Cahan was not to achieve success as a fiction writer until 1917, when he published *The Rise of David Levinsky.*

In the meantime, Cahan founded a newspaper called the *Jewish Daily Forward* in 1897. He left briefly because of disputes among the paper's various socialist factions and worked for Lincoln Steffens on the *Commercial Adverstiser,* but returned in 1899 as editor, a position he held until his death in 1951. Under his leadership the paper became the single most important cultural institution of the Lower East Side. It educated the immigrant to adapt and survive in his new home, acted as spokesman for the Jewish community to the English-speaking world, organized its readers to attack neighborhood problems by political means and served as a center and stimulus for the creation of Yiddish-American literature.

As Samuel Niger, Yiddish cultural historian, noted: "In other languages journalism was at best a branch of literature; in Yiddish all literature stemmed from journalism." Between 1885 and 1914 there were over 150 newspapers in Yiddish, English and other languages on the Lower East Side. The Yiddish press devoted a large share of its columns to literature. There were essays on all subjects — science, philosophy, economics — as well as poetry, short stories and serialized novels. Book publishing was almost superfluous; almost all Yiddish literature originally appeared in newspapers.

As a literary vehicle, the *Jewish Daily Forward* was preeminent. Sholom Aleichem began sending his humorous stories about rural Russia to the *Forward* long before he came to America in 1905. Sholem Asch sent stories from Poland before he arrived in 1914. Although he lived elsewhere in the city, he wrote a novel, *The Mother,* about a Polish family that settles on the Lower East Side. I. J. (Israel Joshua) Singer, whose work had been serialized in the *Forward,* arrived from Poland in 1933. Two years later he brought over his younger brother, Isaac Bashevis Singer, and got him a job on the *Forward,* where he has worked ever since. He first wrote book reviews and human interest stories as a free lance and in 1944 became a staff writer on a regular salary. His introduction to the English-speaking public came in 1953, when Saul Bellow translated his story "Gimpel the Fool" for the *Partisan Review.* Since then Singer has won a series of major literary awards and has become a grand old man of American letters. He always writes in Yiddish and all of his work is first published in the *Forward* and later translated into English with his collaboration. Singer has never written about the Lower East Side and has never lived there, although he sometimes eats at the Garden Cafeteria on East Broadway. Until recently his stories were about Eastern Europe, but they now deal with Yiddish-speaking people on the upper West Side, where he has lived for more than thirty years (see Chapter VIII, The West Side).

Singer was one of the few Yiddish writers to become known outside the Jewish community and his recognition, of course, was directly tied to his publication in English. Another was Morris Rosenfeld, one of a group known as "the sweatshop poets," writers who worked twelve or fourteen hours a day sewing and ironing in the Lower East Side's omnipresent clothing industry. Riis had written that "before you have traveled the length of a single block in any of the East Side streets" you hear "the whir of a thousand sewing machines, worked at high pressure from earliest dawn till mind and muscle give out together." Rosenfeld's most popular poem, "My Boy," told how a child, who rarely saw his father because he worked such long hours, failed to recognize him. Rosenfeld's poems were "discovered" by a Semitic scholar who translated them and had them published as a book, *Songs of the Ghetto*. The success of the book enabled the poet to move to Yonkers, ending a dozen years of work in the sweatshops.

There were many others — journalists, poets, Hebrew scholars — who are unknown today but who, in their time, created a thriving cultural and intellectual life on the Lower East Side. This life was centered in the cafés, a tradition transplanted from Europe; in these meeting places all would gather over the favored beverage, "a glass tea," drunk authentically through a piece of lump sugar held between the teeth. By 1905 there were some 250 to 300 coffee houses dotted all over the area. In his history of Russian Jewish immigration, Moses Rischin describes the function the cafés had in Lower East Side life:

. . . Over steaming Russian tea and lemon, thin slices of cake, and Russian cigarettes, 'confused minds,' disturbed by life's complexities, found respite and tonic in talk. On Rutgers Street and East Broadway, cafés entertained through the night as the journalists of Yiddish Newspaper Row defended their signed columns against the sallies of their challengers . . . Here the admirers of Marx and Kropotkin, Zola and Tolstoy, debated abstruse turns in philosophy and political economy, the purposes of art, and the standards of the theater. Even elderly Talmudists with untrimmed beards and long black coats drank honey cider, chewed lima beans, and disputed the finer points of the Law in their favorite cafés.

The cafés where the newspapermen met clustered around Rutgers Square, which today is Straus Square. The *Forward* Building overlooked the square directly at 175 East Broadway, the *Tageblatt* was at 187, and the *Day* was at 183, in a building still marked by a decaying sign. The *Forward* staff favored a café called Herrick's at 141 Division Street, now replaced by the Seward Park housing project.

It was in Sachs's Café nearby on Suffolk Street that Emma Goldman, who would play a literary as well as political role with her journal, *Mother Earth*, met Alexander Berkman on the first day she arrived in New York in 1889. Berkman, an anarchist most famous for his attempt to assassinate Pittsburgh industrialist Henry Clay Frick, became her lover and lifelong friend. Goldman continued her political education at Justus Schwab's saloon, an anarchist hangout at 50 First Avenue, and lived with Berkman at the upper limits of the Lower East Side at 210 East 13th Street. The apartment, called "the home for lost dogs" because those who had no money and no place to stay often ended up there, became an intellectual gathering place. One room, decorated with a picture of Prince Kropotkin, served as an all-purpose living room, dining room, bedroom and office for *Mother Earth*. The journal was the first to publish the work of Strindberg and Ibsen in this country and it was in its pages that Eugene O'Neill, then a high school student, discovered their work. The other room was a kitchen with a stove that provided the apartment's only heat. The crumbling brown brick building is still standing today.

The animated intellectual life around the cafés was brought to the attention of the larger community by Hutchins Hapgood, a reporter for the *Commercial Advertiser,* who, between 1898 and 1902, wrote a series of articles on the Lower East Side. Hapgood had become acquainted with the intellectual side of Lower East Side life through Abraham Cahan during Cahan's period on the same paper. Hapgood talked with the sweatshop poets and the Hebrew scholars and investigated the Yiddish theater and Jewish customs and family life. He joined the discussions in the cafés and discovered both the intellectual vigor of the immigrants and the difficulties they faced in preserving their ancient customs in the new world. Cahan said that Hapgood was "the only Gentile who knows and understands the spirit of the ghetto."

Hapgood's articles were published as a book, *The Spirit of the Ghetto,* in 1902, with illustrations by a nineteen-year-old immigrant named Jacob Epstein. Epstein, who was to become one of the world's greatest sculptors, lived in a tumbledown building at 102 Hester Street. "When my parents moved to a more respectable and duller part of the city," Epstein wrote in his autobiography, "it held no interest whatever for me. I hired a room in Hester Street in a wooden, ramshackle building that seemed to date back at least a hundred years and, from my window overlooking the market, made drawings daily." The market Epstein sketched, called the "Pig-market," had been described by Riis in 1890. "The name was given to it probably in derision, for pork is the one ware that is not on sale in the Pig-market. There is scarcely anything else that

The Hester Street market, which Jacob Epstein sketched around 1888.

can be hawked from a wagon that is not to be found, and at ridiculously low prices." Today a descendant of this great market, crowded with sidewalk stalls filled primarily with clothing, can be found in the several blocks of Orchard Street stretching south of Delancey Street.

Hapgood was not the first to be drawn to the Lower East Side. His editor, Lincoln Steffens, had written of a slightly earlier period: "I at that time was almost a Jew. I had become as infatuated with the Ghetto as eastern boys were with the wild west, and nailed a mazuza on my office door . . ."

Nor would Hapgood be the last. Van Wyck Brooks often "spent the whole of a Sunday at a café on East Houston Street, reading and writing at one of the marble-topped tables. I was surrounded there by the real mysteries of the ghetto and by Yiddish actors and newspapermen playing chess and drinking tea like figures from the Russian novels I was greedily absorbing." Later, in the twenties, the Lower East Side drew other writers. E. E. Cummings recorded the pleasures he found there in a poem that begins "My eyes are fond of the east side." He wrote of the peddlers of "smooth fruits of eager colours" and "little, huddling nuts" and the pleasant torture of the "L's" roar.

On Saturday nights, John Dos Passos and his friends gathered at Moscowitz's "Rumanian Broilings" near Second Avenue. The restaurant had originally been located on Rivington Street, where it was a wine cellar popular with the Rumanians. Moscowitz played the gypsy cymbalon in a long narrow basement painted with scenes of Rumanian life. At one end, under the American flag, was a picture of Theodore Roosevelt at San Juan Hill; at the other, a Zionist flag draping a picture of Theodor Herzl. Steaks were grilled on a spit over an open charcoal fire. The Café Royale, at 12th Street and Second Avenue, where Cummings and Dos Passos also went, attracted an uptown crowd

that mixed with the actors and playwrights who paru. .
the Yiddish theater, then thriving on Second Avenue.

In the thirties, books written by those who had grown up in
the ghetto began to appear. Michael Gold, who was the leading
spokesman of the Communist party in this country during that
decade, opened his book, *Jews Without Money,* with a description of the street where he had lived: "A tenement canyon
hung with fire-escapes, bed-clothing, and faces. Always these
faces at the tenement windows. The street never failed them.
It was an immense excitement. It never slept. It roared like
a sea. It exploded like fireworks." One of the books became
a classic. Henry Roth's *Call It Sleep,* a novel that portrays the
experience of a six-year-old immigrant boy named David, was
first published in 1934 but was ignored until it was reissued
in 1960. Through the child's perceptions, the East Side neighborhood at 9th Street and Avenue D, where his family comes
to live, is seen as "an avalanche of sound" — the conglomerate
noises of beer wagons, garbage carts, coal trucks and boat horns.

Roth wrote the one novel and began a second, which he
destroyed unfinished even though Maxwell Perkins of Scribner's had approved its opening pages. In the years since, he
has worked as a substitute teacher, a precision metal grinder,
a state hospital attendant, a tutor in mathematics and Latin
and, finally, a farmer of ducks and geese in Augusta, Maine.
Asked in 1971 why he had stopped writing, he answered,
speaking of himself in the third person, in an article for the
New York Times:

> Continuity was destroyed when his family moved from snug,
> orthodox 9th Street, from the homogeneous East Side to rowdy,
> heterogeneous Harlem . . . That which informed him, con-
> nective tissue of his people, inculcated by *cheder,* countenanced
> by the street, sanctioned by God, all that dissolved when his
> parents moved from the East Side to Mick Harlem. The struts

went and the staves. It would have to follow that the personality became amorphous, ambiguous, at once mystical and
soiled, at once unbridled, inquisitive, shrinking. No longer at
home. I guess that's the word, after this smother of words.
No longer at home.

Roth's experience — moving out of and up from the ghetto
— was a typical one for the great majority of families on the
Lower East Side. With time, those who could leave did until,
by the fifties, the neighborhood's characteristic Jewish accent
was almost entirely silenced. In 1974 the *Forward* Building,
perhaps the most significant landmark of the Jewish Lower
East Side, was sold to a Chinese-American organization, sym-
bolically marking the changes already long established in the
neighborhood. Meanwhile, however, a new character had
come to the section of the Lower East Side above Houston
Street. Instead of the cafés where the immigrant intellectuals
had gathered, there were now coffee houses where young
avant-garde poets read their work. The Yiddish theater, which
once had flourished on Second Avenue, was replaced by a
burgeoning of experimental playhouses. Even painters, lured
by inexpensive studio and gallery space, came to inhabit the
area. Once again the Lower East Side had an artistic life.

The East Village

In the early fifties, as rents rose ever higher in Greenwich
Village, writers began to find homes on the Lower East Side.
Although Allen Ginsberg, Jack Kerouac and Norman Mailer
drank in the San Remo on Bleecker Street or the White Horse
on Hudson, they went home to the region east of Third Avenue. Gradually the migration into the area north of Houston

and south of 14th Street swelled until the neighborhood came
to be known as the East Village. Its tenement-lined streets,
where rents were among the cheapest in the city, provided
an incubating ground for the writers of the "Beat Generation." Later, in an outcast tradition exemplified by these
writers, the East Village became the center of the counterculture
of the sixties, producing its most avant-garde poetry and theater
and representing its lifestyle at its most extreme.

Much of the East Village was originally the farm of Peter
Stuyvesant, which stretched from Broadway to the river and
from 5th to 17th streets. In the early nineteenth century the
land was broken into lots, and prosperous New Yorkers lived
in the brick houses that still stand on 10th Street, Stuyvesant
Street, St. Mark's Place and other blocks on the area's western edge. Washington Irving lived in historic Colonnade
Row at 428 to 434 Lafayette Street (the Astor Place Theatre
now occupies 434), in 1836; and James Fenimore Cooper rented
6 St. Mark's Place in 1834. Later the tenements Henry Roth
described were built farther to the east. More recently the area
has been a patchwork of ethnic enclaves — Poles, Ukrainians,
Italians, Puerto Ricans and Jews living in clusters side by side —
and it was not until the arrival of the Beats that it began to take
on the literary dimension it has today.

The Beat Generation is sometimes said to have been made
up of four people — Allen Ginsberg, Jack Kerouac, William
Burroughs and Gregory Corso. Although Ginsberg, Kerouac
and Burroughs had met around Columbia University and
Ginsberg traces the birth of the Beat sensibility to an apartment on 115th Street and Morningside Drive (see Chapter
VIII, The West Side), they came to be most strongly associated with the Lower East Side. It is tempting to link the
"beatness" of the movement with the current desolation of
the neighborhood, but Ginsberg says there is no connection.

Allen Ginsberg's photograph of Jack Kerouac on the fire
escape of Ginsberg's East 7th Street apartment, 1953.

"New York was Charlie Chaplin-land then," he said. "You'd walk around the city hearing 'Rhapsody in Blue' in your head."

The term *Beat* referred to a certain sensibility rather than a physical state or surroundings. It was Kerouac who gave it a name. In an article called "The Origins of the Beat Generation," he wrote, "John Clellon Holmes . . . and I were sitting around trying to think up the meaning of the Lost Generation and the subsequent existentialism and I said, 'You know, this is really a beat generation' and he leapt up and said 'That's it, that's right.' " According to Holmes, who also wrote an article on the subject, Kerouac described Beat as meaning "being right down to it, to ourselves, because we all *really* know where we are — and a weariness with all the forms, all the conventions of the world." Whatever Beat may have meant exactly — Kerouac later said it was "beatific"; Holmes likened it to Kierkegaardian rather than Sartrean existentialism; and Ginsberg and Kerouac had originally heard the term from a Times Square junkie named Herbert Huncke — it came to represent a revolt against both the political and literary establishments in favor of a glorification of spontaneous, personal and mystical, rather than academic, experience.

Ginsberg was the first of the Beats to move to the Lower East Side. He had been hanging out in Village bars since 1948 and in 1951 took an apartment at 206 East 7th Street, which rapidly became an outpost for his friends. Here he regularly received letters from Burroughs, who was in South America and Mexico. In 1953, two years after Burroughs accidentally killed his wife (he tried to shoot a glass off her head in an imitation of William Tell, he came back to New York and moved in with Ginsberg. Burroughs assembled his letters as two books — *The Yage Letters* and *Queer* — and Ginsburg, in one of the first of his endless activities as agent, publicist, promoter, mediator and exchange bureau for poets and writers,

set out to get them published. Earlier, he had been successful
with *Junkie,* which he sold to his friend Carl Solomon at Ace
Books. (Ginsberg had met Solomon, to whom he later dedicated *Howl,* when both were patients at Columbia Psychiatric
Institute.) *Junkie,* set in part in a tenement apartment on
the Lower East Side, told the story of Burroughs's addiction
to morphine and heroin. It was originally published as *Junkie*
by "William Lee." Meanwhile, Ginsberg was writing the
first three poems of *Reality Sandwiches.*

Jack Kerouac often stayed at the 7th Street apartment and
it was there that he met the woman he would depict as Mardou
Fox in *The Subterraneans.* The relationship that ensued was
more intense than his generally superficial affairs with women.
For two months he spent a great deal of time in her apartment
at 501 East 11th Street, a glorified tenement building with an
inner courtyard known to the Beats as "Paradise Alley." After
the affair was over, Kerouac went home to Queens and wrote
The Subterraneans in "three full moon nights" of October
1953, typing at his mother's kitchen table.

Like all of Kerouac's books, *The Subterraneans* is a barely
disguised retelling of his own experience. Kerouac is Leo
Percepied, Allen Ginsberg is Adam Moorad, William Burroughs is Frank Carmody and Gregory Corso is Uri Gligoric.
Kerouac shifts the scene from Paradise Alley to a fictional
Heavenly Lane in San Francisco. But the novel is an exact
description of the Lower East Side scene of the time, with its
parties, jazz and drugs. He describes

> the Pierre-of-Melville goof and wonder of it, the dark little
> beat burlap dresses, the stories you'd hear about great tenormen
> shooting junk by broken windows and starting at their horns, or
> great young pads with beats lying high in Rouault-like saintly ob-
> scurities, Heavenly Lane the famous Heavenly Lane where
> they'd all at one time or another the beat subterraneans lived

. . . seeing it for the first time . . . the wash hung over the court, actually the back courtyard of a big 20-family tenement with bay windows, the wash hung out and in the afternoon the great symphony of Italian mothers, children, fathers BeFinneganing and yelling from stepladders, smells, cats mewing, Mexicans, the music from all the radios whether bolero of Mexican or Italian tenor of spaghetti eaters or loud suddenly turned-up KPFA symphonies of Vivaldi harpischord intellectuals performances boom blam the tremendous sound of it . . .

In invoking the "Pierre-of-Melville" comparison, Kerouac makes the link the Beats frequently did between themselves and other writers once outcast and in disrepute like Melville and Whitman. John Clellon Holmes, in an essay on Kerouac called "The Great Rememberer," draws a direct parallel: "Melville, armed with the manuscript of *Typee,* must have struck the Boston Brahmins in much the same way. Stocky, medium-tall, Kerouac had the tendoned forearms, heavily muscled thighs and broad neck of a man who exults in his physical life." And Ginsberg, like Kerouac, compares life on the Lower East Side in the fifties with the society of poets and outcasts Melville had depicted in *Pierre* a hundred years earlier. "Like *The Subterraneans,*" said Ginsberg, "*Pierre* depicts the gnostic, garbage culture of its time." With the Lower East Side experience, Beat broadened its dimensions. Said Ginsberg: "This was the loam or soil out of which a lot of it grew . . . the apocalyptic sensibility, the interest in the mystic arts, the marginal leavings, the garbage of society . . . the beginning of Department of Sanitation culture."

Beat, therefore, was a social stance first — an attitude of protest against the establishment. It was a protest, again, as a literary movement — the Beats stood in opposition to the writing and criticism of the academy in favor of the literature drawn

from their own spontaneous experience. Seymour Krim reduces it to the simplest terms: "The real thing to remember
is that they were people . . . who had respect for their own
experience and wanted to write from it."

Technically, William Carlos Williams was the Beats' major
poetic influence. They took his dictum, "No ideas but in
things," as a starting point ("Williams' precise real images are
such a relief after affected iambics," said Ginsberg) and learned
from his use of the natural breath in the poetic line. But
they went on from there to develop a kind of prosody that Ginsberg has sometimes compared to jazz and called "spontaneous
bop prosody," the syntax and rhythms arising out of the attempt
to "transcribe the thought all at once so that its ramifications
appear on the page."

And there was always the extraliterary influence of drugs.
Burroughs's *Naked Lunch* was written on cannabis; Kerouac
did virtually all his work on benzedrine; Ginsberg wrote *Howl*
on peyote for visions. Later, there would come experimentation with the altered states of consciousness, which Ginsberg
recorded in a series of poems named for the drugs under which
they were produced, like "Lysergic Acid" and "Mescaline."

In the third poem in *Reality Sandwiches,* "The Green Automobile," Ginsberg wrote: "If I had a Green Automobile/I'd
go find my old companion/in his house on the Western ocean."
The poem was addressed to Neal Cassady, who had been Ginsberg's lover and who was the hero of Kerouac's *On the Road.*
Cassady occupied a rather mythic position in the Beat pantheon,
both as hero and as muse, and it was he rather than any literary
scene that drew Ginsberg and Kerouac to California. There
were, however, a number of poets living in the San Francisco
area — Michael McClure, Gary Snyder, Philip Whalen, Philip
Lamantia and, from an older generation, Kenneth Rexroth —
and Ginsberg's great organizational energies and publicity

instincts catalyzed what was to be called the San Francisco
Renaissance. In 1955, two years after arriving in California,
Ginsberg organized a reading of six poets and there first read
Howl. The poem, which launched the Beat poets in the
public mind, recalled the Lower East Side experience of those

> who ate fire in paint hotels or drank turpentine in Paradise
>   Alley, death, or purgatoried their torsos night after night
> with dreams, with drugs, with waking nightmares, alcohol and
>   cock and endless balls . . .

While the Beats were in California, Norman Mailer was
living out another Lower East Side experience. In 1951, after
returning to New York from Hollywood, he had moved to a
simple, cold water flat on Pitt Street, "way over on the Lower
East Side beneath the Williamsburg Bridge, a grim apartment,
renovated in battle-ship gray," as he described it in *Advertisements for Myself.* He was trying to write stories for magazines,
without much success, and at the same time thinking discon-
nectedly about a long novel. One morning he woke with the
plan in his mind for a prologue and eight-book work concerning
the adventures of a mythical hero named Sergius O'Shaugh-
nessy. Mailer plunged into part one, *The Deer Park,* and
when he finished the first draft decided to forget the eight-novel
concept. *The Deer Park,* said to be about Mailer's second wife,
Adele Morales, draws on his experience in Hollywood and ends
with its protagonist living in a "hole in New York, a cold-water
flat outside the boundary of the Village."

Mailer's next address was 39 First Avenue, the top floor of a
five-story red brick tenement. Dan Wolf, who later founded
the *Village Voice* with Mailer and Ed Fancher, lived on the top
floor of the house next door and would walk over the roof to
visit. "There was a kosher brewery or winery on the ground
floor and its odor permeated the building," recalled Wolf.

Mailer's next address was a huge loft on Monroe Street — "you needed a bicycle to go from one end to another," says Wolf. Here Mailer held enormous parties attended by hundreds of people, some of them celebrities. "It was a very rough neighborhood, and at one of the parties — I remember Montgomery Clift was there that night," said Dan Wolf, "a bunch of toughs came in. They began hitting Norman over the head with a hammer. It was the stunned and silent fifties and nobody rose to the occasion and helped him." After this experience Mailer left the Lower East Side for the more civilized East Fifties.

In 1957, with his essays "The White Negro" and "Reflections on Hip," Mailer charted his own variant of Beat, which he called "hip." Later he differentiated between the two attitudes in "Hipster and Beatnik." "The Beat Generation," he wrote, "is probably best used to include hipsters and beatniks . . . Still, it must be said that the differences between hipsters and beatniks may be more important than their similarities, even if they share the following general characteristics: Marijuana, jazz, not much money, and a community of feeling that society is the prison of the nervous system." Mailer went on to distinguish between the hipster as coming out of "a muted rebellion of the proletariat" and the beatnik as coming from the middle class and choosing not to work as a "sentence against the conformity of his parents." While hipster and beatnik agreed on "the first tenet of the faith: that one's orgasm is the clue to how well one is living," their bodies were not the same: the hipster moves like a cat and dresses with chic while the beatnik is slovenly and has less body with which to lift himself by his sexual bootstraps. For a time, Mailer allied himself with the hipsters and classified Ginsberg and Kerouac in a hybrid group, the "hipniks and beatsters."

In 1957 Allen Ginsberg and Jack Kerouac came back east and found, like prophets who leave their own countries and achieve recognition, that California had made them famous. Strangely, they were now referred to as "San Francisco poets," which both they and the true San Franciscans found insulting. But succcess was finally theirs. *Evergreen Review* published a special issue on the San Francisco Renaissance, which included *Howl* and a piece by Kerouac. Malcolm Cowley, one of Kerouac's early supporters, had finally aroused enough enthusiasm at the Viking Press for the publication of *On the Road,* and *The Subterraneans* was scheduled for publication by Grove Press. *Howl* was sold out at the Eighth Street Bookshop and the Gotham Book Mart. The *Village Voice* heralded the writers' arrival with an article headlined WITLESS MADCAPS COME HOME TO ROOST. But they did not roost long. Kerouac, Ginsberg, Corso and Peter Orlovsky, whom Ginsberg had met in San Francisco, all left for Tangier to visit William Burroughs.

Kerouac was back in New York within three months but Ginsberg and Orlovsky spent two years in Europe. In 1959 they returned to the Lower East Side and moved into Apartment 16 at 170 East 2nd Street, a red brick building with white stone trim one notch above a tenement. The apartment is the setting for Ginsberg's "I beg you come back & be cheerful," which captures the mixed Spanish-Jewish quality of the neighborhood.

> Tonite I got hi in the window of my apartment
>   chair at 3   :   AM
> gazing at Blue incandescent torches
>   bright-lit street below
> clotted shadows loomin on a new laid pave
> — as last week Medieval rabbiz
>   plodded thru the brown raw
>   dirt turned over — sticks
>   & cans
>   and tired ladies sitting on spanish
>   garbage pails — in the deadly heat . . .

Here Ginsberg wrote "Kaddish" and edited Burroughs's
Naked Lunch (the title was originally *Naked Lust* but Kerouac
misread it and Burroughs liked his version better). Ginsberg
found himself at the center of the scene, which had expanded to
include such writers as Diane di Prima, Tuli Kupferberg, Seymour Krim, LeRoi Jones and Hubert Selby. The Cedar Street
Tavern at 24 University Place between 8th and 9th streets,*
which had been a hangout for abstract expressionist painters
like Jackson Pollock, Franz Kline and Willem de Kooning, who
had studios and galleries on the Lower East Side, also became
the watering place of the Beats. "Who was there?" asked
Seymour Krim. "Well, everybody you might expect — Holmes,
Ginsberg, Corso and occasionally Kerouac and then others that
might be thought of more as the Black Mountain crowd —
[Hubert] Selby, Gilbert Sorrentino, and for a while Robert
Creeley."

Also "there" was the poet Frank O'Hara, who linked painters
and writers through his work as an associate curator of the
Museum of Modern Art. "John Ashbery, Barbara Guest, Kenneth Koch and I, being poets," he wrote, "divided our time
between the literary bar, the San Remo, and the artists' bar,
the Cedar Tavern. In the San Remo we argued and gossiped:
in the Cedar we often wrote poems while listening to the
painters argue and gossip. So far as I know nobody painted in
the San Remo while they listened to the writers argue." In 1957
O'Hara moved downtown to 90 University Place, an old three-
story gray brick building. The apartment appears in one of
what he called his " 'I do this I do that' poems":

> I live above a dyke bar and I'm happy.
> The police car is always near the door
>   in case they cry

* The Cedar, its original building torn down to make way for an apartment
house, moved up the street to 82 University Place.

Allen Ginsberg and Frank O'Hara at 791 Broadway during a party
for the Italian poet Giuseppe Ungaretti, May 1964.

or the key doesn't work in the lock. But
   he can't open it either. So we go to Joan's
and sleep over,
     Bridget and Joe and I.
I meet Mike for a beer in the Cedar as
the wind flops up the Place, pushing the leaves
against the streetlights . . .

In 1959 O'Hara moved deep into the East Side to 441 East 9th Street. This apartment was "a tenement dump, a two-room flat," said Patsy Southgate, poet, translator and close friend of O'Hara's. "Frank preferred to spend his money on cabs, restaurants, liquor, cigarettes, rather than living quarters." Among O'Hara's close friends were Ginsberg, Koch and LeRoi Jones. "People just dropped by," said Southgate. "They drank at his house and then went out to a restaurant to eat — Il Bambino, El Charro, John's on East Tenth Street and Second Avenue, Joe's, Angelina's or the Cedar bar. Once at Ninth Street and Avenue A I spent a whole evening trying to convince LeRoi than James Baldwin had a point and wasn't really so radical. LeRoi had nothing but white friends."

In 1964 O'Hara moved to 791 Broadway, across from Grace Church. "The apartment was a sort of elegant big loft facing the rose window of the church. It was all painted white, including the floor," said Patsy Southgate. "There were paintings by De Kooning, Frankenthaler, Motherwell, Franz Kline, Mike Goldberg and Joan Mitchell. It was his first sort of 'grand lodgings.' Usually the TV set would be on and Frank would be on the phone and probably the record player would be on and the icebox would be empty. I never saw anything in it except orange juice for making screwdrivers and maybe a prune whip yoghurt."

One night O'Hara, Jones and the painter Larry Rivers were to be on a television panel together. "LeRoi turned up at Frank's with a lot of blacks and all of a sudden fought with Frank over a glass," remembered Southgate. "When we got to the TV program he gave his famous speech in which he said 'the only good white man is a dead white man.' Then he moved up to Harlem."

LeRoi Jones, now known as Amiri Baraka, had lived first in a one-and-a-half-room apartment on the top floor of 7 Morton

Street in the West Village, where he and his wife, Hettie, put out a magazine called *Yugen,* financed on her salary as manager of the *Partisan Review.* The magazine, which published many of the Beat writers, was named for a Zen term that meant "flower of the miraculous." Hettie prepared the magazine on an old IBM electric typewriter. "The people in San Francisco said 'Oh, it's such a messy thing,' " she recalled. "No one had considered amateurism before. We didn't have any money but we thought these things were valuable to put out." At one point a controversy regarding the nature of poetry between those Hettie Jones called "the crazy faction — Allen, Gregory, Peter and Jack" and "the Black Mountain plus New York people — Frank, Kenneth Koch, John Ashbery" raged over several issues. During its course O'Hara wrote "Personism: A Manifesto" in which he stated that the poem should be "between two persons instead of two pages." In writing, "you just go on your nerve. If someone's chasing you down the street with a knife you just run, you don't turn around and shout, 'Give it up! I was a track star for Mineola Prep' . . . As for measure and other technical apparatus, that's just common sense: if you're going to buy a pair of pants you want them to be tight enough so everyone will want to go to bed with you."

At this time the Joneses also published books in collaboration with Eli Wilentz of the Eighth Street Book Shop under the imprint of Totem Books. The most important of these was Charles Olson's *Projective Verse,* in which he outlined the concepts that would dominate the poetry of the sixties. There were three main principles: "A poem is energy transferred from where the poet got it . . . by way of the poem itself to, all the way over to, the reader. FORM IS NEVER MORE THAN AN EXTENSION OF CONTENT. And, ONE PERCEPTION MUST IMMEDIATELY AND DIRECTLY LEAD TO A FURTHER PERCEPTION."

In the fall of 1958, the Joneses moved to 402 West 20th Street and then in 1960 to 324 East 14th Street — the parlor floor of a Victorian house that has since been radically remodeled. "It was huge, baronial and a bitch to clean," said Hettie. "This home soon became a center for people who would stay overnight, like Joel Oppenheimer who lived in the Bronx and Gilbert Sorrentino who lived in Brooklyn or those like John Wieners and Gary Snyder who came from out west and stayed longer." There were immense parties: "I could feed hundreds on one pot of spaghetti."

By the sixties, said Hettie, "the Lower East Side had become a 'scene.' There was the Cedar bar, happenings and the beginning of black bohemia." The writers also hung out at the Five Spot, where owner Iggy Tormini let musicians like Billie Holiday perform without cabaret cards, and writers and artists listen without paying. On July 17, 1959, on reading of the death of Billie Holiday in the newspaper, O'Hara wrote "The Day Lady Died," which ended with the lines:

> then I go back where I came from 6th Avenue
> and the tobacconist in the Ziegfeld Theatre and
> casually ask for a carton of Gauloises and a carton
> of Picayunes, and a NEW YORK POST with her face on it
> and I am sweating a lot by now and thinking of
> leaning on the john door in the 5 SPOT
> while she whispered a song along the keyboard
> to Mal Waldron and everyone and I stopped breathing . . .

In the winter of 1962 the Joneses moved again, this time to 27 Cooper Square. They installed heating in what had previously been a "cold-water flophouse for bums with upward mobility" and here LeRoi wrote *Blues People* before moving uptown to Harlem.

Unaffiliated with Beat, hip or any of their variants, W. H. Auden lived quietly on the Lower East Side from 1953 to 1972 at 77 St. Mark's Place, where Trotsky had printed *Novy Mir* in

Christopher Isherwood and W. H. Auden in Central Park, 1938.

the basement. Auden's ties were with the academics and West Side intellectuals whom the Beats opposed. In fact, one evening at the Trillings', Auden chided Diana Trilling for having been moved by a Ginsberg reading. A visitor described Auden's second-floor walkup as it was in 1971: "Auden writes on a new portable typewriter ('the best money can buy') in his small, windowless living room, which is cluttered with books, phonograph records and manuscripts. Off the living room are a sleeping alcove with a rumpled bed, a kitchen where he cooks gourmet meals . . . for himself and his friends and another room, also cluttered, which overlooks St. Mark's Place." Al-

though not a presence on the neighborhood poetry scene, Auden
was a parishioner at his local church, the historic St. Mark's-in-
the-Bouwerie, and a familiar figure to local shopkeepers.

In 1963, when Allen Ginsberg and Peter Orlovsky returned
after traveling in South America, Europe and India, they found
the Lower East Side in full swing. The media had discovered
the area's intense poetic activity and made it the subject of a
publicity explosion. Poetry readings had begun in 1960 at the
10th Street Coffee-House, owned by Mickey Ruskin. On Mon-
days there were open readings and on Wednesdays a guest poet
was invited. In 1961 Ruskin bought Les Deux Megots [sic]
Coffeehouse on East 7th Street and the poetry readings moved
there. At the end of '62 Ruskin gave up Les Deux Megots and
the readings were re-established in the winter of 1963 at the
Café Le Metro. Generally 125 people would be allowed in and
another twenty-five or fifty waited outside. During 1964, readings held on radio, in bars, theaters, art galleries and churches
diversified and proliferated.

There were many little magazines and a number of important
subcommunities. One of these was a group of black poets called
the Society of Umbra, which set up its own workshop and
magazine. Among those originally involved were Calvin Hern-
ton and David Henderson. *Umbra* was still publishing as
recently as 1970–71, when Larry Neal, Ishmael Reed, Toni
Cade, LeRoi Jones, Langston Hughes and Nikki Giovanni were
among the writers represented in an issue edited by David
Henderson.

Another group formed around Diane di Prima and Alan
Marlowe's American Theatre for Poets, which presented happenings, dance programs and a series of new one-act plays,
including works by Diane di Prima, Robert Duncan, LeRoi
Jones, Frank O'Hara, and Michael McClure. Di Prima, who
lived at 31 Cooper Square, also published a large and varied

selection of books through the Poet's Press, which she founded, and *The Floating Bear,* a magazine that she had cofounded with LeRoi Jones in February 1961.

Although he was not involved with the East Village scene, one of the most important figures in the experimental theater lived for several years on the Lower East Side. Jack Gelber had come to New York from San Francisco in 1955 and found a "rundown smelly apartment" at 435 East 5th Street. He paid $11.20 a month for the place, which he shared with a saxophone player whose acquaintances were constantly coming and going. Next he went to live at 11 Pitt Street, where he wrote the *Connection,* based mostly on San Francisco experiences but set in a "shooting gallery" that had something of the atmosphere of his 5th Street apartment.

After the Le Metro poetry readings ended in 1965, the Lower East Side "community climate," as poet and editor Allen de Loach called it, began to ebb. Strangely enough, it was only after it was all over that one of the foremost Beats, Gregory Corso, came to live in the area. In 1967 he lived on 5th Street and Avenue C, "right in the heart of the horror," as he described it. "Oh how oppressive it was!" In the late sixties, in a mass fulfillment of the Beat ethos, the Lower East Side became New York headquarters of the psychedelic counterculture. For a brief period the East Village was a colorful center of rock music and hippie life; ethnic dance halls became discotheques and Yiddish theaters were transformed into rock auditoriums. But the runaways who flocked to the area from all over the country were unprepared for the harshness of tenement life. Today many of the poets, of necessity, still live on the Lower East Side — many others have moved to Westbeth in the West Village — and regular poetry readings at St. Mark's-in-the-Bouwerie maintain the tradition. But the increasing viciousness of the neighborhood has created an atmosphere inhospi-

table to the vital communal scene that existed in the sixties. Of
the major figures only Ginsberg, truly indifferent to material
comfort, has remained in the neighborhood. He and Peter Orlovsky lived in the East 10th Street apartment they took in 1965
until 1975 and then moved several blocks away.

Lower East Side Tour 1

Houston Street provides a convenient dividing line for the
Lower East Side area. Starting at Houston and Mulberry, one
can retrace Jacob Riis's route. The area above Canal Street is
still the Italian section, as it was in his day. South of Grand
Street at 149 Mulberry (1) stands the 1816 house that once

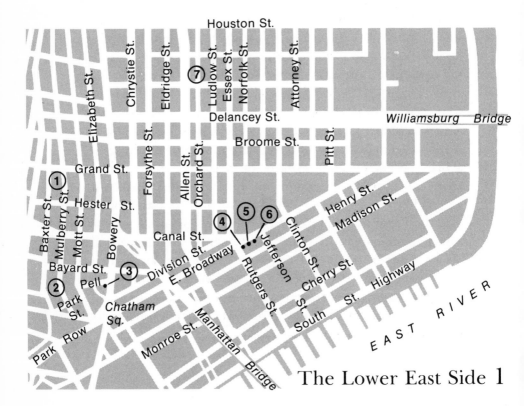

The Lower East Side 1

belonged to Stephen Van Rensselaer. Originally at 153 Mulberry, it was moved to its present location in 1841 and is now Paolucci's Restaurant. The street still curves at "Mulberry Bend" (2) between Bayard and Park streets, although the pushcarts and tenements are gone. On the southwest corner of Pell Street and the Bowery (3) is the oldest surviving house in Manhattan, built in about 1785 by Edward Mooney.

Across Chatham Square, East Broadway leads into what was once "the great ghetto." Very little of the Jewish neighborhood survives. At the corner of Rutgers Street and East Broadway is the Garden Cafeteria (4), once frequented by writers for the *Jewish Daily Forward* and still sometimes visited by Isaac Bashevis Singer. The *Forward* Building itself still stands at 175 East Broadway (5), although it now belongs to a Chinese-American organization. Several steps farther on at 183 (6) is the building, still marked by a dilapidated sign, once occupied by the *Day*. On Orchard Street, between Delancey and Houston streets (7), is an outdoor market reminiscent of the Hester Street Market that existed in Riis's time.

Lower East Side Tour 2

The square mile or so of the East Village is a study in ethnic diversity. At its northern end, where LeRoi and Hettie Jones lived from 1960 to 1962, the neighborhood is strongly Spanish in flavor. The Joneses lived on the parlor floor at 324 East 14th Street (1). Victorian in style before it was radically remodeled, the house was a meeting place for poets and the scene of large communal parties.

Walking toward Jack Kerouac's "Paradise Alley" (2) at 501 East 11th Street, one sees vestiges of the Italian culture Kerouac described in *The Subterraneans* in 1953. Paradise Alley is

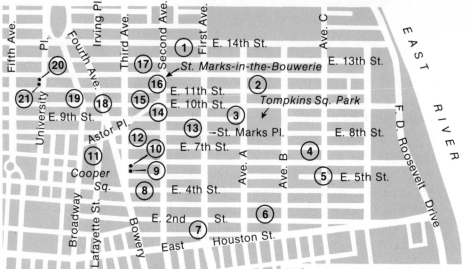

really the courtyard of the rambling tenement building now called Cesce Court. There are gargoyles of Bacchus, a Greek frieze and a statue of Hera inside the brick-paved court.

By 441 East 9th Street (3), where Frank O'Hara lived from 1959 to 1964 in a six-story brick tenement, the neighborhood has become Eastern European — specifically, Ukrainian — in flavor. O'Hara could see St. Brigid's Church, diagonally across Tompkins Square Park at 8th Street and Avenue B, from his window and described it in his poem, "Weather Near St. Bridget's Steeples."

> You are so beautiful and trusting
> lying there on the sky
>   through the leaves
>   you seem to be breathing softly
>   you look slightly nude, as if the clouds had parted

Diagonally across the park, past St. Brigid's, is 206 East 7th Street (4), a six-story brick tenement where, in 1951, Allen Ginsberg started the movement of writers to the Lower East Side. William Burroughs came to live with Ginsberg here in

1953 and Jack Kerouac was a frequent visitor. South on Avenue C at 5th Street (5) is where Gregory Corso lived. This neighborhood, now primarily Puerto Rican, has a bombed-out quality, as if it had been visited by some dire desolation. The neighborhood changes again in the area of 170 East 2nd Street (6), a red brick building with white stone trim, where Allen Ginsberg lived with Peter Orlovsky and wrote "Kaddish." One block south on Houston Street are the delicatessens and "appetizing" stores of the Jewish Lower East Side. Norman Mailer's old address is 39 First Avenue (7), where he lived when there was a kosher brewery in the basement.

Fourth Street between Second and Third avenues (8) is a theater street, the heart of Off-Off-Broadway. The Truck and Warehouse is at 79 East 4th, the La Mama at 74A East 4th and Diane di Prima's East End Theater was at 85 East 4th. North on Third Avenue are the old brick houses at 31 Cooper Square (9), where Diane di Prima lived, and 27 Cooper Square (10), where LeRoi Jones lived before moving up to Harlem. Hettie Jones, now writing children's books, continues to live at 27.

A number of fine nineteenth-century landmarks still remain in this area and some of them have literary associations. The Astor Place Theatre at 434 Lafayette Street (11) occupies another landmark, the series of houses known as La Grange Terrace or Colonnade Row. With its Corinthian columns, the row is considered one of the finest examples of the treatment of a series of houses as a single architectural unit. Washington Irving lived here when the houses were first built.

The house James Fenimore Cooper rented in 1834 stands at 6 St. Mark's Place (12). It is now the St. Mark's Baths. Down the street at 77 St. Mark's Place (13) is the old brick tenement where W. H. Auden spent his winters for twenty years and where earlier Trotsky had published *Novy Mir*. North on Second Avenue is "the beautiful way" at 149 (14), a vegetarian restaurant and health food store that, when it was the Café Le Metro, was the scene of numberless poetry readings. At 117 East 10th Street (15) between Second and Third avenues is the white-painted brick house where Dwight Macdonald lived and where many gatherings of the *Partisan Review* staff, whose offices were nearby at 45 Astor Place (now torn down), were held (see Chapter II, Greenwich Village). One block north is the historic St. Mark's-in-the-Bouwerie (16), where Auden was a parishioner. The tenement where Emma Goldman published *Mother Earth* stands at 210 East 13th Street (17). Fourth Avenue from 9th to 14th streets is the famous old Bookseller's Row (18). The shops, dealing in used and sometimes rare books, that once lined the street are now disappearing.

And exceeding the boundaries of the neighborhood somewhat are the gray-painted brick building at 791 Broadway (19), in which Frank O'Hara had his white-painted loft, and 90 University Place (20), where he "lived above a dyke bar and was happy." The new Cedar Tavern is at 82 University Place (21).

IV. Gramercy Park

IN THE 1850s, Edith Wharton records, "the pioneers of the younger set were just beginning to affect" the area around Gramercy Park. By "younger set" Wharton meant the aristocratic younger set, of course, and descendants of the old Knickerbocker families were to be found in the new neighborhood. Theodore Roosevelt was born in 1858 in a black-shuttered brownstone at 28 East 20th Street, and Washington Irving's nephew John Treat Irving, Jr., lived in another brownstone at 46 East 21st Street. Among the new residents were some with literary connections. Horace Greeley had bought a three-story brick house at 35 East 19th Street in the early fifties. More accustomed to the wilds of Turtle Bay, where he had lived earlier, Greeley found the row unfamiliar and often tried his key at other doors in his block. Perhaps to preserve a little of the country atmosphere he was used to, he kept a goat in the backyard. Encouraged by Greeley, the Cary sisters, Alice and Phoebe, came to New York from Cincinnati and established something of a salon at their house at 52 East 20th Street. The

The Cary sisters' house
at 52 East 20th Street.

sisters were poets (the 1850 city directory lists "Alice Cary, authoress"), and for over fifteen years they held Sunday evening receptions attended by literary New Yorkers.

Although the Roosevelt, Irving and Greeley houses survive, they are overwhelmed by the warehouses and tall commercial buildings that now crowd around Fifth Avenue and Broadway. Scarcely noticeable, they are anomalies in an area given over to manufacture and shipping. One must go east to Irving Place and the region immediately surrounding Gramercy Park to recapture the quality of the neighborhood as it was in the nineteenth century. Lazy and residential, Gramercy Park and, even farther east, Stuyvesant Square have given literature little in the way of subject matter but they occasionally have provided writers with homes.

Among the writers who might have been found at the Cary sisters' for a time was Herman Melville, by birth a New Yorker qualified to move in Wharton's set. Melville had moved into the area in 1862 and was briefly at 150 East 18th Street before buying the house at 104 East 26th that was his residence until his death in 1891. In this period of his life Melville's fortunes were in decline. The public had not appreciated *Moby-Dick* or *Pierre* after the simpler South Sea adventure tales that had made his early reputation. He was largely forgotten and was unable to earn a living by his art. "If I wrote the Gospels in this century I should die in the gutter," he lamented, and was forced to earn his living working as a customs inspector, a job he had described in *Redburn* as "a most inglorious one; indeed worse than driving geese to water."

The house in which Melville lived, replaced by the Armory that would house the famous 1913 Armory Show of postimpressionist art, was yellow-painted brick with brownstone trim. "Our home," wrote Melville's granddaughter Frances Thomas Osborne, "was one of a long row of houses on East 26th Street, each exactly alike except for the number on the door, or perhaps for the tawny color of the cat walking on the iron fence in front." There was mahogany furniture in the parlor and a print of the Bay of Naples hanging in the front hall. Lewis Mumford, one of the critics who began the rediscovery of Melville in the 1920s, noted in his biography that the house had "a quiet interior of its own, an interior like Herman Melville's, acquired before the débâcle of the Civil War. The brown wallpaper and the black iron bed in the wan north light of Herman Melville's room almost alone indicate that a day has dawned that is somewhat darker than a starless night."

Melville customarily took walks to Madison Square with his granddaughter, but on days that were stormy they used the "dusty, chill back porch" instead.

> Grandpa would walk back and forth, I trotting alongside in this uninteresting sport until I suppose enough energy had been worked off to warrant going inside again. One of the redeeming features of the piazza walks was the sight of a blue and red china butterfly . . . It was high in one corner and, looking very life-like to me, I always hoped it would fly lower one day so that we could touch it. The other intriguing thing was the music of the Aeolian harp on the windowsill. The wind blowing through it must have reminded grandpa of the wind in the rigging at sea. In *White Jacket* he mentions an Aeolian harp as a cure for the blues.

Finally, in 1885, Melville's wife came into an inheritance and he was able to retire from the customs house and devote his days to writing again. Here, at the end of his life, he produced one last masterpiece, *Billy Budd*.

While Melville was at East 26th Street, Henry James, who had been abroad, came to live almost back to back at 111 East 25th. James had decided to try New York to see whether it would allay his craving for Europe. He spent six busy months in the city completing *Roderick Hudson,* which was running in the *Atlantic Monthly,* and reviewing books, drama and art for the *Nation.* He decided that New York had turned him into a literary hack and confirmed for himself that it was better to live in Europe. In 1881, when he returned again briefly for a visit, he stayed at 115 East 25th Street with Edwin Godkin, his former editor at the *Nation.* Like Melville's house, both of James's addresses have been swallowed up by the Armory.

While Henry James was explaining the American to Europe, as Van Wyck Brooks expressed it, William Dean Howells was explaining the American to America. For about three years, from late 1888 to 1892, Howells was living on Stuyvesant Square, first in a two-floor apartment in a huge old house overlooking the park at 330 East 17th Street and later in a handsome brownstone at 241 East 17th Street. Howells had begun to work at Harper's, and the area was convenient to his office at Franklin Square. He could take the elevated straight down Third Avenue, an experience he described in *A Hazard of New Fortunes.* His hero, Basil March, finds "the variety of people in the car as unfailingly entertaining as ever." Howells wrote: "New York is still popularly supposed to be in the control of the Irish, but March noticed in these East Side travels of his what must strike every observer returning to the city after a prolonged absence: the numerical subordination of the dominant race. If they do not outvote them, the people of Germanic, of Slavonic, of Pelasgic, of Mongolian stock outnumber the prepotent Celts . . ."

Howells wrote *A Hazard of New Fortunes* in the "uppermost room" of the house at 330 East 17th Street. The novel, which deals with a gentle, middle-class couple based on Howells and his wife, documents the author's growth in social consciousness. March comes to New York from Boston to become the editor of a literary publication whose offices are on West 11th Street.

Exposed to the anticapitalist ideas of his old tutor, whom he encounters again in the city, the editor moves from a position of complacent liberalism to guarded sympathy. The climax of the book is a confrontation in Union Square based on the Haymarket Square riots in Chicago, where members of labor organizations clashed with the police. As the headquarters of the periodical that March edits could not have been located anywhere else (its publisher says, "There's only one city that belongs to the whole country, and that's New York"), so *A Hazard of New Fortunes* could not have been set in any other place. New York as a wide-open city — a place of opportunity where the poor and the rich, the capitalist and the revolutionary, mingle and clash — is essential to Howells's purposes. As such, *A Hazard of New Fortunes* is the first novel to deal with the city's characteristics in a significant way. The novel stands firmly in the tradition of realism Howells advocated, a revolt against romanticism with an emphasis on the didactic rather than the emotional. "If a novel flatters the passions, and exalts them above the principles, it is poisonous," he stated. "It may not kill, but it will certainly injure." Howells wanted to be realistic in both the presentation of physical details and lives as they were really lived. "We must ask ourselves before we ask anything else, is the novel true? — true to the motives, the impulses, the principles that shape the life of actual men and women?"

In 1893 a young man named Stephen Crane had paid for the publication of his first novel, *Maggie: A Girl of the Streets,* under the pseudonym Johnston Smith. Crane sent a copy of the book to Hamlin Garland, then living on 105th Street in Harlem (in 1897 he would be at 23 Gramercy Park), and Garland suggested he send a copy to Howells. Howells, who had moved uptown to 59th Street, read the novel — it was just the realism he had been waiting for — and invited Crane to

Stephen Crane in a friend's studio, 1893.

tea. Meanwhile, Crane had moved into Howells's old neighborhood and was living with three friends in a studio in the building at 143 East 23rd Street that had housed the Art Students League. Crane's roommates were painters and he described their life in his novel *The Third Violet,* the story of a poor artist who falls in love with an aristocratic young woman. "Occasionally one could hear the tramp of feet in the intricate corridors of the begrimed building which squatted, slumbering and old, between two exalted commercial structures which would have had to bend afar down to perceive it. The northward march of the city's progress had happened not to overturn this aged structure, and it huddled there, lost and forgotten, while the cloud-veering towers strode on." When the gas was lit in the room, "the flood of orange light showed clearly the dull walls lined with sketches, the tousled bed in one corner, the masses of boxes and trunks in another, a little dead stove, and the wonderful table. Moreover there were wine-coloured draperies flung in some places, and on a shelf, high up, there were plaster casts, with dust in the creases . . ." Three of the young men slept in the "tousled" double bed, taking turns in the middle, and the fourth used a cot. They bought their food at a delicatessen named Boeuf-à-la-Mode, nicknamed the Buffalo-Mud. Here Crane completed *The Third Violet*. Almost concurrently, Howells was publishing *The Coast of Bohemia*, set in the same 23rd Street Art Students League. In his notebook Crane wrote an Emerson quotation he had seen chalked in the "topmost and remotest" studio in the building: "Congratulate yourselves if you have done something strange and extravagant and broken the monotony of a decorous age." It was a motto Crane would amply fulfill. Although he left the studio in May 1893, he returned periodically for brief stays and it was here that he finished *The Red Badge of Courage*. One of his roommates, R. G. Vosburgh, recorded that "Every incident and phase of character in *The Red Badge* was discussed fully and completely before being incorporated in the story."

The literary figure most strongly associated with the Gramercy Park area is William Sydney Porter, who went to live at 55 Irving Place in 1903, a year after he arrived in the city. He had signed a contract to produce a story a week for $100 under his pen name, O. Henry, for the *Sunday World,* and his new-found financial security enabled him to take a spacious, comfortable room there. He had a large bay window, in which he would sit for hours watching the people go by along the street, and his room had a white marble fireplace and an old-fashioned chandelier with glass beads and prisms, under which stood a long library table.

Porter turned all the characteristics of his new neighborhood to account. Diagonally across Irving Place was Healy's Café, also known as the Club, which he described in a story called "The Lost Blend." Wearing a slouch hat and a black bow tie, Porter would arrive every night about midnight at the red brick café (today called Pete's Tavern) and stand alone at the end of the bar. Never speaking to anyone, he would drink a few beers and then be gone. A German beer hall and restaurant at Third Avenue and 17th Street was the locale of his story "The Halberdier of the Little Rheinschloss." Called in Porter's time Scheffel Hall, the restaurant is now named Tuesday's; in the story Porter called it the Old Munich. "The big hall with its smoky rafters, rows of imported steins, portrait of Goethe, and verses painted on the walls — translated into German from the original of the Cincinnati poets — seems atmospherically correct when viewed through the bottom of the glass," he wrote. The restaurant still has the smoky rafters, the imported steins and the verses painted on the walls.

Near Fourth Avenue at 15th Street was the Hotel America, and Porter found the Latin Americans who frequented it good inspiration for the characters of his stories. In "The Gold That Glittered," the hotel appears as the Hotel Español. Porter was told that Washington Irving had lived in a yellow house at 17th Street and Irving Place, and he was proud to live "three doors from Irving's old home." Unfortunately, Porter, like many others, was mistaken. The house on 17th Street belonged to a merchant named Edgar Irving. This, and the fact that Irving Place *had* been named for the Knickerbocker writer, may have been responsible for the error memorialized in a misplaced plaque today. When Washington Irving visited the city from Sunnyside in Tarrytown, he stayed with his nephew John Treat Irving at East 21st Street. When the poet Orrick Johns came to live at 53 Irving Place in 1911, he in turn mistakenly believed O. Henry had lived in his house.

Fourth Avenue, now Park Avenue South above 14th Street, was one of Porter's favorite streets and he describes it in "A Bird of Bagdad":

Fourth Avenue — born and bred in the Bowery — staggers northward full of good resolutions.

Where it crosses Fourteenth Street it struts for a brief moment proudly in the glare of the museums and cheap theatres. It may yet become a fit mate for its high-born sister boulevard to the west, or its roaring, polyglot, broad-waisted cousin to the east. It passes Union Square; and here the hoofs of the dray horses seem to thunder in unison, recalling the tread of marching hosts — Hooray! But now come the silent and terrible mountains — buildings square as forts, high as the clouds, shutting out the sky where thousands of slaves bend over desks all day. On the ground floors are only little fruit shops and laundries and book shops . . . And next — poor Fourth Avenue! — the street glides into mediaeval solitude. On each side are the shops devoted to "Antiques."

With a shriek and a crash Fourth Avenue dives headlong into the tunnel at Thirty-fourth and is never seen again.

When Porter died, a funeral service was held at a neighborhood landmark, the Little Church Around the Corner at Fifth Avenue and West 29th Street.

In the late teens and twenties, the *Dial* had several outposts in the area around Gramercy Park. Sibley Watson, who financed the magazine, lived in Rochester but his wife had a house at 140 East 19th Street, one of the area's loveliest blocks. There was a bronze nude by Gaston Lachaise in the two-story living room and expressionist canvases by E. E. Cummings lined the staircases. Down the block at 77 Irving Place lived Paul Rosenfeld, who was the *Dial*'s music critic for seven years. (He had previously lived in an apartment at 20 Gramercy Park, where his friends Waldo Frank, Van Wyck Brooks and Randolph Bourne visited; Bourne died there after being cared for by Rosenfeld in his last illness.)

The *Dial* was a magazine primarily run by mail. What socializing did take place among members of the staff and contributors was likely to occur in Rosenfeld's apartment. Alyse Gregory, the managing editor, described it as "an interior that might have been lifted out of some European capital — Vienna, Paris, Florence — and without disarranging a single picture, or overturning a single vase, set down on the chill, dusty sidewalk of Irving Place, New York. It was an interior both intimate and spacious, an interior for pleasures that were grave and thought that was gay, for conversation witty and civilized." Edmund Wilson remembered it as a place where "poets read their poetry and composers played their music" and recalled conversation "beneath his little collection of Hartleys and O'Keeffes and Marins, surrounded by his shelves full of Nietzsche and Wagner, Strindberg, Shaw and Ibsen . . ." Among the guests who gathered here were Darius Milhaud, Aaron Copland, Edgar Varèse, E. E. Cummings, Hart Crane, Marianne Moore, Alfred Stieglitz, the Stettheimer sisters and Allen Tate.

In 1926 the Irving Place apartment became the unofficial offices of the *American Caravan,* an annual magazine that published new American writers. Rosenfeld and Alfred Kreymborg had conceived the idea and asked Van Wyck Brooks and Lewis Mumford to join with them in selecting manuscripts. Each Saturday afternoon the editors, with the exception of Brooks, who was having a nervous breakdown, gathered at Irving Place to read the manuscripts that had been submitted during the week. Often they would take writers to lunch at Lüchow's on 14th Street, the area's most prominent restaurant, which was also a favorite of Dreiser and Mencken and George Jean Nathan when they were in town.

Robert Penn Warren, then a graduate student at Yale, met Rosenfeld in 1927. He would visit New York on weekends and Rosenfeld took him to exhibits and taught him about art. "The really important thing for me, however," Warren said, "was not the mere fact that Rosenfeld introduced me to modern painting. The important thing was that he managed to set it for me in relation to the impulse behind modern literature." Rosenfeld encouraged Warren, who had been writing poetry, to try fiction. He did, and wrote "Prime Leaf," a novelette about rural Kentucky life, which was published in *American Caravan IV*. When the depression came, Rosenfeld's private income was diminished and he moved to a small apartment on West 11th Street.

During the twenties, writers must have bumped into one another coming and going on 19th Street. Carl Van Vechten and Ernest Boyd, whose homes were also gathering places, were living on the same block as the Sibley Watsons. In 1923 Van Vechten was at 151 East 19th Street in an apartment on the top floor. Although the place was tiny — there was a two-burner stove on top of the icebox — the Van Vechtens made it distinctive by covering the living room walls with red, gold-dotted Chinese tea paper. Ernest Boyd, a critic and litterateur who had come from Ireland, lived at 131 East 19th Street, where he entertained frequently. At one dinner party Scott and Zelda Fitzgerald arrived an hour late, after the others had finished eating, and fell asleep at the table over their soup. "Someone gathered Zelda up, with her bright cropped hair and diaphanous gown, and dropped her on a bed in a room nearby . . ." Van Wyck Brooks wrote. "Scott slumbered in the living room, waking up suddenly again to telephone an order for two cases of champagne, together with a fleet of taxis to take us to a night-club."

Several blocks away, in contrast to the high intellectual and social life of 19th Street, a struggling young writer was making an unexceptional hotel a gathering place of quite a different sort. In 1927, through the aid of a rich uncle, Nathanael West got a job as night manager of the Kenmore Hall Hotel at 145 East 23rd Street. West's biographer, Jay Martin, describes the hotel: "Badly designed, with small rooms, no restaurant, and neither conference rooms nor a mezzanine, it was saved by its faults; in some ways, it had been planned as a kind of glorified rooming house, its small rooms renting at low rates, its lobby and drugstore, where all the guests naturally congregated, be- coming popular as unostentatious meeting places for young men and women."

With little to do after midnight, West read for long hours and entertained his fellow writers — Quentin Reynolds, Dashiell Hammett, Maxwell Bodenheim, Michael Gold and S. J. Perel- man — in the early morning hours. Often West, who was called Pep by his friends, would let them stay at the hotel without paying. One night Reynolds discovered that Hammett was half- way through a serial for a pulp detective story magazine called *Black Mask* and was about to be thrown out of his room at another hotel. Reynolds called up West to tell him about it and make a suggestion.

" 'Register him under a phony name,' I said. 'When he fin- ishes his serial he can run like a deer and you can say that he was some skip artist who just blew the joint.' There was silence at the other end of the line. 'What is it, Pep?' I asked anxiously. 'I was just trying to think of a good name to register him under,' Pep said mildly. 'How do you like "T. Victrola Blueberry"?' "

Reynolds took Hammett to the hotel and the three drank a bottle of gin together. The serial was *The Maltese Falcon.* As Reynolds recalled, he and West read *Black Mask* avidly because Hammett was the first writer either of them knew who had actually sold his stories.

West worked on *The Dream Life of Balso Snell,* a fantasy about the adventures of a man who enters the Trojan Horse through its "Anus Mirabilis," in the hotel office from 1927 to 1929. In 1930 one of the owners of the Kenmore bought stock in the Sutton Club Hotel on East 56th Street and West moved uptown to become manager there.

Since the twenties, the Gramercy Park area has played little part in the lives of writers or their work. However, two landmarks with literary associations have remained through the years. The Players Club, an actors' club founded in 1888 by Edwin Booth, occupies an old brownstone house, remodeled by Stanford White, at 16 Gramercy Square. Booth thought actors should mix with those in other professions and a number of writers, including Mark Twain, Booth Tarkington, Edgar Lee Masters and Vachel Lindsay, were made members. Next door at 15 Gramercy Square is the National Arts Club. Founded in 1898 to provide exhibition facilities for the visual arts, it has also numbered literary people among its members, including Richard Watson Gilder, editor of the *Century,* S. S. McClure, Padraic Colum and W. H. Auden. Currently, however, neither club serves any important function for writers. Like the neighborhood, both institutions are only reminders of a literary past.

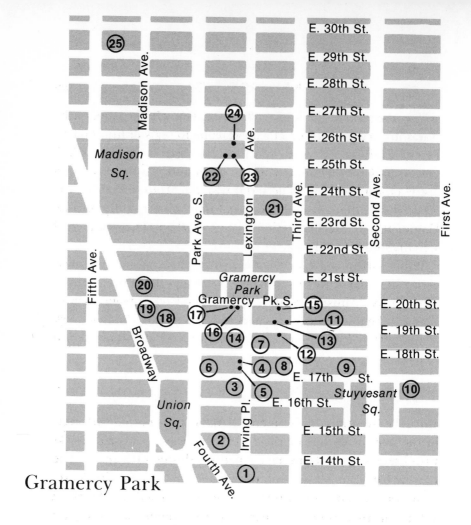

Gramercy Park

Gramercy Park Tour

Lüchow's, 110 East 14th Street (1), at the southernmost extreme of the area, has long been a New York institution. With its immense high-ceilinged, dark-paneled rooms, it resembles a German banquet hall. H. L. Mencken and George Jean Nathan often dined here with Theodore Dreiser, and it was a favorite luncheon spot for the editors of the *American Caravan* — Paul Rosenfeld, Alfred Kreymborg and Lewis Mumford.

The area one block east and west of Irving Place is O. Henry country. The Hotel America (2), which found its way into his stories as the Hotel Español, stood seventy-five yards east of Fourth Avenue (now Park Avenue South) on 15th Street. O. Henry, like many others, believed that the house at the corner of Irving Place and 17th Street, 122 East 17th Street (3), had once been Washington Irving's. Although a plaque to that effect marks the house, Irving never lived there. He did stay frequently with his nephew John Treat Irving, at 46 East 21st Street (20). O. Henry lived from 1903 to 1907 at 55 Irving Place (4) and the poet Orrick Johns lived at 53 Irving Place (5) in 1911. The three houses at 51 to 55 Irving Place have been remodeled, with a new brick façade, to form one apartment building. A restaurant, Sal Anthony's, occupies the same spot as the front parlor-floor room in which O. Henry used to sit, watching the passing scene.

Down 17th Street at 201 Park Avenue South is the Guardian Life Insurance Building (6), where Theodore Dreiser rented an office in 1925 while he was finishing *An American Tragedy*. He also used the office to rendezvous with women. Diagonally across Irving Place from O. Henry's home is the five-story brick house that in his time was Healy's Café, or the Club (7). Today it is Pete's Tavern and O. Henry memorabilia hang on its walls. Around the corner at 170 Third Avenue is Scheffel Hall (8), which O. Henry described in "The Halberdier of the Little Rheinschloss." Although the beer hall now has a modern overlay in its incarnation as Tuesday's, much of the atmosphere of the old restaurant remains.

East on 17th Street at number 241 (9) is the handsome brownstone house where William Dean Howells lived in 1891. Set back from the street behind an iron grillwork fence, the four-story house is ornamented by a second-floor balcony. The house faces Stuyvesant Park, an island of serenity on busy Second Avenue. Earlier, Howells had lived in a house at 330

East 17th Street (10). Beth Israel Hospital now occupies the entire block.

East 19th Street is known as "the Block Beautiful." During the 1920s its mid-nineteenth-century houses and former stables were remodeled and it has been maintained as an attractive architectural unit to this day. During the twenties the homes of three 19th Street residents served as gathering places for the artistic elite. Carl Van Vechten lived in the small six-story apartment house at 151 East 19th Street (11); Sibley Watson, who provided the main financial support for the *Dial,* lived at 140 East 19th (12); Ernest Boyd lived in the five-story brick building with bay windows at 131 East 19th Street (13) and Paul Rosenfeld had an apartment in the five-story red brick building on the corner of 19th Street and Irving Place, 77 Irving Place (14). Rosenfeld had lived earlier in the lovely wisteria-covered brick house at 22 Gramercy Park South (15).

Gramercy Park was planned as a fashionable residential development in the 1830s. In 1888 Edwin Booth, the actor, bought the Gothic Revival house at 16 Gramercy Park South (16), which had been built in 1845, and had it remodeled by Stanford White to serve as a club for those associated with the theater. To this day the brownstone house with its two-story balcony supported by columns is the Players Club, whose literary members have included Mark Twain and Booth Tarkington. Next door at 15 Gramercy Park South (17) is the National Arts Club, founded in 1898 as a haven for artists and writers. Originally two connecting houses built in 1845, the building was remodeled in the Victorian Gothic style by Calvert Vaux. Bay windows and studios adorn the topmost floors.

West of Park Avenue South are three of the addresses from the 1850s when the neighborhood was at its height. Horace Greeley's house, much changed, still stands at 35 East 19th Street (18). The three-story brick house now has a commercial

Horace Greeley's house at 35 East 19th Street, as it
looked in 1905 when the lower floor was a café.

façade, but an identical building is standing next door. The
house in which Theodore Roosevelt was born at 28 East 20th

Street (19) is open to the public from 9:00 A.M. to 4:40 P.M., Monday through Friday. John Treat Irving lived at 46 East 21st Street (20) and his uncle Washington Irving often visited there. The house, a four-story brownstone, its lower portion converted to a brick storefront, still stands.

Nathanael West worked as night manager at the Kenmore Hall Hotel, a nondescript brick building at 145 East 23rd Street (21). Several literary landmarks were lost when the Armory was constructed on Lexington Avenue between 25th and 26th streets. Henry James lived for six months in 1875 at 111 East 25th Street (22). In 1881, when he came to America for a visit, he stayed with Edwin Godkin, his former editor at the *Nation,* at 11'5 East 25th Street (23). Herman Melville lived from 1863 until his death in 1891 at 104 East 26th Street (24). A funeral was held for O. Henry at the Little Church Around the Corner at Fifth Avenue and West 29th Street (25).

V. Chelsea

As a NEIGHBORHOOD with a literary past, Chelsea is dominated by one overshadowing landmark, the Hotel Chelsea. Standing impressively at the midpoint of the area's main thoroughfare, between Seventh and Eighth avenues on 23rd Street, this Victorian Gothic anomaly, with its slate roof, gables and ironwork balconies, has housed artists and writers since it opened in 1884. Boasting a roster of residents that includes William Dean Howells, O. Henry, Edgar Lee Masters, Thomas Wolfe and Arthur Miller, it has, perhaps, been home to more writers than any other single New York building.

Yet long before the hotel's clientele drew attention to it, the neighborhood was rich in literary associations. Edith Wharton was born two blocks east at 14 West 23rd Street in 1862, when the area around Madison Square was at its most fashionable. The rich lived in houses made of the brownstone quarried primarily in Portland, Connecticut. A rich man was known as a "brownstone" and what today is the silk-stocking vote was then the brownstone vote, but Wharton found the architectural fashion oppressive. "One of the most depressing impressions of my childhood," she wrote, "is my recollection of the intolerable ugliness of New York, of its untended streets and the narrow houses so lacking in external dignity, so crammed with smug and suffocating upholstery . . . this little low-studded rectangular New York cursed with its universal chocolate-coloured coating of the most hideous stone ever quarried, this cramped horizontal gridiron of a town without towers, porticoes, fountains or perspectives, hide-bound in its deadly uniformity of mean ugliness . . ."

It was this New York and the passing of the older society that Wharton chose to chronicle in *The Age of Innocence*. Her hero, Newland Archer, lived on West 28th Street and the world he found so stifling, where society "cultivated ferns in Wardian cases, made macramé lace and wool embroidery on linen, collected American revolutionary glazed ware, sub-scribed to *Good Words*, and read Ouida's novels for the sake of the Italian atmosphere," was the same one that oppressed her. Born Edith Jones and as a child called Pussy, she spent most of her time reading and writing in the library of her home, where the collected works of an old family friend, Wash-ington Irving, adorned the shelves "in comely type and hand-some binding." In 1882, after her father died, she moved with her mother to 28 West 25th Street. She was married from the church that still stands across the street; it was then called Trinity Chapel.

Even in Wharton's time, the neighborhood a short block to the west created a striking contrast to the upper-class respecta-bility of Madison Square. All along Sixth Avenue from 14th Street to 42nd was the Tenderloin, an area of shops and de-partment stores by day, and bars, dance halls, brothels and gambling houses by night. The district was said to have earned its name because it was so rich in graft; in 1876 when Alexander "Clubber" Williams became precinct captain he told a reporter that from then on tenderloin was all he meant to eat. The area was as prime a territory for two writers — Stephen Crane and O. Henry — as it was for the police. Crane lived in the area, in the peripatetic way characteristic of him, for a month at a time from 1893 to 1895. Then, after *The Red*

Badge of Courage had made him famous, he moved to 165 West 23rd Street to research a series of sketches for the *New York Journal*. A reporter visiting the apartment in 1896 described it as decorated with impressionistic landscapes and war trophies Crane had collected on a trip to the Fredericksburg battlefield. It was while living here that Crane had one of his most notorious experiences. He was with three women one evening, and while he escorted one of them to a streetcar another was arrested for streetwalking. Crane came to her defense and said he had spent the evening interviewing her and her two companions for his articles and had not observed her soliciting. During the trial, in an attempt to discredit Crane as a witness, the prosecution implied that he was a libertine, drug addict and pimp. Two weeks later he jumped at an offer from William Randolph Hearst to cover the insurrection in Cuba.

Several sketches describing Tenderloin life survive to record Crane's stay. In "When Every One Is Panic Stricken" Crane describes a fire in "one of those ancient dwellings which the churning process of the city had changed into a hive of little industries," a variety of building surviving in the district that is now part of the garment center. "The Duel That Was Not Fought" takes place in a Sixth Avenue bar, and "A Detail" describes the daytime Sixth Avenue shopping district, "where from the streams of people and vehicles went up a roar like that from headlong mountain torrents."

Close upon Crane's heels came William Sydney Porter, who arrived in New York in 1902 after having served three years in prison on an embezzlement conviction in Columbus, Ohio. Katharine Anne Porter told the story this way: "He was my father's second cousin — I don't know what that makes him to me. And he was more known in the family for being a bank robber. He worked in a bank, you know, and he just didn't seem to find a talent for making money; no Porter ever did. But he had a wife who was dying of TB and he couldn't keep up with the doctor's bills. So he took a pitiful little sum — oh, about three hundred and fifty dollars — and ran away when he was accused. But he came back, because his wife was dying, and went to prison."

In the city Porter found his ideal subject and described the lives of its inhabitants lovingly. "Silent, grim, colossal," he once wrote, "the big city has ever stood against its revilers. They call it hard as iron; they say that no pulse of pity beats in its bosom; they compare its streets with lonely forests and deserts of lava. But beneath the hard crust of the lobster is found a delectable and luscious food." His first address here was the far from glamorous Marty Hotel at 47 West 24th Street. He had a small room on an air shaft with a bed and chair and used his trunk as a writing table. Although he moved the following year to the East Side when a contract with the *Sunday World* gave him a steady income, he continued to patronize his West Side haunts. His favorite among these was Mouquin's, at 38th Street and Sixth Avenue, a popular gathering place for artists and writers, who called it Mook's. In "Cosmopolite in a Café" Porter describes the atmosphere generally attributed to the restaurant although he does not refer to it by name. (He usually altered a few details of the settings he used in order to prevent positive identification.) "Invoke your consideration of the scene — the marble-topped tables, the range of leather-upholstered wall seats, the gay company, the ladies dressed in demi-state toilets, speaking in an exquisite visible chorus of taste, economy, opulence or art; the sedulous and largess-loving *garçons,* the music wisely catering to all with its raids upon the composers, the mélange of talk and laughter — and, if you will, the Wurzburger in the tall glass cones that bend to your lips as a ripe cherry sways on its branch to the beak of a robber jay." In search of material, Porter also frequented the Haymarket, a dance hall at Sixth Avenue and 30th Street, where he sometimes paid the prostitutes their usual rates to sit and talk with him at his table.

From 1906 until his death in 1910, Porter's office and sometime home was a room at the Caledonia Hotel, a tan brick building that stands at 28 West 26th Street. To avoid people he didn't want to see, he gave his friends a secret number, which he frequently changed, to be repeated to the hotel operator or clerk. He lived at the Chelsea Hotel briefly in 1907 and again in 1910, when he had a six-room apartment furnished only with a work table, a chair and a bed. Finally, after a lifetime of heavy drinking, he died at the Caledonia of cirrhosis of the liver. Nine empty whiskey bottles were found under the bed.

At the time of Porter's death, the area of the Tenderloin from 23rd to 33rd streets between Sixth and Seventh avenues was a Negro bohemia. It was to this neighborhood that the protagonist of James Weldon Johnson's *Autobiography of an Ex-Coloured Man* first came when he left his native South. "New York City," wrote Johnson, "is the most fatally fascinating thing in America. She sits like a great witch at the gate of the country, showing her alluring white face and hiding her crooked hands and feet under the folds of her wide garments — constantly enticing thousands from far within, and tempting those who come from across the seas to go no farther. And all these become the victims of her caprice." "The Club," a meeting place for Negro writers, entertainers, musicians and composers, which was in fact located on West 53rd Street, is set in the novel in a three-story house on 27th Street near Sixth Avenue.

Although the Hotel Chelsea had existed before the time of Crane and O. Henry, its literary reputation came later. It was originally an apartment house and among its first occupants was William Dean Howells, who took a four-room suite when he arrived in the city in 1888 after leaving Boston. The same year Mark Twain stayed there while on a lecture tour. The Chelsea became a hotel in 1905. "This is not a bourgeois hotel that has gone artistic," said contemporary resident Virgil

Edgar Lee Masters on the roof of the Chelsea Hotel in the 1940s.

Thomson, the composer. "It started as an expensive artistic hotel." John Sloan had a studio there and O. Henry had been in residence in 1907 and 1910. But it was not until the thirties, when Edgar Lee Masters moved into the hotel, became interested in its past and gave it a social focus, that it came into its heyday. Masters even glorified the hotel in a poem:

> . . . Then who will know
> About its ancient grandeur, marble stairs,
> Its paintings, onyx mantels, courts, the heirs
> Of a time now long ago?

> Who will remember that Mark Twain used to stroll
> In the gorgeous dining room, that Princesses,
> Poets and celebrated actresses
> Lived here and made its soul . . .

Late in 1937 Thomas Wolfe stopped by the Chelsea to look at the rooms and met Masters, who urged him to stay and vouched for him at the desk. Wolfe took a corner suite on the eighth floor with a foyer, bedroom, living room, office and bath. He had just left his publisher, Scribner's, and spent the next few months trying to decide on a new one. He frequently sat in the hotel bar, now a Spanish restaurant named El Quijote, and often ate at Cavanaugh's, a famous restaurant, now defunct, down the block at 256. He had a special table in the rear, from which he watched the other patrons.

Wolfe eventually settled on Harper's and on December 31, 1937, his editor, Edward Aswell, brought the contract to him at the Chelsea. Aswell described Wolfe's apartment: "The rooms were dark and dingy, but they had the advantage of ceilings high enough so that he ran no risk of bumping his head. The most impressive feature of the suite was the bathroom, which was quite large, with a toilet set on a raised platform: Tom called it 'The Throne Room.'"

In May 1938, Wolfe put together the manuscripts that were to become *The Web and the Rock* and *You Can't Go Home Again* from the four thousand pages he kept in packing cases in the middle of the living room floor. He left for a trip to the West where he became ill and died four months later in Baltimore.

In the fifties, the Chelsea's famous literary residents included James T. Farrell, Mary McCarthy and Dylan Thomas. Farrell lived here from June 1951 to December 1953, while he was writing the last volume of *Yet Other Waters,* a semiautobiographical novel in his Bernard Carr trilogy, which describes a writer's involvement with the Communist party. In *Judith,* published in 1969, he chronicled the affair he had with a celebrated pianist when he lived at the Chelsea. Mary McCarthy was in residence during the winter and spring of 1952–53 and the spring of 1954. Dylan Thomas made a practice of staying at the Chelsea when he came to America, and in November 1953 was taken from the hotel to St. Vincent's Hospital, where he died. Another writer in the hard-drinking tradition, Brendan Behan, went to the Chelsea in 1961 after being asked to leave the Algonquin, where, it is said, he chased the maids through the halls. In *Brendan Behan's New York,* he wrote: "I would hope that Mr. Bard, the proprietor, and his son Stanley . . . would leave space on their plaque for myself. I am not humble enough to say that I do not deserve one, but I hope it does not come too soon, because of all the names on the plaque, as far as I know, James T. Farrell is the only one that's alive and kicking very much." Behan had his wish and a plaque bearing his name was affixed after his death in 1964. Arthur Miller maintained an apartment in the hotel for seven years in the early sixties. "It is the only hotel I know which has no class lines," he said.

Throughout the years there have been other notable literary visitors — Nelson Algren, William Burroughs, Vladimir Nabokov, Gregory Corso and Julius Lester. Most recently, Edgar Lee Masters's old rooms were occupied by Clifford Irving, who achieved notoriety by writing a bogus biography of multimillionaire Howard Hughes. Today the grandeur Masters described is largely gone, but here and there vestiges remain. The hotel office, once the ladies' sitting room, still boasts an ornate fireplace and ceiling decorated with cherubs hand-painted on canvas. And Virgil Thomson's apartment recaptures the elegant past. The oak floor is polished and covered with Persian rugs. The fireplace, one of many in the Chelsea rooms, is in its original condition, with carved rosewood mantel, deep green glazed tile facing and brass trim and fender. Rosewood Victorian gingerbread decorates each window and the archway between rooms. At one end of the long living room there are built-in rosewood bookcases and cupboards with beveled mirrors. Here the old Chelsea lives.

•

To the west beyond the Tenderloin lies yet another Chelsea, the true Chelsea, which gave the rest of the area its name. In the eighteenth century Chelsea was the estate, named after the Chelsea district in London, of Captain Thomas Clarke. It reached from 14th to 27th streets and from Seventh Avenue to the Hudson River. In the early nineteenth century the property descended to Clarke's grandson, Clement Clarke Moore, a scholar of the Bible and of Hebrew and Greek literature, who is best remembered for his poem, "A Visit from St. Nicholas." As the implementation of the New York City grid plan progressed, Moore took steps to plan Chelsea as an elegant residential neighborhood. He divided his property into lots but controlled its development by covenants written into the deeds. Chelsea never became as fashionable as Fifth Avenue but its streets of middle-class homes, many of which remain and are now protected by designation within the Chelsea Historic District, were of high architectural quality and imparted a harmony found in few other sections of the city.

Several writers found this area a pleasant way station in the early decades of the present century. Edwin Arlington Robinson was a habitué of the Café Francis on West 23rd Street, a haunt, like Mouquin's, of artists and writers. When the proprietor learned that Robinson was penniless and couldn't pay his rent, he offered him a room on the top floor of his house, a four-story brownstone that can be seen at 450 West 43rd Street. Robinson stayed there throughout most of the period between 1901 and 1906. From 1909 until he moved to Hartford in 1916, Wallace Stevens lived at 441 West 21st Street, a red brick house that stands today. After a short-lived job as a reporter for the *Tribune,* Stevens entered New York University Law School. He remarked in later life that "he had been no more serious about poetry during his early days in New York than he had been at Harvard." His first important publication did not come until 1914.

Sherwood Anderson lived in the area in the fall of 1918. "I got a cheap room," he wrote in his *Memoirs,* "somewhere over on the West Side in the twenties between Ninth and Tenth avenues, and there I worked . . . It was a good room. There was the hoarse cry of steamers in the river at night. I was in the back of the house, upstairs, and looked across little city back yards into many other people's rooms. At night I could turn off my lights and sit by my window. There were people making love, dining, quarreling." The room was in a house at 427 West 22nd Street, a brownstone painted gray that even now has the air of a rooming house. Anderson was much older than most of his literary acquaintances in New York — Van Wyck Brooks, Waldo Frank and Paul Rosenfeld

— and wondered whether he had a place in their world. "And so there I was," he wrote, "an American rapidly approaching middle life, sitting in my room over in west Twenty-Second street at night after a day spent listening to the talk of the new men and trying with all my might to be one of the new men myself." With the publication of *Winesburg, Ohio* in 1919, Anderson's standing in the world of letters was established. He had a place in the New York world but he did not choose to live there.

Among Anderson's "new men" was Van Wyck Brooks, soon to become one of the dominant figures in criticism of the twentieth century. As a young man, he had lived one block north of Anderson in the row of houses called London Terrace from 1909 to 1911. The houses, since replaced by a mammoth apartment complex bearing the same name, were noteworthy for their design when they were built in 1845. They were set back about thirty-five feet from the street with gardens in front and were uniformly pilastered to give the effect of a colonnade. Brooks wrote of his house:

> There were three big trees in the front yard, with a cast-iron fountain and a bench, and, within, the kind of furnished rooms that O. Henry so often described with half-broken chairs and the odour of mildewed woodwork. It was kept by a brawny Scotswoman with a drunken husband, and there was an ancient libidinous chambermaid, always dressed in rusty black, who might have stepped out of an eighteenth-century novel. It was a discouraging household, especially in winter, when the trains of "Death Avenue" [Ninth] at the corner ploughed through the snow and one had to resort to the free-lunch counter at the saloon across the street that was one of Edwin Arlington Robinson's haunts. For Robinson had lived eight years before in a brownstone house a hundred yards away . . ."

During this period Brooks often went to a small French

John Sloan's *Yeats at Petitpas*, 1910. Sloan's identifications were, from left to right around the table: Van Wyck Brooks, John Butler Yeats, Alan Seeger, Dolly Sloan, Robert W. Sneddon, Anne Squires, Fred King, John Sloan, Mrs. Charles Johnston and, serving, Mlle. Celestine Petitpas.

hotel at 317 West 29th Street run by three sisters from Brittany named Petitpas. William Butler Yeats's father, the painter Jack Yeats, was in residence there from 1908, when he first visited New York and decided to stay, until his death thirteen years later. W. B. Yeats visited his father at the hotel in 1911 and again in 1914. Conrad Aiken, who lived in London Terrace one summer while an undergraduate at Harvard, remembered encountering Jack Yeats, "who invariably, when asked if he was the father of the great Yeats, replied, '*I* am the great Yeats!' "

There was a restaurant in the backyard at Petitpas' where Yeats would sit at the end of one of the long tables surrounded by the men who were to become the most important American painters of the period — Robert Henri, John Sloan, George Bellows, William Glackens and the Prendergast brothers — and a number of young writers, including Brooks, Alan Seeger, and Padraic and Mary Colum. Yeats's talk "abounded in recollections not only of 'Willie' but of Æ and Synge, Lady Gregory, the Abbey Theatre, George Moore, Dunsany," wrote Brooks. "We had special reasons for our interest in this, for we felt we were on the verge of a not dissimilar movement of our own, the first phase of another revival that expressed an American coming-of-age, an escape from our old colonial dependence on England. Yeats himself said, 'The fiddles are tuning all over America' . . ."

In 1914 the *New Republic* started publication in three old houses at 419 to 423 West 21st Street. Unfortunately, this is one of the few buildings that has been replaced on an otherwise architecturally intact, tree-lined block. The magazine began to achieve literary distinction in 1928 with Edmund Wilson as literary editor. Malcolm Cowley became his assistant in 1929 and when Wilson left to travel around the country reporting on the depression, Cowley replaced him. Cowley lived nearby at 360 West 22nd Street in a sixty-five-dollars-a-month studio from 1930 to 1934. It was under his direction that the magazine reached its height as a literary force. As Alfred Kazin, who began his career as a reviewer for the magazine, remembered, "The lead review in the *New Republic,* a single page usually written by Cowley himself, brought the week to focus for people to whom this page, breathing intellectual fight in its sharp black title and solid double-columned lines of argument, represented the most dramatically satisfying confrontation of a new book by a

Malcolm Cowley reading a *New Republic* manuscript in
the bathtub at 360 West 22nd Street in the early 1930s.

gifted, uncompromising, critical intelligence." Lunch for staff
members and distinguished guests was served in a dining room
on one of the lower floors, and in the thirties, after work, the
staff drank gin and lime and played quoits and deck tennis
in the garden.

In the fifties Chelsea gained yet another literary dimension
when Jack Kerouac wrote the first complete version of *On the
Road* in a loft at 149 West 21st Street in 1951. His friend
Lucien Carr brought home a 120-foot roll of teletype paper from
United Press, which enabled Kerouac to type nonstop. He
claimed he had originated "spontaneous prose," which involved
writing without pausing to calculate or revise. But, in fact, he
had begun *On the Road* in 1948 and was to rework it consider-

ably before it was published in 1957. Later in the decade another writer who, like Kerouac, would come to be associated
with the East Village, lived in Chelsea. In the fall of 1958 Le-
Roi Jones moved to 402 West 20th Street and stayed there for
about a year.

All in all, Chelsea has been a neighborhood of immense
diversity. During the last decades of the nineteenth century
an area only five blocks wide included the fashionable residential district of Madison Square, the gambling halls and brothels
of the Tenderloin and the middle-class respectability of Chelsea
Square. Its literary history has been similarly diverse, encom-
passing Edith Wharton's commentary on New York society,
descriptions of the city's underside by Stephen Crane and
O. Henry, the influential criticism of the *New Republic* and
Jack Kerouac's Beat prose. Today the old houses in the Chelsea
Historic District have been restored and form one of the most
attractive enclaves on Manhattan. But the larger area is now
New York's garment center and is primarily given over to

LeRoi Jones at 402 West 20th Street, around 1959.
(Allen Ginsberg on bongos.)

commercial uses. In terms of the neighborhood's literary associations only the Hotel Chelsea, which still houses an occasional writer, remains.

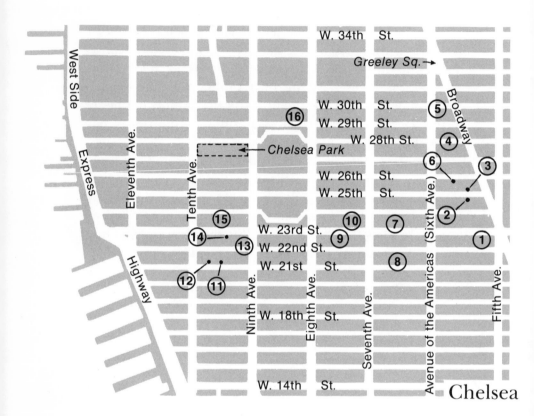

Chelsea Tour

Madison Square, once a fashionable residential area, borders Chelsea on the east. Edith Wharton was born at 14 West 23rd Street (1) in a house replaced by a cast-iron building, one of the many commercial structures that now dominate the neighborhood. She lived two blocks north at 28 West 25th

A glimpse of Edith Wharton's birthplace, the house on the right. This is the only existing photograph of 14 West 23rd Street.

Street (2) at the time of her marriage. This house, as well, has been supplanted by a commercial building but the church where Wharton was married in 1885 still stands across the street (3). At that time the newly completed church was known as Trinity Chapel and served the uptown parishioners of Trinity Church. Currently the Serbian Orthodox Cathedral of St. Sava, it was built in the English Gothic Revival style and has been designated a landmark. Along either side of 28th Street (4) a few brownstones and brick houses remain from the era Wharton described in *The Age of Innocence*. Wharton's brother lived here as well as her fictional characters, the Archers.

Going west to Sixth Avenue one enters the area once known as the Tenderloin. Many of the grand department stores, where the shopgirls O. Henry wrote about worked, are standing but have been converted to other uses. At night the action shifted to the street's dance halls and gambling houses. On the southeast corner of Sixth Avenue and 30th Street stood the Haymarket (5), the famous dance hall painted by John Sloan and visited by O. Henry and Eugene O'Neill.

At 28 West 26th Street (6) stands the Caledonia Hotel, where O. Henry had a room he used for writing from 1906 until his death in 1910. Stephen Crane lived several blocks away at 165 West 23rd Street (7) for eleven months while researching city life for a series of articles for the *New York Journal*. In a loft in the brownstone at 149 West 21st Street off Seventh Avenue (8) Jack Kerouac wrote *On the Road*.

The Hotel Chelsea at 222 West 23rd Street (9) is one of the few remaining Victorian Gothic apartment houses once common in New York. French doors open onto balconies richly decorated with ironwork leaves and flowers. The building has been designated both a historical and an architectural landmark. In the lobby, vestiges of a former elegance can be seen in the marble floor and the ornately carved fireplace mantel. Paintings and sculpture by former and present Chelsea residents, such as Larry Rivers, are now displayed there. Across the street is the YMCA (10) where William Saroyan stayed at the age of nineteen when he first came to New York. He had lost his luggage, including $100, all the money he had, and paid one dollar in change as an advance on his room. Among the various Chelsea residents who used the YMCA pool were Brendan Behan and Edgar Lee Masters.

The Chelsea Historic District, with its lovely tree-lined blocks of nineteenth-century houses, runs mainly between 20th and 22nd streets and Ninth and Tenth avenues. At 419 to 423 West 21st Street (11) is the site of the three houses that

The original London Terrace in Chelsea.

served the *New Republic* as offices. In 1938 they were replaced by a brick apartment building. Wallace Stevens lived here in a pleasant brick house at 441 West 21st Street (12) from 1909 to 1916. Sherwood Anderson lived in an old brownstone rooming house at 427 West 22nd Street (13) in 1918.

Edwin Arlington Robinson lived at 450 West 23rd Street (14), one of a row of brownstone houses, from 1901 to 1905. Across the street once stood a row of four-story houses named London Terrace (15), in which Van Wyck Brooks and Conrad Aiken lived at various times. A vast apartment complex bearing the same name now occupies the site.

At 317 West 29th Street (16), in what was once a French neighborhood, stands the house that was the famous Petitpas', where J. B. Yeats lived and where John Sloan, Van Wyck Brooks, Alan Seeger and others visited.

VI. Midtown

WALT WHITMAN once noted that "while New York was a bad place for literary farming, it was a good market for the harvest." Although he would eventually be proven wrong on the first part of his proposition as more and more good writing came out of New York, he was prescient on the second. Around 1900 the center of publishing moved from Boston to New York. The old nineteenth-century firms were joined in the twentieth by new companies that would change the cast of publishing and shift the balance of influence. Where the New England Brahmins had taken a conservative moral, political and literary tone, the new firms launched the publication of works by Continental European authors, writings about radical politics, literature that was experimental in style, and books whose breakthroughs in subject matter would often plunge the publishers into battle with the censors.

At the same time New York, in its role as capital of style and sophistication in America, was producing a series of publications that kept the fashionable abreast of the latest in art, theater and writing and provided a steady diet of highly literate entertainment. The prototype of such magazines, the *Smart Set,* was followed by *Vanity Fair,* the *American Mercury* and, still thriving today, the *New Yorker.* By the twenties, Midtown — the business district of the city extending from 34th Street to West 59th Street — was bustling with literary activity, mostly of

the harvest but sometimes of the farming variety. Like the Park
Row area in the mid-nineteenth century, Midtown was the
center of both the theater and commercial publishing. Authors
came to do business with their publishers and stayed in the
great hotels. Journalists, playwrights, critics and celebrities so-
cialized in Midtown restaurants, speakeasies and living rooms.
And some writers even came to write.

One of the area's earliest residents symbolized the rise in the
city's literary significance. When William Dean Howells moved
from Boston to New York, his action was viewed as a sign that
the country's literary center had shifted. As editor, critic and
novelist, Howells was considered so much the representative sensibility of his time that the last third of the nineteenth century
has often been called "the Age of Howells." A native of Ohio,
Howells had worked for the *Atlantic* in Boston, eventually becoming editor and enjoying a wide influence on American writing. In 1886, however, he contracted with *Harper's Magazine* in
New York to write "The Editor's Study," a column he called "a
symposium of one," in which he used reviews of current books
as a springboard for discussing his critical ideas. For a while he
commuted between Boston and New York, finally moving here
in the early nineties. Although he wrote about the Stuyvesant
Square area in *The Coast of Bohemia* and *A Hazard of New
Fortunes* (see Chapter IV, Gramercy Park), he spent his years
as America's pre-eminent literary figure in a series of addresses
on or near West 59th Street. Here, where tall hotels and apartment buildings have replaced a row of smaller hotels and brownstones, he wrote *The Coast of Bohemia, A Traveler from Altruria* and *Literary Passions.* The mansions of the rich lined
nearby Fifth Avenue. Around the corner between 57th and
58th streets stood "Marble Row." This series of houses with
shimmering white façades had been built by Edith Wharton's
great-aunt, Mary Mason Jones, in 1870. Mrs. Jones appears in

The Age of Innocence as Mrs. Manson Mingott, an eccentric aristocrat who had "put the crowning touch to her audacities by building a large house of pale cream-coloured stone (when brown sandstone seemed as much the only wear as a frock-coat in the afternoon) in an inaccessible wilderness near the Central Park." The old Plaza Hotel was on its present site at the corner of 59th Street, and the columned Hotel Savoy and the Romanesque Netherland Hotel, the predecessor of the present Sherry-Netherland, were across the way. Howells would have been fairly well at home, at least economically, in this district of fabulous mansions and elegant hotels. One biographer, Kenneth S. Lynn, estimates that the 1970 equivalent of his income during the 1890s would have been around $120,000 a year, which he earned through his great productivity and his acumen in negotiating royalties up to 25 per cent. At the same time, he reflected on the disparity between the rich dashing by in their carriages and the poor seated on the benches of Central Park, whom he could see from his window.

In 1908 Howells moved to 130 West 57th Street, his address until his death in 1920. Van Wyck Brooks, then twenty-three-years old, interviewed him there in 1909 for a publication called *The World's Work*. Howells was seventy-two. "He goes into his little study after breakfast, and sits down at a very clean, plain writing-table, and writes. It is a habit of half a century . . ." Frank Norris, another author who had met Howells in the late nineties, represented him as Trevor in "The Lost Story." "He was a short, rotund man," wrote Norris, "rubicund as to face, bourgeois as to clothes and surroundings, joyful in manner, indulging even in slang. One might easily set him down as a retired groceryman — wholesale, perhaps, but nonetheless a groceryman."

A few other literary people lived nearby. Lincoln Steffens had a seven-room apartment at 341 West 56th Street in 1897.

William Dean Howells at 130 West 57th Street in 1909.

The décor of the apartment was eclectic; a samovar from the Lower East Side and a silver tea service presented to his wife's father during the Civil War shared the dining room sideboard. James Weldon Johnson lived several blocks south in the Marshall Club at 260 West 53rd Street. In the early 1900s, the area around West 53rd was a center for black writers, musicians and performers. The Marshall was the most popular meeting place and Johnson portrayed it as "The Club" in his *Autobiography of an Ex-Coloured Man*. There was a restaurant and ragtime music but no bar. The main floor had lace-curtained windows and pictures of every Negro who had attained distinction — athletes, performers, political leaders. Some whites went "slumming" at the club, but many of those who came were theatrical performers of Negro roles; they based their characterizations on what they saw there. Johnson, who was a successful songwriter at the time, lived on the second floor of the Marshall for a while, using the back rooms as a studio.

The area around the Art Students League, which had moved from East 23rd to its present site on West 57th Street, was a center for artists, who lived in small rooms near the school. Vachel Lindsay came to New York to study there with Robert Henri in 1905. He had rooms with a friend on the top floor of a building on 57th Street. There was a trap door in the ceiling leading to the attic, where he lived when he had no rent money. Around 1908 Lindsay began to turn his energies to poetry. He had very little money and, to test the idea that ordinary people could appreciate his poetry, he decided to sell it on the street. "About eleven o'clock in the evening in accordance with a plan matured for some weeks," he wrote ". . . I put twelve copies of the 'We Who Are Playing' in my overcoat pocket, and made a plunge for Tenth Avenue . . . Well, I tried a sleepy big shock-headed baker first. I tried to give the poem to him. He considered the thing for some time as I explained it, but finally handed it back saying he had no use for it . . . So the next place I said to the proprietor, 'I will sell you this for two cents.' At once I saw the thing take . . ." After selling several poems on Tenth Avenue, Lindsay went over to Ninth, where he sold only to druggists — "the confectioners and delicatessens refused." He concluded that "there is more poetry in the distribution of verse than in the writing of it."

·

In 1902 Howells wrote: "New York society has not taken to our literature. New York publishes it, criticizes it, and circulates it, but I doubt if New York society much reads it or cares for it, and New York is therefore by no means the literary centre that Boston once was, though a large number of our literary men live in or about New York . . . New York is a vast mart, and literature is one of the things marketed here . . ."

New York's importance as a literary market was reflected in the fact that the *Smart Set* had become the proving ground for literary careers. The magazine came into its most important period in November of 1914, when H. L. Mencken and George Jean Nathan took over as its editors. Nathan's function was administrative: he ran the office and supervised the daily routine; Mencken dealt with authors and selected manuscripts for publication. Each also wrote a column, Nathan on theater and Mencken on books. Through his column and his editorial power on the magazine, Mencken was the most influential voice in American letters for fifteen years. Before the tenure of Mencken and Nathan, the *Smart Set* had helped found the careers of O. Henry and James Branch Cabell. Now it was to introduce its readers to a whole new era in literature. It "discovered" Eugene O'Neill by publishing three of his plays; it gave James Joyce his first exposure in the United States with two of his Dubliners stories; and it bought the work of F. Scott Fitzgerald regularly enough to enable him to quit his advertising job and complete his first novel, *This Side of Paradise*. In addition, Mencken popularized a new standard in literature. He praised Mark Twain, Conrad and Melville and was the first prominent critic to champion Walt Whitman. He introduced Americans to Flaubert, Stendhal and Goethe.

Mencken himself was never a New Yorker and it is a measure of the primacy of the city that, despite his hatred of it, he came here regularly from Baltimore to do his work on the *Smart Set*. "I thoroughly detest New York, though I have to go

there very often," he said. "Have you ever noticed that no
American writer of any consequence lives in Manhattan.
Dreiser tried it . . . but finally fled to California." Mencken
was discounting the new bohemians in Greenwich Village. He
told a young writer, "Don't ever, if you can possibly help it,
go below Fourteenth Street. The Village literati are scum."
He and Nathan would venture that far downtown only to
visit Dreiser and take in dinner at Lüchow's.

Mencken's visits to New York gradually settled into a
routine. He would arrive at the Algonquin Hotel at 59 West
44th Street late Sunday afternoon, check in, call Nathan across
the street at the Hotel Royalton and join him for an evening
out at a bar or a party. (Nathan maintained an apartment on
the top floor of the Royalton from 1908 until his death in
1958.) Monday morning Mencken would go to the *Smart Set*
office, which occupied various addresses on Fourth, Fifth and
Eighth avenues before finally settling down at 25 West 45th
Street. The reception room was decorated with original art
work for covers and had a golden oak church pew as a visitors'
bench. There was a yellow tea cosy woven from hundreds of
cigar bands, cigars being Mencken's trademark, and a tapestry
depicting a Newfoundland dog rescuing a baby — thrown over
a claw-foot gilt chair. The tapestry also served as a cover for
a table made from saw horses and an alabaster slab that
Mencken had filched from a Maryland graveyard. During the
long work sessions when he was in town, immense lunches
sent in from a nearby German café were served here with a
sign saying POETS' FREE LUNCH tacked above the slab.

In between the serious writing, the *Smart Set* sprinkled its
pages with fillers, epigrams, quotes and inane news stories
reprinted without comment, divertissements later to be taken
up by the *New Yorker*. Eventually, however, the lightness
infected the whole periodical and came to undermine it. By

1923 Mencken and Nathan concluded that the *Smart Set* had become too frivolous, and decided to leave it and form a more serious magazine, the *American Mercury*, published by Alfred Knopf. Unfortunately, they could never agree on what to be serious about. Nathan stepped down as coeditor in 1925 and became a contributing editor, withdrawing entirely in 1930. Mencken once characterized their difficulty in a letter to Nathan: "*The Smart Set* went to pot because it was too trivial — because it interested intelligent readers only intermittently, and then only when they were in trifling moods — when they were, so to speak, a bit stewed intellectually." Dreiser had voiced the same criticism years earlier when Mencken had asked him for a promotional blurb. "Under you and Nathan the thing seems to have tamed down to a light, non-disturbing period of persiflage and badinage . . . Everything, apparently, is to be done with a light, aloof touch, which to me is good but like a diet of soufflé."

The *American Mercury* took offices first at the Heckscher Building at 730 Fifth Avenue (57th Street) , where Knopf had his publishing company. The office was so drab that Mencken called it "the undertaking parlor." To save the space of files, no carbons were made and there was a house rule that only in cases of emergency did anyone speak to anyone else before 11:00 A.M.

While the *Smart Set* found itself becoming too smart, another magazine was making a virtue of taste and fashion. *Vanity Fair* had some of the same contributors — Edna St. Vincent Millay, Theodore Dreiser, D. H. Lawrence, Elinor Wylie — but set them in a different context. On its heavy satin pages it published the newest writers alongside reproductions, often in color, of avant-garde paintings and photographs of personalities, actors and celebrities that today recall a gentler, more civilized and optimistic era. Here is the young Gary Cooper photo-

Neysa McMein's
portrait of
Dorothy Parker.

graphed in all his lanky elegance by Cecil Beaton next to
Matisse's *White Plumes*. Here is the luminous Garbo side by
side with the latest from the pen of Gertrude Stein. Interspersed are the wittiest efforts of Dorothy Parker and Robert
Benchley. Before it was through, *Vanity Fair* had published
the work of virtually every important new writer and painter of
the 1920s and 1930s. At its offices at 19 West 44th Street, three

who were to become midtown literary celebrities were employed. Robert Benchley was managing editor, Robert Sherwood was drama editor and Dorothy Parker filled in as drama critic for P. G. Wodehouse. Benchley, who had written a paper on undertaking when he was in school, subscribed to two undertaking magazines. Parker cut out a picture illustrating how and where to inject embalming fluid and hung it over her desk until editor Frank Crowninshield asked her to take it down. When the office manager sent around a memo forbidding the discussion of salaries, Parker, Benchley and Sherwood wrote theirs on signs, which they wore around their necks. Finally, when Parker was fired in January 1920 for panning three plays in a row, Sherwood and Benchley resigned in protest. Sherwood got a job reviewing films for the humor magazine *Life,* and Parker and Benchley went off to free-lance from an office they shared together. They took a room on the third floor of the Metropolitan Opera House studios for thirty dollars a month and discussed using "Parkbench" as a cable address. Benchley said the room was so small that "one cubic foot less of space, and it would have constituted adultery." It was widely rumored, though apparently not true, that Parker had a sign saying MEN lettered on the door. Three months later Benchley left and went to *Life* as drama editor. Parker left soon afterward.

Dorothy Parker and Robert Benchley were among the few writers to make homes of sorts in Midtown. Parker had been born in the West Seventies and had lived in a boarding house at 103rd Street and Broadway when she took her first job at *Vogue* at ten dollars a week. In 1917 she went to *Vanity Fair.* She was briefly married to Edwin Pond Parker II but separated from him in 1920 and took a small apartment at 57 West 57th Street, where her friend Neysa McMein, a magazine illustrator and artist, had a studio. According to her biographer,

John Keats, Dorothy Parker had "a cheaply furnished room, utterly without taste, as anonymous as a room in a traveling salesmen's hotel . . . She was so seldom home that her private life was, in a sense, nonexistent."

Benchley had left his family in Scarsdale and went to live first at the Algonquin and then at the Royalton, where he had a two-room suite. With its mahogany trim and cross-latticed windows, the place looked Victorian. "Oh, so they think they're Victorian," he said. "I'll show them something Victorian, if that's the way they want to play." He furnished the room with a dark red rug, red draperies, a red velvet tasseled cover on an oak table, brass student lamps with green shades and three pictures of Queen Victoria. He collected books for their titles alone — such works as *Forty Thousand Sublime and Beautiful Thoughts, Success with Small Fruits, Talks on Manure* — and acquired so many oddities — a cello and music stand, a model of the Erie steamboat, a collection of beer mugs and Brueghel prints — that his motto became "Dig It Up, Dust It Off, and Give It to Benchley."

In his long career as a drama critic, first for *Life* and later for the *New Yorker,* Benchley spent most of his time out on the town. A typical day consisted of breakfast at eleven-thirty, fooling around at the typewriter for a while, late lunch at the Algonquin, answering mail, telephoning his wife or visiting friends in the afternoon. At six or seven he would go for drinks to Jack and Charlie's Puncheon Club, the forerunner of the "21" Club at 42 West 49th Street, or Tony's, a speakeasy where Heywood Broun and Franklin P. Adams also gathered, then to the theater, then back to Jack and Charlie's for dinner and, after it closed, on to Harlem to Dickie Wells', the Nest or the Savoy Ballroom. He even went out to write and sometimes rented a room at Polly Adler's, the "house" run by the well-known madam. When he died, a wake, presided over by Marc Connelly, was held at "21," and a plaque reading "Robert Benchley, His Corner, 1889–1945" was placed over the table where he customarily sat.

Benchley and Parker were two of the regulars in a group called the Round Table, which began to gather at the Algonquin Hotel in 1919. The group is said to have originated when press agent John Peter Toohey took *New York Times* drama critic Alexander Woollcott to the Algonquin to sample the angel cake. Woollcott, Franklin P. Adams, who under the byline F. P. A. wrote a famous column for the *New York World* called "The Conning Tower," and Heywood Broun, then a sportswriter for the *Tribune,* formed a weekly luncheon habit. Others joined them. The story goes that the midgets from the Hippodrome across the street teased Robert Sherwood, who was extremely tall, whenever he left the office of *Vanity Fair.* "As a result," records Nathaniel Benchley, "Sherwood wouldn't go out to lunch alone, and he took to asking Robert [Benchley] and Mrs. Parker if they would mind walking on either side of him, at least until they got past the midgets. This led to the three of them having lunch together every day." So Sherwood, Parker and Benchley joined Toohey, Woollcott, Broun and Adams and soon they were all meeting daily first in the Pergola Room (now the Oak Room) , then in the Rose Room at a long table and finally at the round table from which the group drew its name. Eventually the group also included Edna Ferber, George S. Kaufman, Marc Connelly, Harold Ross, his wife, Jane Grant, and others, and became known to the public through F. P. A., who would report the group's witticisms in his column.

Woollcott's biographer, Samuel Hopkins Adams, explained that "leadership in the group went, by tacit consent, to F. P. A., due to his reputation, already national, his wit, and in some degree to his financial status as by far the highest paid newspaperman of the lot. He was . . . a lean, sinewy man, faintly

demonic of expression, with a passion for Horatian odes and
base-line tennis; fast as a boxer on his mental feet, and endowed
with an intolerant manner masking a tolerant mind."

Edna Ferber wrote of the group: "Their standards were high,
their vocabulary fluent, fresh, astringent and very, very tough.
Theirs was a tonic influence, one on the other, and all on the
world of American letters. The people they could not and
would not stand were the bores, hypocrites, sentimentalists
and the socially pretentious. They were ruthless toward charla-
tans, toward the pompous and the mentally and artistically
dishonest. Casual, incisive, they had a terrible integrity about
their work and a boundless ambition." Still, this collection
of witty critics, playwrights and journalists should not be confused with writers in a more serious literary tradition. "People
romanticize [the Round Table]," said Dorothy Parker. "These
were no giants. Think of who was writing in those days —
Lardner, Fitzgerald, Faulkner, and Hemingway. Those were
the real giants. The Round Table was just a lot of people
telling jokes and telling each other how good they were."

Today the round table stands in the Oak Room, where it is
occasionally reserved by Marc Connelly, one of the few surviving members of the group. The Rose Room, restored some
years ago by theatrical designer Oliver Smith, is much as it was
in the twenties. *New Yorker* people still lunch there regularly — editor William Shawn usually sits at table number one
— as do editors from the nearby publishing houses. The lobby,
with its dark wood paneling, Chinese lamps, grandfather clock,
velvet-covered sofas and wing chairs, has never been changed,
except for new upholstery, and is a favorite cocktail place for
literary people.

On Saturday nights in the early twenties, the Round Table
extended itself into a poker game called the Thanatopsis Pleasure and Literary Club, a name taken from Sinclair Lewis's
Main Street, later modified to the Thanatopsis Poker and In-

side Straight Club. The poker game, which included Harold Ross, Raoul Fleischmann, an heir of the baking family, and Herbert Bayard Swope, editor of the *New York World,* as well as Kaufman, Toohey, Connelly, F. P. A., Broun and Woollcott, had its origins in a wartime game in Paris. Ross, who was to found the *New Yorker,* promoted the resurrection of the game at his 11th Street apartment. Later the players moved to an upstairs room at the Algonquin and later still to Ross's 47th Street house, "21," and the Colony restaurant.

The founding of the *New Yorker* magazine in 1925 can be seen as a product of Harold Ross's association with the people of the Round Table and the Thanatopsis Club. From 1917 to 1919 Ross had worked in Paris with Woollcott and F. P. A. as editor of *Stars and Stripes,* the armed services magazine. When he came back to New York he started *Home Sector,* an unsuccessful stateside version of the magazine. In 1920 he married Jane Grant, a reporter for the *New York Times,* and on the day of the wedding signed a contract to edit the *American Legion Weekly.* The two lived on her salary and saved his for a publishing venture.

After the *American Legion Weekly,* Ross briefly edited a humor magazine called *Judge.* Then in 1924 he met Raoul Fleischmann over the Thanatopsis poker table. He sold Fleischmann on his idea for a weekly magazine of humor and satire that would incorporate the Algonquin's sophisticated, debunking attitude toward life. With $25,000 from Fleischmann and $20,-000 from Ross and Grant, the *New Yorker* (the name was contributed by John Peter Toohey) began publication at 25 West 45th Street, the building that had housed the *Smart Set.*

If the *Smart Set* had started out as a serious literary forum and ended as a "soufflé," the *New Yorker* took the reverse direction. The first issue, one critic remarked, looked as if "it had been made up by the office cat's knocking over the wastebasket." It was filled with sophomoric humor and half-baked Broadway gossip. Gradually, however, Ross assembled the staff that would give the magazine its distinctive quality. E. B. White arrived in 1926 and took over the lead "Notes and Comment" column. James Thurber came in 1927 and set the tone for "The Talk of the Town," editing and rewriting the offerings of amateurs and several reporters. The editorial influence of the two extended far beyond their departments. Both contributed pieces regularly and so much set the tone of the magazine as to be considered its soul. And both also fulfilled Ross's dream of publishing humor of such high caliber that it could be called literature. A third staff member helped to establish the *New Yorker*'s literary importance. Katharine Sergeant, who later married E. B. White, came to the *New Yorker* as a reader in 1925. She eventually became managing editor and took responsibility for the literary aspects of the magazine. Of the Algonquin group, Robert Benchley wrote "The Wayward Press" and later covered the theater, and Alexander Woollcott contributed a weekly column, "Shouts and Murmurs."

In the mid-thirties, some members of the editorial staff complained that Ross, who had invested in some outside ventures, had lost interest in the magazine and should be replaced. The story goes that Fleischmann invited Thurber to the Algonquin and asked whom he would suggest. This so incensed the humorist that he picked up the baked potatoes from an adjoining table and began to hurl them across the room. When they were gone, he turned to hard rolls. In *Here at the New Yorker*, Brendan Gill questions the accuracy of the story and suggests that Thurber made it up. "No restaurant keeps baked potatoes in baskets on tables . . ." he says, "and at that time the Algonquin served not hard rolls but popovers . . . It is just possible that a drunken Thurber . . . tossed a single warm popover in Fleischmann's direction . . ."

It was Thurber who best described the *New Yorker* in its

early days. "The new magazine reflected the reckless detachment of the period," he wrote.

> It wore no armor and it sought no grail; it did not carry a sword cane or even an umbrella. Since neither trumpet nor banner had called it into existence, it was not going anywhere to do anything about anything. It was just walking along, like any other visitor from out of town, looking into the expensive store windows, gazing up at the tall buildings, widening its eyes and dropping its jaw at impressive statistics or unusual facts. The amiable periodical tiptoed away from disputes and disturbances, since it had nothing particularly in mind to prove or disprove, to attack or defend. Now and then it jostled the celebrated, or thumbed its nose at the powerful, but all in a spirit of gay mockery. The *New Yorker* was not really angry. It just didn't give a good goddam.

As Dwight Macdonald, who was later to become a member of the *New Yorker* staff, observed in 1937 in a highly critical essay called "Lie Down and Laugh," this position already represented a radical change from the magazine's purposes at its founding. "The *New Yorker*," he remarked, "was established to exploit commercially two groups of sophisticated readers: those who followed Mencken and Nathan and those who looked to the Manhattan wits centering around the Algonquin Hotel . . . The brash Menckenians and the aggressively sophisticated Algonquins have been superseded by the timorous and bewildered Thurber." In recent years, however, the *New Yorker* has changed again, most noticeably perhaps in the editorial "Notes and Comment," which has become decidedly angry and has taken as strong stands on such issues as the Vietnam War and the impeachment of President Nixon as any periodical with a popular following. As Macdonald later reported in 1966, the magazine had begun to be weightier and more thoughtful when William Shawn became managing editor. "Do we have to run that in our funny little magazine?" Ross would ask when presented with something he considered too serious. When Shawn succeeded to the editorship after Ross's death in 1951, the change became more pronounced, with a shift to what Macdonald called "elaborately researched reportage and 'intellectual stuff' . . . The different temperaments of the two editors were responsible," he wrote. "Also the difference between the pre-war and the post-war periods. By 1940, Ross, Benchley, Thurber, White, Dorothy Parker and the other original 'New Yorker wits' found themselves in a less clement atmosphere."

Today the *New Yorker* has come to represent the highest standards in literature and journalism. It survives as the major mass market for serious fiction and poetry and each year publishes important nonfiction books in advance of publication. It now occupies offices on the eighteenth, nineteenth and twentieth floors of 25 West 43rd Street, where writers, editors and artists work out of a series of warrens identified only by numbers handpainted in the same curving style as the typeface used on the magazine's cover. The atmosphere has been described as "donnish," an impression reinforced by the old wooden desks and threadbare carpets that furnish the rooms. With the exception of a Fabian Bachrach photographic portrait of Ross, the halls are decorated only with maps — subways maps, a Hammond International World Map, a postal zone map, "Sorties de Paris" — each so commonplace that finally, taken as a whole, they transcend their ordinariness, like a work of conceptual art.

·

The crowd that gathered at the Algonquin had two additional Midtown meeting places. One was Neysa McMein's studio on 57th Street. Edna Ferber, who modeled her character Dallas O'Mara in *So Big* on McMein, described the apartment: "At her untidy hospitable studio you might encounter, any day between three and six, anyone from Irving Berlin to the reigning Vanderbilt; from Father Duffy to H. G. Wells. And in the midst of the talk, and the music made by someone at the piano, and the roar of the L train on Sixth there was Neysa working calmly away at her canvas in the middle of the room, her hair wrung into a careless knot at her neck, her smock smeared with paint, her face smudged but wreathed in lovely smiles." Although the Round Table group was present en masse at every McMein party, her circle was a wider one. Alexander Woollcott noted:

> The population is . . . wildly variegated. Over at the piano Jascha Heifetz and Arthur Samuels may be trying to find what four hands can do in the syncopation of a composition never thus desecrated before. Irving Berlin is encouraging them. Squatted uncomfortably around an ottoman, Franklin P. Adams, Marc Connelly and Dorothy Parker will be playing cold hands to see who will buy dinner that evening. At the bookshelf Robert C. Benchley and Edna Ferber are amusing themselves vastly by thoughtfully autographing her set of Mark Twain for her. In the corner, some jet-bedecked dowager from a statelier milieu is taking it all in, immensely diverted. Chaplin or Chaliapin, Alice Duer Miller or Wild Bill Donovan, Father Duffy or Mary Pickford — any or all of them may be there.

The second address where the Algonquin crowd gathered was a kind of commune far west on 47th Street. Hawley Truax, a lawyer who had been Woollcott's classmate at Hamilton College and helped to finance the *New Yorker,* bought twin brick houses at 412 and 414 West 47th Street and, in partnership with Harold Ross and Jane Grant, set about modernizing them to be used as a joint residence. Woollcott invited himself into the cooperative. The houses had no electricity but were heated by potbellied stoves and fireplaces in every room. The two original kitchens were combined and made into a communal dining room, which opened into a backyard in which they installed a large fountain. There was a Chinese cook and anyone could bring guests for dinner as long as advance warning was given. The dining room, furnished with a black lacquered sideboard and walnut tables, was the headquarters for the weekly Thanatopsis poker games.

The Rosses had an apartment with a sitting room on the first floor, Truax and Woollcott were on the second (Woollcott characterized his apartment as "a small and disordered flat in the Gas House district") and Kate Ogleby and William Powell, friends of Woollcott's from Cleveland, had apartments on the third floor. A housewarming was held in 1923; playwright Charles MacArthur had invitations printed and passed them out on the street. Along with Dorothy Parker and Harpo Marx, he rented a merry-go-round and gave the neighborhood children rides. Also present were F. Scott Fitzgerald, Edna St. Vincent Millay, who read her poems, and George Gershwin, who played a new composition called "Rhapsody in Blue." The house acquired various names — Chinaman's Chance and the Speakeasy, because of a mysterious-looking peephole in the door, Wit's End, coined by Dorothy Parker, and the Gash House, Woollcott's favorite. Life consisted of periods of guerrilla warfare between truces — Woollcott disrupted the household by invading the Ross apartment at any hour of the night, crashing noncommunal parties and raiding gatherings to carry guests off to his own apartment. He left in the spring of 1926 and the following year both Ross and Grant moved when their marriage broke up.

Two other Midtown living rooms served as literary and intellectual centers in the twenties and thirties. Carl Van Vechten, who arrived in New York in 1906 to be assistant music critic for the *New York Times,* made his home, no matter how modest, a gathering place from the very beginning. His first address was "a large room at 39 West 39th Street where Sinclair

Lewis occupied an adjoining chamber." The two would nod to
one another in passing. In 1907 Van Vechten was at 528 Seventh
Avenue near 40th Street. Although he had only a single room
without bath or kitchen, he entertained regularly, usually serving grapefruit, which was then "as exotic as pomegranates." It
was not until the early twenties, when Van Vechten and his
wife, the actress Fania Marinoff, moved to 150 West 55th Street,
that their celebrated parties began. Van Vechten had by this
time begun his association with and sponsorship of the writers
and other figures of the Harlem Renaissance. So many prominent Negroes attended his parties that they were reported as a
matter of course in black society columns and Walter White
called his apartment the Midtown branch of the NAACP. In
addition, many white writers — Somerset Maugham, Hugh Walpole, Witter Bynner, Arthur Davison Ficke, Louis Untermeyer
— visited at various times. The double apartment had a black
and orange cubist study, a sea green, purple and raspberry
drawing room, and was "full of silver fishes and colored glass
balls and ceiling-high shelves of gaily-bound books." Here after
all-night parties or jaunts to Harlem, Van Vechten worked as
long as twelve hours a day on his most controversial book,
Nigger Heaven (see Chapter IX, Harlem) .

Emily Clark, who wrote *Innocence Abroad,* a literary memoir, described one party "with George Gershwin at the piano
playing and singing bits from his current musical show to a
crowd of people, among whom Theodore Dreiser sat, heavy and
brooding, the direct antithesis, almost a contradiction, of all that
Gershwin means. And Elinor Wylie sat, aloof and lovely, a
contradiction and denial of all that both Dreiser and Gershwin
mean. Later some woman danced, and later still Paul Robeson
sang. Last of all, James Weldon Johnson recited his 'Go Down,
Death' and Carl hovered about in doorways, his face, as always
on such evenings, benevolent and shining."

Carl Van Vechten, Alfred A. Knopf, Jr., and James Weldon
Johnson at a joint birthday party in the 1930s.

For several years Van Vechten gave an annual party for himself, James Weldon Johnson and Alfred A. Knopf, Jr., because
their birthdays all fell on June 17. In 1936 the Van Vechtens
moved to Central Park West, where Van Vechten continued
his unique role in the artistic life of New York. As Edward
Lueders wrote in the *New Republic:* "In the fifty years since
he took up residence in New York, Van Vechten has been

friend, host, adviser, champion, and appreciative audience to three generations of celebrities in society, literature, and the arts. In the process, he has become perhaps the most successful dilettante in the land, a sophisticated ringleader among the intelligentsia and a genial patron of the arts."

Near Van Vechten's 55th Street address, in the Alwyn Court, an apartment building with an extraordinary, ornate façade cast in terra cotta, lived the three Stettheimer sisters, Ettie, Carrie and Florine. Ettie wrote two novels, Florine was a painter and Carrie worked for twenty years on a ten-room doll house, decorated with miniature but authentic works of art by William Zorach, Archipenko, Gaston Lachaise and others, now in the Museum of the City of New York. At their home, recalled Virgil Thomson, who was one of the visitors, gathered "a selection of New York's rather fine intellectual life." The apartment was done in "the marble and gold and red velvet German-royalty style with a fluffy overlay of modern Baroque," wrote Thomson. "There were crystal pendants everywhere and gold fringes and lace and silk curtains so much longer than the windows that they stood out in planned puffs and lay no less than two feet on the waxed floors." In the evenings Ettie usually wore red taffeta with puffy skirts tightly closed around each ankle, Carrie wore gold and white and Florine wore black velvet.

•

The Algonquin's reputation as a literary hotel had predated the Round Table group, going back to Mencken's visits there in 1914, and was to continue after the famous wits stopped meeting. When Heywood Broun ran for Congress on the Socialist ticket in 1930, he had his campaign offices at the hotel. When Gertrude Stein visited America in 1934 after an absence of twenty-five years, she and Alice B. Toklas took a three-room suite at the Algonquin. On her first evening in the city Stein took a walk to Times Square and saw the lights of the Times Building repetitiously announcing her arrival in New York. The same year, James Thurber went to live at the Algonquin after the breakup of his marriage. One evening he met F. Scott Fitzgerald, who was also staying there. They spent the night drinking at Tony's and drove up to the hotel in a cab at daylight. When they discovered they had something in common — they were nearly the same age and both had daughters — they got back in the cab. They drove around the park, discussing Ring Lardner. Thurber was also a habitué of Costello's Bar and Grill at 44th Street and Third Avenue and there, in ninety minutes one night, he drew a mural depicting the battle of the sexes. When the drawings were painted over, Thurber did another set. Since then Costello's has moved twice, murals and all, and is now at 225 East 44th Street.

From the thirties to the fifties, William Faulkner frequently stayed at the Algonquin when he came to New York to see his publishers. One year his wife and friends were unable to reach him and finally found him unconscious on the floor of his Algonquin room. He had been drinking and had burned his back leaning against a steam pipe. When he won the Nobel Prize in 1949, he wrote his acceptance speech on Algonquin stationery. Parts of "Barn Burning," *Requiem for a Nun, A Fable, The Mansion* and *The Reivers* were written at the hotel.

There is a myth that anything written at the Algonquin must be a success. Perhaps in hope, if not belief, many writers — including Tennessee Williams, John Updike, Bruce Catton, Peter De Vries, Gore Vidal, Graham Greene, Günter Grass, Art Buchwald, Thornton Wilder and John Osborne — still stay at the hotel.

Other Midtown hotels have, to a lesser degree, acquired

something of a literary history. Amy Lowell stayed at the St. Regis at Fifth Avenue and 55th Street in the early years of the century and at the Belmont in the twenties. She always reserved a suite of five rooms — a bedroom with vacant rooms on either side, a sitting room and a room for her companion, Ada Russell. She ordered all the clocks to be stopped and any objects that reflected light covered with dark cloths. She worked at night, slept from 6:00 A.M. to 2:30 P.M. and saw visitors only after 5:00. She was astute at the "harvesting" end of publishing, which she conducted in New York. She would call all the major newspapers and magazines to find out who was reviewing her latest book. Then she invited each reviewer to tea, explained her intentions in the book and insisted he write as he pleased. This usually assured the success of the review.

William Saroyan had a special affection for the Great Northern Hotel at 118 West 57th Street, where he stayed in 1935 after his first book was published. "I loved being at The Great Northern Hotel," he wrote, "and I went back to the hotel again and again when I was in New York — until at last it just wouldn't do any more: the hotel had changed, I had grown more worldly, I had become wealthy, and the world itself had changed, so I moved on and up, as the saying is." Most recently he has stayed at the Royalton.

Ernest Hemingway rewrote the galley proofs of *For Whom the Bell Tolls* in the Hotel Barclay at 111 East 48th Street in ninety-six consecutive hours, never leaving his room. In later years he always stayed at the Sherry-Netherland because he liked the "good protection" — no name on the register, phone calls screened, newsmen and photographers thrown off the scent. But in 1959 he gave up the hotel for a three-room pied-à-terre at 1 East 62nd Street, a once luxurious town house that had been divided into apartments.

F. Scott Fitzgerald conducted most of his New York life in

hotels and portrayed the city as the visitor's glamorous mecca of public places rather than the homes and offices where people lived and worked. "To this day," Alfred Kazin has written, "Fitzgerald remains the only poet of New York's upper-class landmarks . . . New York was a dreamland to Fitzgerald. It represented his imagination of what is forever charming, touched by the glamour of money, romantically tender and gay." His characteristic view is expressed in the first pages of *This Side of Paradise,* in which he describes the city as seen by Amory Blaine:

> New York burst upon him on Washington's birthday with the brilliance of a long-anticipated event. His glimpse of it as a vivid whiteness against a deep blue sky had left a picture of splendor that rivalled the dream cities in the Arabian Nights; but this time he saw it by electric light, and romance gleamed from the chariot-race sign on Broadway and from the women's eyes at the Astor, where he and young Paskert from St. Regis' had dinner. When they walked down the aisle of the theatre, greeted by the nervous twanging and discord of untuned violins and the sensuous, heavy fragrance of paint and powder, he moved in a sphere of epicurean delight.

Amory Blaine's New York is compounded of afternoons at the Plaza, the theater, dinner at the Ritz or the Princeton Club and cocktails at the Biltmore bar, as was Fitzgerald's. Scott and Zelda were married in the rectory of St. Patrick's Cathedral in April 1920 and spent their honeymoon in Room 2109 of the Biltmore. When they were asked to leave because of their disruptiveness — Fitzgerald did handstands in the lobby, for instance — they moved to the Commodore. Late in 1920 they took an apartment at 38 West 59th Street and had their meals delivered from the Plaza Hotel. They held parties attended by H. L. Mencken, George Jean Nathan, Edna Ferber, Dorothy Parker, John Peale Bishop and Edmund Wilson. It was during

this period that Zelda took her famous dips into the Pulitzer
Fountain opposite the hotel. Then they were off to Europe and
St. Paul, Minnesota. In September 1922 they stayed at the
Plaza while looking for a place to settle in New York, finally
choosing a house in Great Neck. *The Great Gatsby,* set against
the Great Neck background, also used the Plaza for the critical
scene in which Gatsby and Daisy confront Tom Buchanan with
their love for one another.

·

Among the publishers the writers came to visit, the most colorful was Horace Liveright, whose offices in a four-story brownstone at 61 West 48th Street became another of the gathering
places of the era. Liveright had started in publishing with
Albert Boni, who had run the Washington Square Book Shop
in Greenwich Village (see Chapter II, Greenwich Village).
In 1917 Boni and Liveright was founded with headquarters at
105 West 40th Street. Gradually the established nineteenth-
century publishing firms — D. Appleton and Company; Dodd,
Mead; Doubleday, Page; E. P. Dutton; Harper and Brothers;
Henry Holt; G. P. Putnam's and Charles Scribner's — were
being joined by a new breed. These publishers, who were
generally Jewish (Jews had been excluded from advancement
in the established companies), launched into fresh areas. B. W.
Huebsch, who entered publishing in 1902 and was to merge
with Harold K. Guinzburg in 1925 to form the Viking Press,
found his authors abroad and published H. G. Wells, D. H.
Lawrence and James Joyce as well as translations of Gorky,
Chekhov and Strindberg. Alfred and Blanche Knopf, who
started in 1915, also published Europeans, like Tolstoy, Gogol,
Dostoevsky, Nietzsche and Mann, but added the Americans
Mencken, Nathan and Cather to their lists. But Boni and Live-
right were the first to publish such Village writers as Mary Hea-

ton Vorse, Hutchins Hapgood, Harry Kemp, Max Eastman, Maxwell Bodenheim, John Reed and Eugene O'Neill. In 1928 the two publishers tossed a coin to determine who would control the firm. Liveright won, and with the Modern Library, which Boni had founded, as the backstop of the company broadened out and soon became spectacularly successful. "When I went to work for Horace Liveright in 1924," Bennett Cerf wrote in an article on Liveright's death, "his list included Dreiser, O'Neill, Anderson, George Moore, Atherton, Lewisohn, Jeffers, Van Loon, Rose Macaulay, Sigmund Freud . . . and for good measure he had the Modern Library, which although almost completely neglected, was already selling over three hundred thousand copies a year. What a list for a one-man publishing house!"

Horace Liveright also had an unusually talented staff. In addition to editor-in-chief T. R. Smith, whom he hired away from the *Century Magazine* of which he was editor, there was Cerf, who later cofounded Random House; Richard Simon, who left to form Simon and Schuster; and Donald Friede, who left to start the now defunct Covici-Friede. The readers at various times included Beatrice Kaufman, the wife of George S. Kaufman, who provided a link to the Algonquin group, and Lillian Hellman. Yet in spite of all these assets and a steady stream of best sellers (the firm had six in 1928 alone), Liveright seemed determined to fail. He risked large sums producing plays on Broadway and speculating in the stock market, and, by selling the Modern Library to Bennett Cerf in 1925, committed a suicidal error. Without the steadily selling backlist the Modern Library had provided, the firm was forced to produce best sellers on demand in order to survive. By 1930 Liveright was bankrupt and in 1933 he was dead at the age of forty-six.

While in its heyday, however, the firm occupied a special place in publishing. As Lillian Hellman put it:

A job with any publishing house was a plum, but a job with Horace Liveright was a bag of plums . . . Liveright, Julian Messner, T. R. Smith, Manuel Komroff, and a few even younger men had made a new and brilliant world for books . . . They discovered or persuaded over Faulkner, Freud, Hemingway, O'Neill, Hart Crane, Sherwood Anderson, E. E. Cummings . . . all of them attracted by the vivid, impetuous, high-living men who were the editors. It didn't hurt that Horace was handsome and daring, Julian serious and kind, Tom Smith almost erudite with his famous collection of erotica and odd pieces of knowledge . . . that the advances they gave were large and the parties even larger, full of lush girls and good liquor; that the sympathy and attention given to writers, young or old, was more generous than had been known before, possibly more real than has been known since.

Liveright and his firm occupied the entire brownstone. The stock room and shipping department were in the basement and the business offices on the first floor. At the back of the second floor, reached by a nineteenth-century staircase, was a reception room with an enormous fireplace, three Italian double doors and a bust of Theodore Dreiser. Beyond the doors on the extension roof was an awning-covered roof garden with furniture upholstered in shades of coral, mauve and jade. Here and in the reception room were held the famous parties. In addition to any Liveright authors who were in town, guests might include Otto Kahn, New York Mayor Jimmy Walker, Herbert Bayard Swope, Paul Robeson, John Barrymore, Thomas Wolfe, the Millay sisters, Carl Van Vechten, Elinor Wylie and Sinclair Lewis. The parties sometimes spilled over into Liveright's office in the front half of the second floor, which also served the publisher as a studio apartment. There was a narrow carved Italian desk, a huge Chinese jar for wastepaper, a fireplace, lounging chairs, grand piano and bar and an adjoining zinc-lined shower.

Other publishing offices would fulfill more than the usual function. The former Random House offices in the architecturally historic Villard Houses, designed by Stanford White, on Madison Avenue between 50th and 51st streets, for instance, became one of William Faulkner's favorite writing places when he found he could no longer work well in Oxford, Mississippi. He liked the ornate rooms with their high ceilings, paneled walls and heavy draperies, and would often arrive early in the morning when the doors were still locked and sometimes sleep over in the fifth-floor employees lounge. But no other publishing house would ever approach Liveright's in boldness or in style.

•

One other Midtown institution served as a focal point for literary life from the twenties onward. On the first day of January 1920, Frances Steloff opened a bookstore at 128 West 45th Street. It was called the Gotham Book and Art, and a sign designed by John Held, Jr. — depicting three men in a boat and bearing the store's motto, "Wise Men Fish Here" — was hung outside. In 1923 the store moved to 51 West 47th Street and called itself the Gotham Book Mart. Here Steloff began to stock an impressive number of little magazines and a wide selection of the newest poetry and prose. It became known as "the place where you can buy *transition*," and because young writers were grateful to Steloff for stocking their work, they often came to the store. The poet, novelist and essayist Christopher Morley, who lived across the street at 46 West 47th, helped to make the place a literary hangout when he established the Three Hours for Lunch Club, which was joined by Buckminster Fuller, William Rose Benét, book exporter Bill Hall and others. The members came in the early afternoon, had food passed to them from Chez Maurice next door and ate in

The garden of the Gotham Book Mart, with Paris-inspired book stalls, at 51 West 47th Street, where it was located until 1946. The umbrella at left sheltered the "Three Hours for Lunch Club."

the garden. Mencken visited the store regularly when he was in the city. One day he and Dreiser came in and found some of their own books among the first editions. They embellished them with long inscriptions and then began to dedicate other books, including more than one Bible, which they signed "With the compliments of the authors."

In the thirties the Gotham was used for a series of lectures initiated by Samuel Putnam, editor of the *New Review,* a short-lived international quarterly. He called them the Dog Star evenings, in reference to Pope's *Dunciad.* Another time about a hundred writers, nearly all of whom had lived abroad, met to establish an expatriots' group called the Left Bank Club of America. The store also frequently held publication parties and celebrations for foreign writers. Among the many honored were Edith and Osbert Sitwell, Dylan Thomas, Paul Goodman, Anaïs Nin, Jean Cocteau, Katherine Anne Porter and William Carlos Williams. In 1939 a "wake" was held to celebrate the publication of Joyce's *Finnegans Wake;* clay pipes and tobacco were imported from Belfast and Old Bushmills from Dublin. The Gotham is also the home of the James Joyce Society. When it was organized in 1947, T. S. Eliot bought the first membership.

Frances Steloff went out of her way to help writers and other artists. Edmund Wilson once phoned from Cape Cod to tell her

The invitation to "Finnegans Wake," a 1939 celebration for the publication of James Joyce's book.

The Dead Come to Life at "Finnegans Wake"

Who, confidentially, will be the life of the party

on May 4th at the

Gotham Book Mart

51 West 47th Street

Obsequies will be held in the garden, beginning at 5 p.m.

You are invited to be a mourner   *R.S.V.P.*

At the "wake," from left: Christopher Morley, Frances Steloff, Arthur Davison Ficke, book collector Wilbur Macy Stone, Joyce's biographer Herbert Gorman, Mrs. Steloff's assistant Kay Steele, Mrs. William Carlos Williams (with hat), William Carlos Williams (with hat), actor Albert Hecht.

that John Dos Passos needed $200 to pay his insurance premium. She wired the money and was sent the holograph manuscript of *Manhattan Transfer* as collateral. Wilson himself would sometimes borrow money out of the cash register and leave an IOU. Martha Graham borrowed $1000 to stage her first dance concert. Henry Miller sent regular SOS's for food, clothing, a car, money to go to Mexico, and they were posted on the store's bulletin board. In 1941, this philanthropy was institutionalized in a group called the Writers' Emergency Fund, which loaned money to young writers with no strings attached.

In 1946, when Steloff had to move and couldn't find another shop, Christopher Morley and Mark Van Doren discovered that Columbia University owned the brownstone at 41 West 47th

At a Gotham Book Mart party: front row, from left, Malcolm
Cowley, Marianne Moore, Frances Steloff and Kenneth Burke.
Standing, Allen Tate (left) and Stephen Spender.

Street. They went to see the trustees, who eventually sold her the building. Today the Gotham remains much the same as it always was, cramped and cluttered with half a million books and hundreds of photographs of writers, the great and near great, peering down from the moldings. At eighty-six, Miss Steloff still works in the shop daily, commanding an alcove of works on metaphysics and theosophy. In 1967 she sold the store to Andreas Brown, a bibliographer and appraiser of rare books, who has attempted to preserve the ambiance while making the operation more efficient. Now, once again, the store is planning to move.

•

Midtown remains the center of American publishing and the harvesting continues as it did in Whitman's day. Several of the publishers have new, modern buildings of their own — Random House at 201 East 50th Street, Harper & Row at 10 East 53rd and Harcourt Brace Jovanovich at 757 Third Avenue. The two-hour lunch is the literary institution of the seventies, and the haunts of writers and editors today are likely to be the restaurants that serve an elegant midday meal rather than the nightspots that distinguished the twenties. The names change as the restaurants open and close and as the publishing community tires of the old and goes on to the new. Midtown still has two prime literary landmarks in the Algonquin Hotel and the Gotham Book Mart. It still has the Broadway theater and perhaps the last traces of the urban glamour Fitzgerald cherished. William Dean Howells's observation about the city and literature holds true: New York still publishes it, criticizes it and circulates it — with the important difference that today New York, by far the largest market for serious books, reads it too.

•

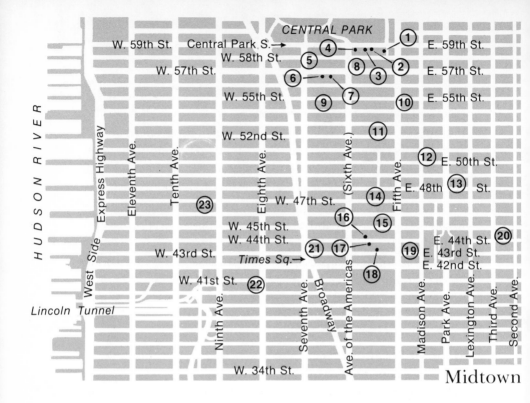

Midtown

Midtown Tour

With the exception of a few interesting houses, Midtown literary landmarks consist primarily of hotels and office buildings. You can sit in the restaurant of the Park Lane and imagine yourself in the apartment of Zelda and Scott Fitzgerald or have a drink at the Café de la Paix at the St. Moritz and enjoy the same view William Dean Howells did at the turn of the century. Or you can patronize the surviving restaurants and bars with literary associations.

The Plaza Hotel at Fifth Avenue and Central Park South (1), immortalized by F. Scott Fitzgerald in *The Great Gatsby*, is one of the city's architectural landmarks. Designed by Henry J. Hardenbergh, it is richly detailed with dormers, balconies and balustrades. The Fitzgeralds lived nearby in a brownstone at 38 West 59th Street, which has now been replaced by the Park Lane Hotel (2). William Dean Howells once lived in a

house at 40 West 59th Street (3) on the site of the present
Harry's Bar, and also in a house at 48 West 59th, now the St.
Moritz Hotel (4).

The Alwyn Court at 182 West 58th Street (5) is where the
Stettheimer sisters lived and entertained culturally eminent
New Yorkers. This unique building, profusely decorated in
terra cotta castings, was designed in 1907 by the firm of Harde
& Short. The decoration consists of French Renaissance detail,
featuring the crowned salamander, symbol of Francis I, king of
France. William Dean Howells also lived at 130 West 57th
Street (6), and William Saroyan's favorite hotel was the now
seedy Great Northern at 118 West 57th Street (7).

The studio of Neysa McMein, once frequented by the Algonquin crowd, was in an old building at 57 West 57th Street (8),
now replaced by an apartment house. Carl Van Vechten gave
his famous parties and wrote *Nigger Heaven* in a double apartment at 150 West 55th Street (9), a nine-story brick building.
Amy Lowell often used the St. Regis Hotel (10) at 5th Avenue
and 55th Street as her New York headquarters. The "21" Club,
at 21 West 52nd Street (11), is the direct descendant of the
49th Street Jack and Charlie's Puncheon Club, where the Algonquin wits and others often met. A plaque over his table
commemorates Robert Benchley. From 1946 to 1969 Random
House had its offices in the historic Villard Houses at 451 to
455 Madison Avenue (12). Four different houses designed to
look like one were modeled on the Palazzo della Cancelleria in
Rome. Random House owned the mansion at the 51st Street
corner but sold it when the firm moved to a new building near
Third Avenue in 1969. The Barclay Hotel at 111 East 48th
Street (13) is where Ernest Hemingway revised the proofs of
For Whom the Bell Tolls.

The Gotham Book Mart, perhaps Midtown's most interesting
literary landmark, occupies an old brownstone house at 41 West

47th Street (14). The first offices of the *Smart Set* and the *New Yorker* were both at 25 West 45th Street (15). The Algonquin, scene of the famous Round Table in the twenties and hostelry today for many writers, is at 59 West 44th Street (16). People in the publishing world gather for drinks in the lobby around cocktail time. Almost directly across the street at 44 West 44th Street (17) is the Royalton Hotel, where, at various times, George Jean Nathan and Robert Benchley maintained permanent suites. The *New Yorker* magazine presently occupies the eighteenth, nineteenth and twentieth floors of an office building at 25 West 43rd Street (18). Zelda and Scott Fitzgerald spent their honeymoon in Room 2109 of the Biltmore Hotel at Madison Avenue and 43rd Street (19). Costello's Bar and Grill has moved twice since James Thurber painted its famous murals, but the murals have moved with it. They can now be seen at 225 East 44th Street (20).

On Midtown's west side, a plaque marks the site of Eugene O'Neill's birthplace, the Barrett House, a family-style hotel at the northeast corner of 43rd Street and Broadway (21). Until it was torn down in 1940, O'Neill liked to point out the exact room where he was born — number 236, third floor, third window from Broadway on the 43rd Street side. During the depression the WPA Federal Writers' Project occupied a huge loft in the Port Authority Building on Eighth Avenue and 41st Street (22). Among the writers on the project were John Cheever, Richard Wright, Muriel Rukeyser, Alfred Kazin, Claude McKay, Ralph Ellison and Philip Rahv. Legmen received $21.67 a week, and editors, $23.86. As a rule those on the project were not allowed to work on their own writing. Their major achievement was the still excellent guide to New York City. When Philip Rahv was asked to do an essay for the book dealing with New York's literary history, he refused the assignment, claiming the city had none. After being told about

Poe, Melville and the rest, he did the job. Several books eventually came out of the Negro unit of the project, including Claude McKay's *Harlem: Negro Metropolis* and *The Negro in New York*, edited by Roi Ottley and William J. Weatherby.

Between Ninth and Tenth avenues, in the neighborhood known as Hell's Kitchen, the double house occupied by Harold Ross, Jane Grant, Alexander Woollcott and others still stands at 412 West 47th Street (23). The four-story brick buildings, covered with old dark gray paint, have bars on the windows and are in bad repair today.

VII. The East Side

IN 1844, shortly after moving to New York, Edgar Allan Poe began a series of letters about the city for the *Columbia Spy,* a newspaper in Pottsville, Pennsylvania. Documenting his wanderings, Poe voiced what would become a perennial protest. He lamented the destruction of the old New York as it made way for urban development. But Poe had more to mourn than the loss of buildings, for what was taking place in his time was the implacable leveling of the island terrain for the implementation of the city's grid plan. He was particularly disturbed by the destruction of the area facing what was then called the Sound on the East Side. For his third letter to the *Spy,* he explored the area around Turtle Bay, a cove that today is the site of the United Nations Park. "A day or two since I procured a light skiff, and with the aid of a pair of sculls . . . made my way around Blackwell's Island, on a voyage of discovery and exploration," he wrote. "The chief interest lay in the scenery of the Manhattan shore, which is here particularly picturesque. The houses are, without exception, frame, and antique . . . I could not look on the magnificent cliffs, and stately trees, which at every moment met my view, without a sigh for the inevitable doom — inevitable and swift."

The leveling Poe anticipated soon took place. The remnants of the magnificent cliffs are barely discernible under the apartment buildings perched on Beekman Place and Sutton Place.

The stately trees have been replaced by frail, constrained city sycamores and oaks surrounded by wickets and ivy. But the East Side today has regained the social ascendancy it had in Poe's time. The region where John Jacob Astor built "Astoria," at 88th Street and First Avenue, and Edith Wharton's first families kept their country homes has been primarily a place for writers to live when their financial standing was assured. And the literature that has used the East Side as its setting has been mainly concerned with society and success.

When Poe was visiting Turtle Bay, Horace Greeley, publisher of the country's most influential paper, the *New York Tribune*, was living there with his family in a spacious old country mansion (see Chapter I, Lower Manhattan). The house, as Greeley wrote, "was located on eight acres of ground, including a wooded ravine, or dell, on the East River, at Turtle Bay, nearly opposite the southernmost point of Blackwell's Island." Accustomed to "the rumble and roar of carriages," Greeley at first found the stillness at night "so sepulchral, unearthly," that he had difficulty in sleeping.

The same year, 1844, Margaret Fuller had published *Summer on the Lakes,* an account of her travels in the "West," which at that time meant Illinois and Wisconsin. Impressed by the book, Greeley invited her to come to New York to write for his newspaper and board at his home. Fuller, who had received, under her father's guidance, the thorough classical education accorded only boys at that time, was a major figure in the New England transcendentalist movement. Famous for her Conversations, discussion groups on high-minded subjects attended first by the best-educated women of Boston and later the men as well, Fuller had edited the *Dial* and moved as an equal in the society of such thinkers as Emerson, Thoreau and Hawthorne. She was reported to have said, "I now know all the people worth knowing in America, and I find no intellect comparable to my own."

Fuller accepted Greeley's offer and arrived at Turtle Bay in December. She described the house:

> Stopping on the Harlem road, you enter a lane nearly a quarter of a mile long, and going by a small brook and pond that locks in the place, and ascending a slightly rising ground, get sight of the house, which, old-fashioned and of mellow tint, fronts on a flower garden filled with shrubs, large vines, and trim box borders . . . Passing through a wide hall, you come out on a piazza stretching the whole length of the house, where one can walk in all weathers; and thence, by a step or two, on a lawn with picturesque masses of rocks, shrubs, and trees overlooking the East River . . . And owing to the currents and the set of the tide, the sails glide sidelong, seeming to greet the house as they pass by.

In New York Fuller became one of the two most important literary critics of her time. She reviewed Carlyle, Browning, Shelley, Tennyson, Longfellow, Hawthorne, Poe, Emerson and Lowell, making judgments that are, for the most part, valid to this day. She also did a series of exposés on New York hospitals and prisons, including the one on Blackwell's Island, and during her stay Greeley published her *Woman in the Nineteenth Century*. This was the first considered feminist statement since Mary Wollstonecraft's *Vindication of the Rights of Women* and the intellectual impetus for the American feminist movement, which would flower in the 1850s. When she left for Europe in August of 1846, she wrote in her farewell column: "New York is the focus, the point where American and European interests converge . . . Twenty months have presented me with a richer and more varied exercise for thought and life, than twenty years could in any other part of these United States."

The other great critic of the era, Edgar Allan Poe, had once written that humanity may be divided into three classes, "men, women, and Margaret Fuller." In the spring and summer of

1846 Poe was also at Turtle Bay, living at a farm belonging to Mr. and Mrs. John L. Miller. The house, at 47th Street and Second Avenue, had an attic with three rooms, where the Poes stayed. They were almost penniless and left a bed behind as payment for their board when they moved to Fordham.

The mansions and farmhouses that Poe, Fuller and Greeley knew were replaced in the 1860s by rows of the brownstones characteristic of New York. After the building of the Second and Third Avenue Els in 1880 and the development of water-front industry, the neighborhood began to deteriorate. By the early twentieth century, it had become the slum, inhabited by a variety of ethnic groups, depicted in Sholem Asch's *East River*. In 1914 the Irish literary critics Padraic and Mary Colum took advantage of the depressed real estate values to find lodgings they liked in the neighborhood. "We rented a furnished apartment in Beekman Place, then an unfashionable and dingy part of the city, though amazingly characterful," Mary Colum wrote.

> For the five-room furnished apartment in a walk-up brown house we paid the sum of 35 dollars a month. All the section east of Third Avenue, around the 50s and below was very foreign and like the moldy and rundown part of a European city — like the Bastille section of Paris, for instance — into which drifted men and women of all European nationalities; in the 50s, Polish and Russian Jews were in the majority. Beekman Place at the time was certainly dingy, but with the bright New York sun shining on the water, the boats and the barges, all the life of the river which we could view from our windows, we felt we had struck the pleasantest living quarters in the City.

The Colums held at-homes with tea and cake on Sundays. J. B. Yeats came often, walking all the way from Petitpas', and John Quinn, the New York lawyer and patron of Irish literature, also visited frequently. One day he was there when Amy Lowell came. "We heard Amy's voice screaming for someone to bring her a chair, as she wanted to rest on the landing before mounting the next flight," Mary Colum recalled. "Quinn bolted down the stairs, and as I followed and introduced them he looked at the bulk of Amy with fairly open astonishment. 'So you are the great John Quinn?' said Amy, rising to the occasion. He should have answered 'So you are the great Amy Lowell?' But he did not."

In the twenties the area began to undergo renewal. One of the most successful efforts was Turtle Bay Gardens, a group of twenty houses back to back on 48th and 49th streets renovated by Mrs. Walton Martin. She painted or stuccoed their brownstone fronts and filled in the swampy backyards to create a communal garden. Still in existence today, the gardens have a central flagstone path, a fountain copied from one at the Villa Medici in Rome and low masonry walls adorned with iron or stone turtles, cobras and snails. Two old willow trees and plantings of holly, laurel, ivy and rhododendron fill the garden. The houses were sold to their owners, among them a number of literary figures, subject to restrictive covenants that have preserved the character of the enclave. The distinguished editor Maxwell Perkins lived at 246 East 49th Street during the thirties.

Perkins, who discovered and launched F. Scott Fitzgerald, Ernest Hemingway, John P. Marquand, Erskine Caldwell, James Jones and others, had a special relationship with Thomas Wolfe. Working almost as a collaborator, he helped Wolfe cut and revise the voluminous drafts of his early books sentence by sentence and line by line. Following conferences at Chatham Walk, an outdoor café at the Hotel Chatham at Vanderbilt Avenue and 48th Street, where the two went after working late, Wolfe would walk Perkins home. They continued talking until

Perkins went out for the early edition of the morning paper. Wolfe's *Of Time and the River* was one of approximately sixty-five books dedicated to Perkins by grateful authors. In 1935 Wolfe moved to a three-room apartment at 865 First Avenue near Perkins's house and spent many evenings at his editor's. There was a break between the two when Wolfe transferred to Harper, presumably to prove he could write his books without Perkins's help. The editor is portrayed as Foxhall Edwards in Wolfe's *The Web and the Rock* and *You Can't Go Home Again*.

Perkins's office at Scribner's, at 597 Fifth Avenue, a few blocks from his home, was the scene of a famous literary confrontation. In 1933 Max Eastman had written an article about Ernest Hemingway, called "Bull in the Afternoon," for the *New Republic*. Four years later Hemingway walked into Perkins's office unexpectedly one afternoon to find Eastman there. Hemingway ripped open his shirt to display his hairy chest, then reached over and opened Eastman's, revealing an expanse of skin that, in Perkins's words, was "bare as a bald man's head." A fight ensued and the two fell to the floor, grappling. Each gave a different version of the story to the newspapers.

Some years later, when writing his memorable appreciation, *Here Is New York*, E. B. White recalled the incident. "I am sitting at the moment in a stifling hotel room in 90-degree heat, halfway down an air shaft, in midtown. No air moves in or out of the room, yet I am curiously affected by emanations from the immediate surroundings. I am twenty-two blocks from where Rudolph Valentino lay in state, eight blocks from where Nathan Hale was executed, five blocks from the publisher's office where Ernest Hemingway hit Max Eastman on the nose, four miles from where Walt Whitman sat sweating out editorials for the Brooklyn Eagle, thirty-four blocks from the street Willa Cather lived in when she came to New York to write books about

Nebraska . . ." and so on. White did not usually live in a hotel room. In fact, of the eight New York apartments he occupied at various times, three were in Turtle Bay: 245 East 48th Street from 1936 to 1938, 239 East 48th during a winter sometime later and 229 East 48th from 1945 to 1957. Here he had what the poet Louise Bogan described as "a dream-duplex." The apartment had "a circle of lemon-colored couches; one fine painting over the fireplace; a broad black cocktail table; and, best of all, four windows (one of them behind a concert grand) onto the communal garden." He chose a tree in the garden as the definitive symbol of New York. "In Turtle Bay," he wrote, "there is an old willow tree that presides over an interior garden. It is a battered tree, long suffering and much climbed, held together by strands of wire but beloved of those who know it. In a way it symbolizes the city: life under difficulties, growth against odds, sap-rise in the midst of concrete, and the steady reaching for the sun. Whenever I look at it nowadays, and feel the cold shadow of the planes, I think: 'This must be saved, this particular thing, this very tree.' If it were to go, all would go — this city, this mischievous and marvelous monument which not to look upon would be like death."

Dorothy Thompson was another resident of Turtle Bay Gardens. In 1941, after her divorce from Sinclair Lewis, she bought the house at 237 East 48th Street. The apartment, decorated primarily in Bauhaus-style, had a vestibule with eight sketches painted on glass of Thompson as she went through the activities of a typical day, a library with some three thousand books, a living room dominated by a black leather couch about eight feet long and a feminine bedroom in pale green satin and ivory. Her studio had "the air of a command post," according to her biographer, Marion K. Sanders. "Walls papered with maps, an illuminated globe, and a short-wave radio enabled her to follow the progress of the war on land, sea, and air." Like White,

Dorothy Thompson on her eight-foot couch with movable
arm rests, in her Turtle Bay house, 1942.

Dorothy Thompson sold her house in 1957. Today, Robert
Gottlieb, editor-in-chief of Knopf, is in Dorothy Thompson's
house; and literary agent Julian Bach lives at 241 East 48th.
Forty-ninth Street is the theatrical side of the Gardens; here
there are houses owned by Ruth Gordon and Garson Kanin,
Stephen Sondheim, and Katharine Hepburn.

With renewal, Beekman Place became even more elegant
than Turtle Bay. In 1937, after winning the Pulitzer Prize for
The Late George Apley, John P. Marquand took a duplex

apartment overlooking the river at 1 Beekman Place. Marquand, whose mother was Margaret Fuller's niece, wrote most often about New England, but two books were set in New York. In *So Little Time,* a writer for the theater married to an independently wealthy society woman (like Marquand's second wife, Adelaide Hooker) lives in an East Side duplex, and *Point of No Return* tells the story of a suburban banker who works in New York. Of its hero, Charles Gray, Marquand wrote: "It did not matter that he had not been born and raised there, because New York belonged almost exclusively to people who had come from other places. New York in the end was only a strange, indefinable combination of triumph, discouragement and memories. It did not matter what the weather was there, or the season of the year, or whether there was war or peace . . ."

Mary McCarthy, then a young free-lance writer, lived across the street in the apartment house at 2 Beekman Place from 1933 to 1936, when she was married to Harold Johnsrud. Kay, the heroine of her novel *The Group,* lived, like her creator, in the east Fifties. In the summer of 1937, after an interlude in the Village, McCarthy was again living on Beekman Place, in a borrowed apartment with Philip Rahv. Two Beekman Place had another literary resident when Antoine de Saint-Exupéry took a six-room suite there in 1941. A visitor described the apartment, which had been decorated for the previous tenant, Greta Garbo, and still held her furnishings: "Tawny wall-to-wall carpeting, large faded mirrors, an old dark green library, a sort of Venetian patina where the ships glide by in front of the windows as though on a level with the carpets." During this period, Saint-Exupéry began writing *Le Petit Prince,* which had come to him when he was entertaining friends with drawings on napkins at the Café Arnold on Central Park South.

The final step in the renewal of the Turtle Bay area was the construction in 1966 of the United Nations Plaza, twin apart-

ment towers rising from what had once been an area of tenements and slaughterhouses. Truman Capote lives there today
in a five-room cooperative apartment with a living room described by Gloria Steinem as "a dusty-plush 'best' parlor in the
South seen through the eyes of Vuillard, and suspended twenty
stories above Manhattan."

.

The rest of the East Side, particularly the area near Fifth, Madison and Park avenues, was not subject to the alternation in
social standing that afflicted Turtle Bay. Edith Wharton, a
social barometer as always, was living in "a little house in
Madison Avenue" after her marriage when her work was first
accepted for publication. Three poems were taken simultaneously by *Scribner's, Harper's* and the *Century* magazines. "As
long as I live," she wrote, "I shall never forget my sensations
when I opened the first of the three letters, and learned that I
was to appear in print. I can still see the narrow hall, the
letter-box out of which I fished the letters, and the flight of
stairs up and down which I ran, senselessly and incessantly, in
the attempt to give my excitement some muscular outlet!"
Later the Whartons moved to a town house at 884 Park Avenue,
which Edith furnished in accordance with the views she had
expressed in her first book, *The Decoration of Houses.* Henry
James, who stayed there on a visit to New York in 1905, called
it "a bonbonnière of the last daintiness naturally." James described the visit to a friend: ". . . She was charming, kind
and ingenious, and taste and tone and the finest discriminations,
ironies, and draperies mantelled us about."

At the close of the twenties a good quotient of the Algonquin
wits, prosperous by now, went to live on the East Side. Edna
Ferber was at 791 Park Avenue, George S. Kaufman was at 14
East 94th and Alexander Woollcott had a penthouse with a

river view at 450 East 52nd Street, then one of New York's most luxurious apartment houses. Woollcott had a valet and a chauffeur, and the St. Regis barber came to shave him every morning. In 1936 he sold the apartment to Noel Coward.

In 1930 Nathanael West again provided a center of poverty in the midst of prosperity, as he had earlier in Gramercy Park. Formerly the night manager of the Kenmore Hall Hotel on 23rd Street, he took the same job at the Sutton Club Hotel at 330 East 56th. Here again he let friends — Erskine Caldwell, S. J. Perelman and his wife (West's sister Laura), Edmund Wilson, and Robert Coates — stay for little or no money. James T. Farrell and his wife were welcomed after they had been evicted from their hotel, and Lillian Hellman and Dashiell Hammett came and occupied the Diplomat's Suite. Hammett had skipped from the Hotel Pierre, wearing, layer upon layer, all the clothing he owned. He was writing *The Thin Man* and put Laura Perelman's dog, Asta, in the novel. Quentin Reynolds often stayed over rather than travel home to Flatbush late at night. "I would go to the Sutton . . . and be given a room and no nonsense about signing the register or paying. Besides this attractive feature, the Sutton had a swimming pool, and many a midnight when the hotel was quiet, Nat would turn over his duties to the head bellboy and we'd go swimming. After that, sitting around with something to drink, we would talk, usually about writing . . ."

West was fascinated by the sordid lives and suffering of the people in the hotel. He referred to the sundeck as "suicide leap," because so many people jumped from it during the depression. He and Lillian Hellman steamed open the guests' letters to see the difference between the reality and the façade of their lives. He was preoccupied with loneliness, fear and desperation, the disease of the spirit W. H. Auden would call "West's Disease," in an essay on his work. Both of West's major works, *Miss Lonelyhearts* and *The Day of the Locust,* draw heavily on the atmosphere of the hotels where he worked.

The same year, 1931, Dorothy Thompson and Sinclair Lewis were living prosperously at 21 East 90th Street. They had two sitting rooms so that each could entertain guests separately. And in 1932 Willa Cather moved to 570 Park Avenue, where all her windows faced the blank wall of the Colony Club.

In the thirties two East Side homes were gathering places of very different kinds. Kirk Askew, a 57th Street art dealer, and his wife, Constance, had at-homes at 166 East 61st Street, known to habitués as the Askew Salon. The salon was held on Sunday afternoons during "r" months from 5:00 P.M. on. There was a large drawing room with tall windows overlooking a garden and a small cork-lined library for more serious discussions. The at-homes were not parties but "a continuing, well-organized operation with a clear and consistent objective" — the advancement of the careers of a group of art dealers and curators to which Askew belonged. In addition to painters and composers, many writers were guests: Carl Van Vechten, Emily Hahn, Glenway Wescott, Elizabeth Bowen, E. E. Cummings, Gilbert Seldes and Archibald MacLeish. Elizabeth Bowen once stayed in the guest bedroom and Virgil Thomson lived there on and off from 1932 to 1935.

Several blocks away, at 220 East 69th Street, Stephen Vincent Benét's home became a haven for young poets seeking help and advice. Like Howells in his day, Benét was one of the few writers who commanded the respect of the young and at the same time made himself available to them. He had won the Pulitzer Prize in 1929 for *John Brown's Body* and wrote his famous story, "The Devil and Daniel Webster," in 1936. Benét said the house on 69th Street "looks like something you build out of those pink stone building blocks when you are a child and has more wasted hall-space than the Grand Canyon."

He and his family lived there until 1939, when they moved to 215 East 68th Street. He took long walks, often through Central Park, every morning before working.

During the late thirties and early forties the war brought a number of expatriates to New York and some of them settled on the East Side. Saint-Exupéry was living on Beekman Place, Thomas Mann was at the Hotel Bedford at 118 East 40th Street and André Maurois was at the Ritz Tower, on the northeast corner of Park Avenue and 57th Street. Maurois had no money but the management allowed him to pay when he could and told his wife to furnish their three-room apartment with French antiques and send them the bills. When he left to spend several months in Kansas City, Maurois wrote:

> I shall miss this tiny New York apartment where there is nothing ugly. On our lamp shades, in transparency, the two pink houses of the Place Royale and the poplars of the Dordogne. On our wall, the Angel of Chartres bending above the Beauce plain. In the morning, at sunrise, the soaring towers of New York, amber or rose, take on the smooth luminous softness of walls by Vermeer or Guardi. I have loved this part of town . . . the Greek grocer who gave me chocolate for my French friends, because I had written a life of Byron; the young salesman, cool and cultured, of the Chaucer Head Bookshop, who preferred fine texts to best sellers; the Canari d'Or restaurant where Monsieur Robert, the French proprietor, always has a corner for us; the florist who, everytime we pass her shop, makes Simone a little gift: a rose or a violet; Klebanoff, the newspaper seller, who also sells books, theatre tickets, cigarettes, cough drops, and is a notary public besides . . .

Maurois and his wife saw other expatriates: Saint-Exupéry, Mann, Jules Romains, Pierre Claudel, Fernand Léger and André Gide.

The forties also brought John Steinbeck, who had come to New York from San Francisco in 1925. Then he had first worked as a laborer pushing wheelbarrows of concrete for the construction of Madison Square Garden. After a stint on a newspaper and a period in which, jobless and weak with hunger, he tried to write stories, he shipped back to San Francisco. "The city had beaten the pants off me," he wrote. "Whatever it required to get ahead, I didn't have. I didn't leave the city in disgust — I left it with the respect plain unadulterated fear gives." With success behind him, he returned in 1943 and took an apartment at 330 East 51st Street. "My new home consisted of the first and second floors of a three-story house and the living room looked out on a small soot-field called a garden. I was going to live in New York but I was going to avoid it. I planted a lawn in the garden, bought huge pots and planted tomatoes, pollinating the blossoms with a water-color brush." In 1951 Steinbeck moved to 206 East 72nd Street, where he lived until his death in 1968. He summed up his feelings about the city in an article called "The Making of a New Yorker": "New York is an ugly city, a dirty city," he stated. "Its climate is a scandal, its politics are used to frighten children, its traffic is madness, its competition is murderous. But there is one thing about it — once you have lived in New York and it has become your home, no place else is good enough. All of everything is concentrated here, population, theater, art, writing, publishing, importing, business, murder, mugging, luxury, poverty. It is all of everything. It goes all night. It is tireless and its air is charged with energy. I can work longer and harder without weariness in New York than any place else."

Eugene O'Neill, who disliked city life, took a six-room penthouse with his third wife, Carlotta Monterey, at 35 East 84th Street in 1946. (The O'Neills had an apartment at 1085 Park Avenue for several months in 1931.) The apartment had a terrace on three sides with panoramic views of the city, and

Eugene O'Neill on the terrace of his penthouse at
35 East 84th Street, around 1946.

the walls of the rooms were painted in strong colors — deep purple, royal blue, Chinese red. In O'Neill's combination bedroom-study there were pictures of clipper ships and an oil painting of Broadway during the theater rush hour. "There's the whole story of the decline of America," O'Neill told a *New Yorker* interviewer, pointing to the pictures, "from the most beautiful thing America has ever made, the clipper ship, to the most tawdry street in the world."

In 1944 Mary McCarthy and Edmund Wilson lived at 14 Henderson Place, a cul-de-sac off 86th Street between York and East End avenues, until the end of their marriage. After their separation Wilson brought Anaïs Nin to visit. She described the experience: "A street lined with old-fashioned English brick houses. Pointed slate roofs, ivy and trees, but all of them so narrow and bleak; the windows long and narrow. He had forgotten his key, so we entered through the basement. The place had an air of devastation. 'Mary took away all the furniture.' We entered the parlor, a deep and narrow room. In the middle of the empty room stood two rocking chairs. On the walls, a series of Hogarth prints."

In 1953 Sylvia Plath spent a brief but traumatic month in New York as a guest editor of *Mademoiselle* magazine. She stayed at the Barbizon, a hotel for young women at Lexington Avenue and 63rd Street, which she called the Amazon in her autobiographical novel, *The Bell Jar*. ". . . It reminded me of my dormitory at college," she wrote. "It wasn't a proper hotel — I mean a hotel where there are both men and women mixed about here and there on the same floor. This hotel — the Amazon — was for women only, and they were mostly girls my age with wealthy parents who wanted to be sure their daughters would be living where men couldn't get at them and deceive them; and they were all going to posh secretarial schools like Katy Gibbs." The visit to New York triggered a depression that culminated in a suicide attempt when Plath returned to Massachusetts. Friends and critics speculated that she found the world of fashion journalism artificial and banal, that she was brought up short before the inadequacy of her preparation for life in New York as an editor and writer and that, despite the protection of the Barbizon, she had some unfortunate sexual experiences, including an attempted rape by a South American playboy.

The same year, Dorothy Parker, who had been in California for most of the preceding two decades, returned to New York to live in a "stark, bare, colorless, and impersonal room" in the Volney, a residential hotel at 23 East 74th Street. After another trip to California, she returned to the Volney in 1963 and lived there until her death in 1967. In her last years she was extremely poor. Her good friend Lillian Hellman took two paintings, presents from Dorothy in more prosperous times, sold them and gave her the money. Hellman was living at this time in a house at 63 East 82nd Street, which she had bought in 1944. In 1969 she sold the house and a year later moved to Park Avenue in the Sixties, where she still lives. Her apartment is furnished with fine furniture: an early American highboy, an Empire love seat, Sheraton chairs, pieces from her plays and paintings by Toulouse-Lautrec, Rouault, Picasso and Ben Shahn. Her parties there are considered among New York's most exclusive literary events.

Other writers currently living on the East Side are Edward Albee, who has a painting-filled apartment on Fifth Avenue; Dwight Macdonald, who, though often associated with the West Side intellectuals, lives on East 87th Street; and Kurt Vonnegut, who lives across from Turtle Bay Gardens on 48th Street. George Plimpton, who, as an expatriate, began the *Paris Review* in 1953, returned to New York in the late fifties to live in a house overlooking the East River on 72nd

A party around 1965 at George Plimpton's for the formation of Film-wrights, a cooperative of playwrights and novelists. Plimpton is at left front. In right foreground with his back to the camera is Arthur Kopit with Frank and Eleanor Perry behind him. Standing to their right are Jack Richardson and, holding a drink, Mario Puzo. Truman Capote is on the couch, his dog at his feet. William Styron is talking to Capote, and Harold L. Humes, a founder of the *Paris Review,* is the man with the pipe listening in. The group at left rear includes (left to right) Jonathan Miller, Gore Vidal and filmmaker Richard Leacock. At far rear, right, Ralph Ellison is talking to Peter Matthiessen.

Street. Norman Podhoretz speculates that Plimpton performed a unique literary function. "He brought writers and intellectuals into contact with the rich, the powerful, and the fashionable for the first time in any of their lives, and thereby did much to increase the standing and power of the former, if not the comfort and happiness of the latter."

In recent years only a few authors of stature have chosen

to write about the East Side. Marquand wrote several novels
set there, but unlike his close dissections of New England
they deal with the city in an abstract way. Truman Capote's
Breakfast at Tiffany's, which he wrote when he lived in Brooklyn Heights, opens in an East Seventies brownstone said to
be based on his first New York apartment. "It was one room
crowded with attic furniture, a sofa and fat chairs upholstered
in that itchy, particular red velvet that one associates with hot
days on a train . . . The single window looked out on a fire
escape. Even so, my spirits heightened whenever I felt in my
pocket the key to this apartment; with all its gloom, it still
was a place of my own, the first, and my books were there, and
jars of pencils to sharpen, everything I needed, so I felt, to become the writer I wanted to be." In the novel Holly Golightly
had occupied the apartment below. John O'Hara came to
New York from Pennsylvania in 1927 and immediately began
to live a dissolute life, to the detriment of his work. "God,
to think that I recognize the faces of scores of cops and doormen
between 42nd Street and 59th!" he said. "Waiters in speakeasies and the Algonquin and Sardi's and B-G sandwich shops
know me by name . . . and in essence I don't like it." In
1934 he wrote about this life in *Butterfield 8,* a book named
for a telephone exchange then serving the fashionable East Side.
He had lived at the Pickwick Arms Hotel at 230 East 51st
Street while writing the football column for the *New Yorker*
and starting *Appointment in Samarra;* and he wrote *Butterfield 8* in a brownstone on East 55th Street. In 1940, after
several stints in Hollywood, he could at last afford Butterfield
8 himself. He rented a ground-floor apartment in a remodeled
town house at 27 East 79th Street, and later, from 1945 to 1949,
he lived at 55 East 86th Street.

Finally, Louis Auchincloss has been the only writer born
and bred on the East Side to chronicle life among old New

York society as Edith Wharton did in the early part of the century. He lived at 66 East 79th Street from 1935–1945. *Portrait in Brownstone,* set on 53rd Street, is based on his grandmother's family, which occupied what was called "Dixon Alley" in the 1890s. There were six Dixons on 49th Street between Fifth and Sixth avenues and one on 48th. After attending Groton, Yale and the University of Virginia Law School, Auchincloss went to work at the law firm of Sullivan and Cromwell. When he resigned in 1952 to devote himself to full-time writing, he was living at 24 East 84th Street. He has long since gone back to another law firm and lives today on upper Park Avenue.

Auchincloss is alone in writing from his own experience about the world of law and business. "No writer today has anything to do with Wall Street," he says. "No major people have anything to do with business at all. Even Marquand didn't come by it naturally; he boned up. Writers don't have to go into business anymore. The universities support them . . . or the magazines." Auchincloss remains the only major writer to use the characteristic upper-class life of the upper East Side as his subject.

East Side Tour

Turtle Bay Gardens (1), which encompasses the houses from 227 to 247 East 48th Street and 226 to 246 East 49th Street, has been designated a historic district. The brownstone houses, most of which have been stuccoed or painted, share a private garden. At various times E. B. White lived in two Turtle Bay houses on 48th Street, the yellow one at 229 and the beige one at 239, and one just outside its limits, the unpainted brown-

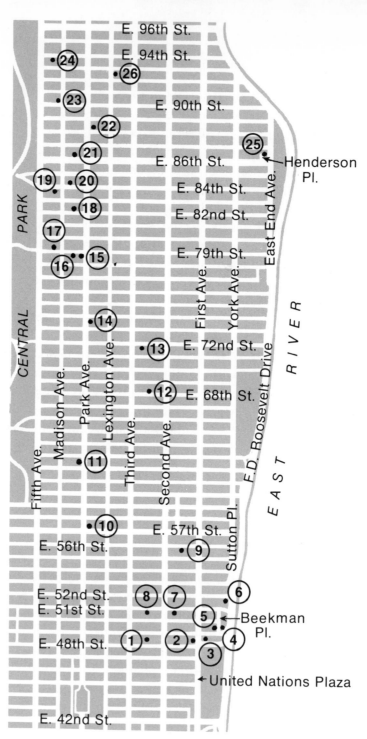

The East Side

stone at 245. Dorothy Thompson lived in the white house at 237 East 48th Street. Theatrical people — Ruth Gordon and Garson Kanin, Katharine Hepburn, and Stephen Sondheim — own several of the houses on the 49th Street side. The great editor Maxwell Perkins lived in the yellow house at 246 East 49th Street. One of his authors, Thomas Wolfe, lived nearby in the apartment building at 865 First Avenue (2) for a while in 1935. In the 1840s Edgar Allan Poe, Margaret Fuller and Horace Greeley lived in the Turtle Bay area. Poe stayed at the Miller farmhouse, located at what is now 47th Street and Second Avenue, and Margaret Fuller boarded with the Greeleys in their house at about 50th Street. Truman Capote lives just north of the location of Turtle Bay itself (filled in and now United Nations Park) at 870 United Nations Plaza (3) .

The area overlooking the river around Beekman Place has become one of the most desirable in the city. Padraic and Mary Colum lived here in the early part of the century, when it was "an unfashionable and dingy part of the city." John Marquand lived in a duplex in the immense apartment building at 1 Beekman Place (4) in 1937. Mary McCarthy had lived in the similar building across the street at 2 Beekman Place (5) from 1933 to 1936 during her first marriage. In the summer of 1937 she was again living on Beekman Place in an unspecified apartment with Philip Rahv. Antoine de Saint-Exupéry took a six-room apartment, previously Greta Garbo's, at 2 Beekman Place in 1941. In the early thirties, Alexander Woollcott lived at 450 East 52nd Street (6) , then and now one of New York's most luxurious apartment houses.

John Steinbeck lived in the three-story brick house at 330 East 51st Street (7) in 1943. In the garden, which he called a "soot-field," he planted a lawn and tomatoes in pots. John O'Hara was living in the Pickwick Arms Hotel at 230 East

51st Street (8) when he began *Appointment in Samarra*. Nathanael West was the night manager of the Sutton Club Hotel, 330 East 56th Street (9), during the depression. So many people jumped from the sundeck that he called it "suicide leap."

Park Avenue and its environs has had its share of literary residents. André Maurois lived in the richly detailed Ritz Tower Hotel on the northeast corner of 57th Street (10) during the war. Willa Cather lived up the avenue at 570 Park (11) from 1932 until her death. The home of Stephen Vincent Benét, first at 220 East 69th Street and later at 215 East 68th, was a gathering place for young poets. Both houses have been replaced by the same gigantic apartment building (12), but the south side of 68th Street suggests what the neighborhood was like in Benét's day. John Steinbeck lived from 1951 until his death in 1968 in an attractive brownstone house with white shutters at 206 East 72nd Street (13). At this writing, the house is vacant and boarded up and may soon be demolished.

Back on Park Avenue at 791 (14) is the apartment building where Edna Ferber went to live at the close of the twenties. Edith Wharton's house, which once stood at 884 Park (15), has been replaced by an apartment building. Louis Auchincloss, a great admirer of Wharton's, grew up around the corner in the brick apartment building at 66 East 79th Street (16). In 1940 John O'Hara lived in a ground-floor apartment in the drastically remodeled town house at 27 East 79th Street (17), today the headquarters of the designer Hanae Mori.

Lillian Hellman owned the lovely brick house at 63 East 82nd Street (18) from 1944 to 1969. Louis Auchincloss was living in the brownstone at 24 East 84th Street (19) in 1952 when he decided to write full-time for a while. Up the block at 35 East 84th (20), Eugene O'Neill had a penthouse apartment in the mid-forties. John O'Hara lived in the fifteen-story brick apartment building at 55 East 86th Street (21) from 1945 to 1949. O'Neill lived briefly at 1085 Park Avenue (22) in 1931. Dorothy Thompson and Sinclair Lewis were living in the apartment building at 21 East 90th Street (23) the same year. George S. Kaufman lived at 14 East 94th Street (24), in a town house now painted white, in the late twenties.

Mary McCarthy and Edmund Wilson lived at 14 Henderson Place (25) in the charming cul-de-sac off 86th Street between York and East End avenues in 1944, when they were married. The group of brick Queen Anne houses along Henderson Place, East End Avenue and 87th Street was built in 1881 for "persons of moderate means" by John C. Henderson. They now comprise the Henderson Place Historic District.

Since the late forties, readings by distinguished American and visiting European poets have been held at the Young Men's and Young Women's Hebrew Association at 92nd Street and Lexington Avenue (26).

VIII. The West Side

NEW YORK today has no thriving literary center like the Greenwich Village of the 1910s and 1920s. There is not one area where writers live in great concentration and share a sense of community, collaboration and mutual stimulation, although various institutions scattered around the city serve as focal points. But if New York has anything approaching a literary center today, it is the upper West Side.

Lionel Trilling wrote that in 1929 he "signalized [his] solidarity with the intellectual life by taking an apartment in Greenwich Village." But most recently, until his death in 1975, Trilling, like many other literary people, lived on the West Side. In part the shift uptown of the literary community is a matter of practicality; the large apartments on West End Avenue and Riverside Drive have provided reasonably priced housing for the writers whose families expanded during the fifties. But additionally, the West Side is the geographic area most closely associated with certain contemporary literary currents. In a time when the New York literary scene is dominated by critics and essayists writing about social and political problems, West Siders encounter these problems with stunning immediacy on their own teeming, anarchic streets. And in a time when a Jewish sensibility dominates New York fiction and criticism, the West Side, once "the golden ghetto" of prosperous immigrants, is an appropriate ground for its flowering.

Yet the West Side is a literary neighborhood with a difference. Unlike the majority of writers of the past who abhorred bourgeois lifestyles, those on the West Side embrace them in massive, impersonal middle-class buildings. And unlike most neighborhoods with large concentrations of literary people, the West Side has no public place — no bar, restaurant or cafeteria — where writers and intellectuals gather. They are most likely to meet in Zabar's, a gourmet delicatessen, where each arrives and departs separately. Although the West Side literati are presumably connected by ephemeral intellectual filaments, they claim hardly ever to see one another.

The West Side, like all of New York, was originally lovely countryside. Washington Irving described it in *A History of New York* as "a sweet rural valley, beautiful with many a bright flower, refreshed by many a pure streamlet, and enlivened here and there by a delectable little Dutch cottage, sheltered under some sloping hill; and almost buried in embowering trees." Several decades later, in the days when John James Audubon recorded catching a 200-pound sturgeon in the Hudson below his house at 156th Street, Edgar Allan Poe was living in a farmhouse on a rocky knoll at what is now 84th Street between Broadway and Amsterdam Avenue. Poe spent the summer of 1844 there while finishing "The Raven." He and his wife lived in a garret under the eaves, but Poe worked in a spacious study on the floor below. The fireplace mantel, where he carved his name, is now in Philosophy Hall at Columbia University.

Residential development on the West Side began in the 1880s. Numerous blocks of row houses were succeeded by luxury apartment houses as the preferred style of building. The first, and forever the most distinguished, was the Dakota, built in 1884 on Central Park West at 72nd Street. Next came the Ansonia, completed in 1904, at 73rd and Broadway. Although the building was constructed in the style of the resort hotels of the French Riviera, the architect and builder, W. E. D. Stokes, kept goats, ducks, chickens and a small pet bear in the roof garden and sold eggs to the tenants at half price. The West Side streets, however, were never to become truly fashionable, with the exception of Central Park West. From the early 1900s the grand buildings overlooking the Park drew a number of literary residents who had achieved financial success. Although the apartment houses sometimes were numbered according to their cross streets, they were all on Central Park West.

First among the literary gathering places was 1 West 87th Street, the home of John Quinn, the New York lawyer who was a patron of Irish literature, a collector of postimpressionist art and defender of the *Little Review* in the obscenity suit

The farmhouse at 84th Street and Broadway where Edgar Allan Poe lived in the summer of 1844.

resulting from its publication of *Ulysses*. William Butler Yeats stayed with Quinn in November of 1903 while on an American lecture tour. He had his own key and treated the apartment as his home in New York; his poem "Never Give All the Heart" grew out of a conversation he had there with Quinn. In later years, when Quinn was living at 58 Central Park West, Yeats, Lady Gregory and Standish O'Grady all stayed with him at various times. The lawyer had an unexpected literary connection through his Paris collector, Henri Pierre Roché, who wrote the apparently autobiographical *Jules et Jim* at the age of seventy-five.

Ellen Glasgow lived at 1 West 85th Street from 1911 to 1916 in an apartment overlooking the Park. She was writing *Life and Gabriella,* a book set on East 57th Street and in London Terrace, where her friend Van Wyck Brooks lived (see Chapter V, Chelsea). In 1917 Sara Teasdale and her husband moved to the Beresford at 211 Central Park West. Teasdale, who considered herself extremely delicate, was almost a recluse and seldom went out. John Hall Wheelock recalls that she was so sensitive she was incapable of saying good-by, and simply went into another room and closed the door when it was time for a guest to leave.

In 1923 Edna Ferber sublet an apartment at 50 Central Park West in an ornate building with cast-iron bay windows. The following year she took a five-year lease on another apartment in the same building, with eight windows facing the Park. Another of the Algonquin wits, Marc Connelly, has been living since 1929 at 25 Central Park West, the Century, a prime example of the art deco apartment houses built in the twenties and thirties.

In 1943 Sinclair Lewis telephoned a rental agency and announced that he wanted an apartment with a view of all the New York bridges and a living room sixty feet long and twenty

feet high. The agent rented him a duplex at the Eldorado
Towers, an orange stone art deco building at 300 Central
Park West. Lewis wrote to a friend: "I have taken a gaudy
flat, a cross between Elizabeth Arden's Beauty Salon and the
horse-stables at Ringling Circus Winter Headquarters: 29 floors
up in the air and commanding a fair view of the Orkney Isles
on the West, of Girard Avenue South on the North and West."
Lewis called the apartment "Big Intolerable" or "Intolerable
Towers." On the upper floor were a living room, dining room
and sitting room with a fireplace. Below, there were bedrooms
and Lewis's study, which was dominated by an enormous map
of Minnesota. The apartment was decorated with pale gray
walls, terra-cotta tile floors, dull green, beige and yellow upholstery and bleached woodwork. The same building would
serve to symbolize the ultimate in nouveau-riche upward mobility as the home of Herman Wouk's Marjorie Morningstar.

Among the most distinctive West Side blocks is 67th Street
from Central Park West to Columbus Avenue. Four of the
buildings on the block were constructed by the same developer,
Walter Russell, who wanted them to be the best possible artists' housing. Most of the apartments have two-story studio
living rooms. The Hotel Des Artistes at 1 West 67th Street,
most magnificent of the buildings, originally had its own
communal kitchen, squash courts, swimming pool, theater
and ballroom. It now has a restaurant on the first floor, the
Café Des Artistes, decorated by Howard Chandler Christy with
murals of nude women against fields of flowers. Fannie Hurst,
the highly successful writer of popular fiction, lived here
from 1932 until her death in 1968. She had a triplex with a
study brought in its entirety, including wall panels and stained-
glass windows, from a sixteenth-century Italian palazzo. She
described the apartment: "Baronial living room, thirty-foot-
high ceiling. Woodburning fireplaces. Balconies. A roof ter-

race halfway across the building. My workroom, overlooking
this terrace, oak paneled, with stained-glass windows, seemed
to have a hush built into it." Other tenants of the Des Artistes
have been Isadora Duncan, Alexander Woollcott and Noel
Coward. In 1929 the building was the scene of a famous
literary murder/suicide; Harry Crosby, publisher of the Black
Sun Press in Paris, killed a woman companion and then himself.
His wife, Caresse Crosby, was at the theater with Hart Crane
when the news came. E. E. Cummings wrote a poem about it:

> 2 boston
> Dolls; found
> with
> Holes in each other
>
> 's lullaby.

The neighborhood behind the elegant façade of Central Park
West has always been primarily middle-class. Theodore
Dreiser used its characteristic ambiance in *Sister Carrie,* which
he began when he was living at 6 West 102nd Street in 1899.
It is evidence of the sparse settlement of the area that Carrie
can see the Hudson to the west and the tops of the trees in Central Park to the east from her third-floor apartment on 78th
Street near Amsterdam Avenue. Dissatisfaction with the
middle-class housewifely life and a yearning for the glamour
of the big city downtown lead Carrie to seek a career in the
theater.

In the winter of 1902, after a trip to Europe with her brother,
Gertrude Stein stayed with three friends in a wooden apartment building overlooking the Hudson on West 100th Street.
Here she started her first novel, *Q.E.D.,* in which the main
character, Adele, returns to New York from London, as Stein
had, and says, "I simply rejoiced in the New York streets, in
the long spindling legs of the elevated, in the straight high un-

decorated houses, in the empty upper air and in the white surface of the snow. It was such a joy to realize that the whole thing was without mystery and without complexity, that it was clean and straight and meagre and hard and white and high." The novel, which discusses a Lesbian affair, was published under the title *Things As They Are* after Stein's death.

In 1916 Louis Untermeyer was living on the West Side, leading what he described as "two separate lives." In frequent visits to the Village, where he was working on the *Masses,* he mingled with the bohemian set. Back home at 310 West 100th Street, he lived the life of "the upper-class bourgeoisie" and entertained Vachel Lindsay, Robert Frost and Amy Lowell — and one exception from downtown, Edna St. Vincent Millay. Often the poets would read their work. Untermeyer recalled that "Frost read with just a slight New England tang, sort of down country." Amy Lowell read "wonderfully, colorfully. When she died her poems died with her because they needed her flamboyant personality; they needed all her feminine-masculine vigor . . . Edna Millay read very well because of her particular quality, her combination of elfin and gamin." Sometimes the Village crowd would come uptown for a cheese and beer party. Untermeyer remembered serving "tea, coffee, fine sandwiches and very good Viennese pastries for the other crowd."

F. Scott Fitzgerald, just discharged from the army, was living in a cheap room at 200 Claremont Avenue in 1919. He was working for an advertising agency and trying to make his way as a writer. At one time he had "one hundred and twenty-two rejection slips pinned in a frieze" around his bedroom. When Zelda broke their engagement because Fitzgerald had no money and could offer her little security, he went home to St. Paul to rewrite *This Side of Paradise.* (They were married as soon as Scribner's accepted the book.) Fitzgerald's own West Side neighborhood may well have provided the setting in *The Great Gatsby* for the apartment Tom Buchanan keeps for assignations with his mistress, in "one slice in a long white cake of apartment-houses" on West 158th Street.

•

The vast middle-class precincts of the West Side were the rearing ground for a number of children who would later distinguish themselves as writers. Young Dorothy Rothschild, later Dorothy Parker, spent her early years in a comfortable house at 57 West 68th Street and attended the Blessed Sacrament Convent on 70th Street. Later, when she began working for *Vogue,* she roomed in a boarding house at 103rd Street and Broadway. She earned ten dollars a week and paid eight dollars for her room and two meals a day. Lillian Hellman came to New York from New Orleans when she was six and lived on the West Side, frequently visiting her mother's family nearby. "The Newhouse apartment," she wrote in *An Unfinished Woman,* "held the upper-middle-class trappings, in touch of things and in spirit of people, that never manage to be truly stylish. Heavy weather hung over the lovely oval rooms." Nathanael West's father, who was a contractor involved in the building boom, wanted his son to go to the progressive Public School 81 on 119th Street between Seventh and St. Nicholas avenues and accordingly built an apartment house a block from the school and moved his family into it. Despite, or perhaps because of, his father's efforts, West was absent as many as thirty times a semester and never got a grade higher than a B. In 1917 his family moved to Tenth Avenue and 59th Street and he attended DeWitt Clinton High School, where his schoolmates included Countee Cullen and Lionel Trilling. Here his grades were spectacularly bad. He left school without graduating and got into college by altering his

high school transcript. Anaïs Nin, who had spent her earliest
years in Europe, lived with her mother and brother on the
first floor of a rooming house at 158 West 75th Street from
1914 to 1919. Here she began the diary, intended as a record
for her father, who had abandoned the family, that would be
her major literary work. A few years later, J. D. Salinger was
growing up on the West Side; he lived at 390 Riverside Drive
on the corner of 111th Street. The childhood he attributes to
the Glass children in *Seymour, Raise High the Roof Beam,
Carpenters* and other works must have been very similar to his
own. Before moving to the East Side, as Salinger's family also
did, the Glasses live in the Hotel Alamac on Broadway and 71st
Street and then in an apartment building at 110th Street and
Riverside Drive with a canopy lit by "bulby bright lights."
They play curb marbles and stoopball. "As we played it,"
Salinger wrote, "a rubber ball was thrown against some architectural granite fancy-work — a popular Manhattan mixture of
Greek Ionic and Roman Corinthian molding — along the
façade of our apartment house, about waist-high." They went
for haircuts in a barbershop "at 108th and Broadway, nested
verdantly . . . between a Chinese restaurant and a kosher
delicatessen" and bought Louis Sherry ice cream from a drugstore at 113th and Broadway.

In 1932 Herman Wouk's family moved from the Bronx to a
"luxurious Manhattan apartment building on the northwest
corner of 101st Street and West End Avenue." His years there,
Wouk said, "furnished the milieu, the story and the characters"
for *Marjorie Morningstar,* although he set his heroine on Central Park West.

•

It was only in the fifties that the West Side began to be viewed
as a place for writers and intellectuals to live. Some observers

speculate that this came about as a result of a child-bearing
trend. "The Village was more radical in the thirties; people
were childless," said Elizabeth Hardwick. "In the nineteen
fifties people were searching for the large house. It was a phenomenon of the Eisenhower era — babies, the stress on family,
have a big apartment, gather your books." Then, too, many
of the fifties writers and intellectuals were Jewish and found
the West Side comfortably familiar. Meyer Levin, Chicago-
born author of *Compulsion,* took a humorous view of the phenomenon. "I was rehabilitating this brownstone — when was
it? Six years ago? Suddenly it came to me. I'm an obsessive-
compulsive! Back in the late twenties I worked in Palestine.
And now I'm doing it all over again on the West Side — re-
claiming ancient Jewish land."

Frederic Morton, in an article on the West Side written
for the *New York Times,* speculated that "the mass migration
of intellectuals to the West Side often implies a frank coming
to terms with the probity of their origins . . . It's *really* all
right to be Jewish." Alfred Kazin put it another way: "If
you're interested in Jewish history, there's no shame to living
on the West Side."

In any case, the West Side has come to be associated with
"New York intellectuals," a group defined primarily by Irving
Howe in his 1968 *Commentary* essay, "The New York Intellectuals, A Chronicle and A Critique," and by Norman Podhoretz, editor of *Commentary,* in his autobiography, *Making It.*
Howe, who lives on Riverside Drive, wrote: "They are, or
until recently have been, anti-Communist; they are, or until
some time ago were, radicals; they have a fondness for ideo-
logical speculation; they write literary criticism with a strong
social emphasis; they revel in polemic; they strive self-con-
sciously to be 'brilliant'; and by birth or osmosis, they are
Jews." Norman Podhoretz added that what he calls "the

Alfred Kazin in his book-lined living room on West End Avenue.

family" has produced its share of books, "but its characteristic form has been the short piece."

In addition to Howe and Podhoretz themselves, members of the West Side intelligentsia include Susan Sontag (Riverside Drive), James Baldwin (470 West End Avenue on occasional visits home from Paris), Barbara and Jason Epstein (West 67th Street), Alfred Kazin (West End Avenue), Murray Kempton (West End Avenue) and Elizabeth Hardwick (West 67th Street). Reports have it that Kempton once quipped, "Only Norman Podhoretz would think that 'making it' and living on West End Avenue and One hundred and fifth Street were the same thing."

The intellectuals, who originally gathered around the *Partisan Review*, now have a variety of forums — Podhoretz's *Commentary*, Howe's *Dissent*, and the *New York Review of Books*. The *New York Review* was conceived one night during the 1963 newspaper strike when Robert Lowell and Elizabeth Hardwick, then married to one another, were having dinner at the Epsteins'. The first issue was dummied up on the dining room table of the Lowell-Hardwick apartment, one of the West 67th Street studio duplexes described by Lowell as "the last gasp of true Nineteenth-Century Capitalistic Gothic." The apartment is still filled with furnishings from Lowell's parents' house in Boston — a red velvet sofa, oriental rugs and American primitive paintings. Lowell described its "oak panels, mantel" and "book ladders on brass rods" in his poem "The Golden Middle."

The *New York Review*'s second issue came from the identically laid-out Epstein apartment several buildings west. As Merle Miller noted in an article called "Why Norman and Jason Aren't Talking," Jason Epstein used to cook on his restaurant stove for the Podhoretzes as well as other West Siders who are no longer on speaking terms since feuding began between *Com-*

mentary and the *New York Review*. Although there was a time when West Side intellectuals got together, it seems there is now no gathering place, to say nothing of a salon. "The reason there are no successful salons is simple," journalist and critic Victor Navasky wrote in 1966. "To have a salon, enemies must at least be friends. But as Columbia English professor Albert Goldman has pointed out, 'We don't have enough social quality. We don't like each other enough . . .' And Irving Kristol theorized, 'A lot of New York intellectuals have roots in Eastern Europe where, unlike England and France, there was no tradition of civility.' "

Alfred Kazin has observed that "until recently, the writers most sensitive to the city were indeed strangers to it." Kazin was thinking back to William Dean Howells, but his observation holds true of the present-day West Side. Although New York area writers Philip Roth, in *Letting Go;* Salinger, in his Glass family stories; and Herman Wouk, in *Marjorie Morningstar,* have made some use of the West Side, the writer who has best absorbed, described and raised it to a level of symbolic significance is Saul Bellow. Bellow, who was born outside Montreal and grew up in Chicago, did not come to New York until the forties. His novel *The Victim* uses New York only as a barely noticeable backdrop although it begins with a vivid description of the city: "On some nights New York is as hot as Bangkok. The whole continent seems to have moved from its place and slid nearer the equator, the bitter gray Atlantic to have become green and tropical, and the people, thronging the streets, barbaric fellahin . . ." From 1950 to 1952 Bellow was a visiting lecturer at New York University, living at least part of the time in the Village at 17 Minetta Lane. Later he moved to 333 Riverside Drive, a beautiful white brick limestone-trimmed house from which he had a view of the river from one room, his bathroom. *Seize the Day,* published in 1956, makes full use of the West Side locale. It is set in the fictional Hotel Gloriana, near the Ansonia, which Bellow described as looking "like a baroque palace from Prague or Munich enlarged a hundred times, with towers, domes, huge swells and bubbles of metal gone green from exposure, iron fretwork and festoons." Bellow is fascinated by the old men and women who live along Broadway in the Seventies, Eighties and Nineties. "Unless the weather is too cold or too wet they fill the benches about the tiny railed parks and along the subway gratings from Verdi Square to Columbia University, they crowd the shops and cafeterias, the dime stores, the tea-rooms, the bakeries, the beauty parlors, the reading rooms and club rooms." In *Herzog*, the protagonist has a small apartment on West 17th Street, but all his women live on the upper West Side. Finally, in *Mr. Sammler's Planet*, the neighborhood itself takes center stage. Bellow's descriptions become more graphic and intense as he raises the city to the level of symbol. Sammler parts his curtain and looks out: "Brownstones, balustrades, bay windows, wrought-iron. Like stamps in an album — the dun rose of buildings canceled by the heavy black of grilles, of corrugated rainspouts . . . Such was Sammler's eastward view, a soft asphalt belly rising, in which lay steaming sewer navels. Spalled sidewalks with clusters of ash cans. Brownstones. The yellow brick of elevator buildings like his own. Little copses of television antennas . . . Westward the Hudson came between Sammler and the great Spry industries of New Jersey. These flashed their electric message through intervening night. SPRY." Bellow writes of upper Broadway: "It was aware of being a scene of perversity, it knew its own despair. And fear. The terror of it. Here you might see the soul of America at grips with historical problems, struggling with certain impossibilities, experiencing violently states inherently static." As one character in *Mr. Sammler's Planet* says, "New York makes one think about the collapse of civilization, about Sodom and Gomorrah, the end of the world." And of all New York, Broadway and 96th Street most forcefully conveys this idea. "By a convergence of all minds and all movements the conviction transmitted by this crowd seemed to be that reality was a terrible thing, and that the final truth about mankind was overwhelming and crushing . . . Sammler could not swear this was really accurate, but Broadway at Ninety-sixth Street gave him such a sense of things."

Though none find it as compelling a subject as the visitor Bellow, a host of other important contemporary writers live on the West Side. Joseph Heller, author of *Catch 22* and *Something Happened,* maintains an apartment on West 80th Street although he spends much of his time in Amagansett, near the tip of Long Island. Jack Gelber, whose play *The Connection* was a turning point in American theater when it was produced in 1959, lives on West End Avenue in the Nineties. (The Living Theatre, which produced the play, had its origins in a large apartment at 789 West End Avenue inherited by Julian Beck from his father. Here he and Judith Malina first put on plays. Later they used a loft at 110th Street and Broadway as a theater.) According to Gelber there is little West Side socialization based on literary affinities. "Most of the interaction I get is on the street, in the supermarket, walking the dog," he has said. "I'll meet someone and he'll say, 'What are you doing, Jack?' Writers don't talk about writing anyway. As far as I can gather, their main topic of conversation is money — what kind of an advance did you get, how many performances did you have."

Isaac Bashevis Singer has lived on the West Side for over thirty years — "as long as I lived in Poland," one of his characters says. "I know each block, each house . . . I have the illusion of having put down roots here. I have spoken in most

Isaac Bashevis Singer at his desk in his apartment
on West 86th Street.

of the synagogues. They know me in some of the stores and in
the vegetarian restaurants. Women with whom I have had
affairs live on the side streets. Even the pigeons know me; the
moment I come out with a bag of feed, they begin to fly toward
me from blocks away." Singer currently lives on 86th Street
between Broadway and Amsterdam Avenue.

·

Merging with the West Side group but having its own distinct identity is the literary circle associated with Columbia University. Young critics, poets and fiction writers who studied there or are on the faculty tend to live in the buildings above 110th Street. And a number of Columbia alumni who left the area have become writers. Harlem Renaissance writer Zora Neale Hurston did graduate study with Columbia anthropologist Franz Boas after graduating from Barnard, and Langston Hughes attended Columbia College, living in Hartley Hall, in 1921. When he came to New York in 1929, Federico García Lorca stayed in John Jay Hall with a friend who was a Columbia professor. Herbert Gold went to Columbia, living for a time in Hartley Hall. Bernard Malamud got an M.A. at Columbia, and J. D. Salinger took Whit Burnett's course in the short story. Historically, a number of Columbia professors have had a literary influence, most notably the Van Doren brothers, Carl and Mark. Although they both lived in the Village, their influence was strongly felt on campus. Carl taught at Columbia from 1911 to 1930, during which time he was also, in succession, literary editor of the *Nation* and of the *Century Magazine*. He played an important part in the rediscovery of Herman Melville, assembling the first bibliography of Melville's work and encouraging Raymond Weaver to write the first Melville biography. Alfred Kazin said that "Carl Van Doren got me to write *On Native Grounds.*" Mark Van Doren taught at Columbia from 1920 until 1959 and succeeded his brother as literary editor of the *Nation*. Among his students were John Berryman, Thomas Merton, Herbert Gold, Allen Ginsberg and Jack Kerouac. Van Doren was particularly influential with the poets; he himself won the Pulitzer Prize for poetry in 1940. On Mark Van Doren's death, Allen Ginsberg remembered that the professor "taught Kerouac Shakespeare and gave him an 'A.' Kerouac quit the Columbia football team to spend more

Allen Ginsberg on the roof of his apartment building
at 114th Street, around 1947.

time studying Shakespeare with Van Doren. Most of the other professors were interested in careers in literature and he was interested in illuminated wisdom."

The Beat movement was born in the forties out of the interaction between Ginsberg and Kerouac and William Burroughs, who met in the area around Columbia. Two young women named Edie Parker and Joan Adams were living in an apartment on 118th Street between Amsterdam Avenue and Morningside Drive. In 1943 Kerouac went to live there with Edie, to whom he was later married for a short time. Burroughs moved in with Joan, whom he married in 1944, and Ginsberg stayed with them all for a while in 1945. "This," said Ginsberg, "was the seminal situation" in terms of the Beat sensibility. "Something happened in Joan Adams's apartment to all of us. Listening to her and Burroughs talk, make fun of the public consciousness. We'd sit around talking very ironically, cynically, about public persons. I guess everyone else was hypnotized by the officialese mentality." In 1945 Ginsberg was suspended from Columbia for letting Kerouac stay in his room in Hartley Hall and for writing an obscenity in the dust on his windowpane. "The dean called me in and said, 'Mr. Ginsberg, I hope you realize the enormity of what you've done.' I took that phrase back to Burroughs and Joan. It represented the official world in which the entire bedrock of economics and foreign policy and law was based. They burst into screams of laughter. I realized the dean of Columbia was crazy, literally crazy; a madman was running the entire college." Here, too, Burroughs did his first writing when Kerouac persuaded him to undertake alternate chapters of a detective novel in the style of Dashiell Hammett. The three spent a great deal of time in a Columbia hangout, the West End Café on Broadway, making it the only West Side saloon with literary connections.

Mark Van Doren in his office at Columbia about 1945.

Since the Van Dorens, the major literary influence at Columbia has been Lionel Trilling. Trilling, who himself had been a student and was later a colleague of Mark Van Doren, held a special significance for the young Jewish intellectuals as the first Jew to be given a permanent appointment in the Columbia English department. He was regarded as the pre-eminent "New York intellectual." In Trilling the two main West Side literary traditions — Columbia and the New York intellectuals — met. And if Greenwich Village in the late twenties had a special literary valuation because Edmund Wilson lived there — "He seemed in his own person . . . to propose and to realize the idea of the literary life," Trilling wrote — Trilling, in turn, conferred that significance on the West Side.

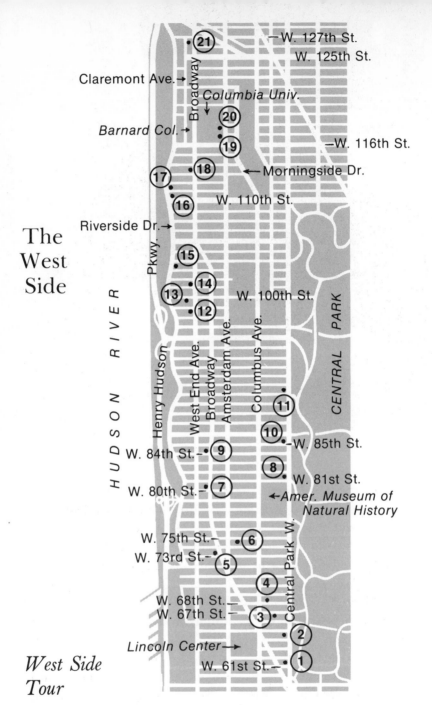

The West Side

The West Side

West Side Tour

The Century Apartments at 25 Central Park West between 61st and 62nd Streets (1) is one of New York's most attractive art deco buildings. Marc Connelly has lived here since 1929. Another member of the Algonquin group, Edna Ferber, lived two blocks north at 50 Central Park West (2). Numbers 1, 15, 25 and 33 West 67th Street (3) were constructed by the same developer, Walter Russell, as housing for artists. All the buildings contain duplex apartments with two-story living rooms that have large expanses of window. The buildings have been popular with writers as well as painters and photographers. The Hotel Des Artistes at 1 West 67th Street has been the residence of Fannie Hurst, Alexander Woollcott and Noel Coward.

Dorothy Parker lived as a child at 57 West 68th Street (4), one in a row of five-story stone houses with bay windows. The Ansonia, at 73rd Street and Broadway (5), a once luxurious apartment hotel, is a West Side landmark. Theodore Dreiser once lived here. Anaïs Nin lived in a brick and stone house at 158 West 75th Street (6) similar to the one in which Dorothy Parker spent her childhood several blocks away. Zabar's, a gourmet delicatessen between 80th and 81st streets (7), is the closest thing to a gathering place that West Side intellectuals have today.

Sara Teasdale and her husband lived at the Beresford at 211 Central Park West (8) in 1917. A plaque on the north side of 84th Street just west of Broadway (9) marks the site of the farm where Edgar Allan Poe spent the summer of 1844. Ellen Glasgow lived at 1 West 85th Street (10) from 1911 to 1916. The red brick and limestone building is called the Orwell House. Sinclair Lewis had a duplex in the Eldorado Towers at 300 Central Park West (11) in the early 1940s. Herman Wouk used the same building as the fictional home of his heroine Marjorie Morningstar.

The Living Theatre first began its productions in a large apartment at 789 West End Avenue (12) on the southwest corner of 99th Street, where Julian Beck had an apartment. The building is one of many large, undistinguished brick apartment houses on the West Side. In 1916 Louis Untermeyer lived at 310 West 100th Street (13), an earlier, more interesting structure with ironwork balconies and decorative grills in front of long casement windows. During his college years Herman Wouk lived in the massive fifteen-story red brick building at 845 West End Avenue (14).

Saul Bellow, who has written frequently about the West Side, lived during the fifties at 333 Riverside Drive (15), a lovely white brick, limestone-trimmed house within the Riverside–West 105th Street Historic District. The houses within the district, which covers Riverside Drive from 105th to 106th and most of 105th Street from Riverside Drive to West End Avenue, were all built from 1899 to 1902 in the French beaux arts style. J. D. Salinger placed his fictional Glass family in an apartment building at 110th Street and Riverside Drive that had a canopy studded with light bulbs. The structure at 380 Riverside Drive (16) fits this description. Salinger himself spent part of his childhood one block north at 390 Riverside Drive (17).

The West End Café, commonly called the West End bar, at 2911 Broadway (18) between 113th and 114th streets was a hangout for the Beat writers during the forties. Several writers lived on the Columbia campus itself. Federico García Lorca stayed in John Jay Hall (19) with his friend and teacher Ferdinando de los Rios when he came to New York in 1929. Langston Hughes, Herbert Gold and Allen Ginsberg all lived in Hartley Hall (20) at various times. Hughes didn't like Columbia because he felt it was too big and "the buildings looked like factories." Ginsberg was suspended for letting Jack Kerouac stay in his room and for writing obscenities in the dirt on his window. F. Scott Fitzgerald lived briefly at 200 Claremont Avenue (21), "a high, horrible apartment-house in the middle of nowhere," while trying to become a writer.

IX. Harlem

FOR MOST OUTSIDERS, Harlem is simply the quintessential ghetto — a precinct riddled with poverty, drugs, crime and violence. Some may temper this image with memories of the speakeasy and cabaret life of the twenties or nostalgia for the jazz era, when Dizzy Gillespie, Charlie Parker and Charlie Christian hammered out their art in Harlem clubs. But for black people, particularly black writers, Harlem is immeasurably more.

In the twenties, while downtown New York used Harlem as its playground, black intellectuals and writers assigned it a far more serious function. To them it was mecca, the big, beautiful capital of the black world. They came from all over the country to write, think and socialize together in the vital community that was developing·in Harlem. Few among them are well-remembered — Countee Cullen and Langston Hughes perhaps are the only widely familiar names — but when the twenties were over and the depression came, they left behind them the beginnings of black American literature.

In the forties, black writers began to document the effects of the depression on the people of Harlem. The neighborhood was never to recover from its heavy toll or to regain the innocence and optimism of the twenties. By the fifties, however, two towering literary figures, Ralph Ellison and James Baldwin, were to come to grips with Harlem, transmuting it in their writing. Today, again in a period of heightened consciousness, black writers are rediscovering their literary past and attempting to build cultural institutions in Harlem that will survive where those of the twenties did not. Although they may not choose to live physically in Harlem, it is in some way their mental residence — a focal point for their artistic consciousness.

Harlem was first settled in 1637 when two brothers named Isaac and Hendrick de Forest bought strips of land in the area, then a wilderness inhabited by wolves, rattlesnakes and hostile Indians. Soon a community developed and by 1658 it was sufficiently large to be established as the village of Nieuw Haarlem. By the early nineteenth century, the farms had been replaced by elaborate estates owned by the most prominent New York families — the De Lanceys, Beekmans, Bleeckers, Rikers and Coldens. One reminder of this era, Hamilton Grange at 141st Street and Convent Avenue, still survives. A gracious country house designed by John McComb, one of the foremost architects of the time, it was built by Alexander Hamilton in 1802. Here, in a finely furnished library and greenhouses filled with tropical and subtropical plants, he spent the last few years of his life.

In the 1840s and '50s Harlem had declined as a farming area; the soil was worn out and many of the estates were sold off. But the press of population northward from downtown was soon to transform the area. With each subsequent improvement in transportation — in 1881 the elevated reached 129th Street, in 1884 it was extended to 145th Street, and in 1901 the IRT Lenox Avenue subway line was constructed — the population grew. One of the builders who participated in the construction boom at the turn of the century was Nathanael West's father, Max Weinstein, known for his large luxury apartment houses adorned with ornamental work in limestone. In 1908 West lived with his family in one of them, the De Peyster, which stands on Seventh Avenue between 119th and 120th streets. During this period more and more Jews began moving to the area between 110th and 125th streets. Among them were Arthur Miller's parents, and in 1915 Miller was born on 111th Street. While he was still an infant his family moved to apartment 6B in the yellow brick building facing the Park at 45 West 110th Street.

The boom of the early 1900s caused overbuilding; many apartment houses were empty, the landlords desperate for tenants, and as a result the rather extraordinary events occurred that made the Harlem Renaissance possible. An enterprising Negro realtor named Philip A. Payton approached several landlords with the proposal that he fill their apartments with black tenants. The landlords accepted and in 1903 several houses on 134th Street were rented. Payton and a partner, J. C. Thomas, later bought two five-story apartment buildings, dispossessed the whites and put in Negro tenants. Other realtors did the same. And after selling its property in the Pennsylvania Station area, St. Philip's Episcopal Church, a Negro congregation, turned around and invested the proceeds in thirteen apartment houses on 135th Street between Lenox and Seventh avenues. By dint of initiative and cooperative effort, Negroes, who had previously lived in the Tenderloin and San Juan Hill areas, were able to do the unprecedented: secure for themselves new housing in one of New York's prime residential areas.

Obviously, Harlem then was not a ghetto in the usual sense of the term. James Weldon Johnson described it as "one of the most beautiful and healthful sites in the whole city." Writing in 1930 he said, "It is not a slum, nor is it a 'quarter' consisting of dilapidated tenements. It is a section of new-law apartment houses and handsome dwellings, with streets as well paved, as well lighted, and as well kept as in any other part of the city."

The desirable community soon attracted the black elite.

W. E. B. Du Bois in the office of the *Crisis* magazine.

W. E. B. Du Bois came to New York from Atlanta in 1910 to edit
the *Crisis,* a publication of the NAACP. James Weldon Johnson
moved to Harlem in 1914 after seven years as a diplomat. And

in 1917 Marcus Garvey, later to lead the Back-to-Africa movement, founded the Universal Negro Improvement Association.
Harlem represented a spirit of protest, militancy and self-as-
sertion — a new kind of identity for the Negro. The new consciousness drew the talented young men and women who were
to create the movement known as the Negro Renaissance. In
literary terms the Renaissance was in fact only an awakening —
the first emergence of black writers in force. Little more than
half a century after the end of slavery, America had produced
only a few Negro writers, among them Paul Laurence Dunbar,
Charles W. Chestnutt, James Weldon Johnson and W. E. B.
Du Bois. But in a larger sense, the term "Renaissance" characterized a rebirth of the race, as in the phrase "the New Negro."
And as a social phenomenon it involved not only writers, but
musicians, actors, dancers and a hitherto unprecedented exchange with white people that was expressed both on a personal
level and in a wholesale influx of sight-seers, curiosity-seekers

"The New Negro Has No Fear" reads the sign carried in a Harlem parade
in the twenties.

and speakeasy habitués to Harlem. Langston Hughes captured
the uniqueness and extravagance of the Renaissance when he
wrote:

> It was a period when, at almost every Harlem upper-crust dance
> or party, one would be introduced to various distinguished
> white celebrities as guests. It was a period when almost any
> Harlem Negro of any social importance at all would be likely
> to say casually: "As I was remarking the other day to Hey-
> wood —," meaning Heywood Broun. Or: "As I said to
> George —," referring to George Gershwin. It was a period when
> local and visiting royalty were not at all uncommon in Harlem.
> And when the parties of A'Lelia Walker, the Negro heiress, were
> filled with guests whose names would turn any Nordic social
> climber green with envy . . . It was a period when every
> season there was at least one hit play on Broadway acted by a
> Negro cast. And when books by Negro authors were being
> published with much greater frequency and much more pub-
> licity than ever before or since in history.

The beginnings of the literary strands of the Renaissance,
as most beginnings, are vague and subject to dispute. Most
seem to recognize West Indian poet and novelist Claude McKay
as forerunner of the movement, whether they mark its start
with his poem "Harlem Dancer," which appeared in *Seven
Arts* under the pen name Eli Edwards in 1917, or his sonnet
"If We Must Die," two years later. In any case, the movement
was well under way when the anthology *The New Negro,* edited
by Rhodes Scholar and Howard University professor Alain
Locke, was published in 1925.

The movement had an old guard and a new: elder statesmen
and gurus as well as fresh, young talent. "Jessie Fauset at the
Crisis, Charles Johnson at *Opportunity,* and Alain Locke in
Washington, were the three people who midwifed the so-called
New Negro literature into being," wrote Langston Hughes in a
capsule description. "Kind and critical — but not too critical

for the young — they nursed us along until our books were born. Countee Cullen, Zora Neale Hurston, Arna Bontemps, Rudolph Fisher, Wallace Thurman, Jean Toomer, Nella Larsen, all of us came along about the same time."

The Renaissance writers did not constitute a school in the sense of possessing a common style, political attitude or subject matter, though many critics generalized about "primitivism and exoticism." If anything, it was marked by extraordinary diversity. What could be more disparate than Cullen's Keatsian sonnets, Jean Toomer's experimental prose, Langston Hughes's jazz rhythms and Zora Neale Hurston's rediscovered folk tales? What the writers of the Renaissance had in common was that they were the first to focus on the question of Negro identity. Venturing into areas of Negro life previously ignored or denied, they were attempting the self-description that is the first step toward the independence and autonomy of mind necessary to create art.

Alain Locke, who taught philosophy at Howard, is often credited with being the "father" of the Negro Renaissance. Zora Neale Hurston, who was a member of the Stylus, the literary club he advised, suggested that more of the credit should have been shared with Charles Johnson, editor of *Opportunity*, the magazine of the Urban League, and later first Negro president of Fisk University. Johnson, who arrived in Harlem in 1921 and founded *Opportunity* in 1923, saw a story she had written for the Stylus and asked her to send something to him. She sent "Drenched in Light" and he published it. "He wrote me a kind letter and said something about New York. So, beginning to feel the urge to write, I wanted to be in New York. This move on the part of Dr. Johnson was the root of the so-called Negro Renaissance. It was his work, and only his hush-mouth nature has caused it to be attributed to many others." Langston Hughes concurred: "Mr. Johnson, I believe, did more to encourage and develop Negro writers during the 20s than anyone else in America. He wrote them sympathetic letters, pointing out the merits of their work. He brought them together to meet and know each other. He made the *Opportunity* contests sources of discovery and help."

Jessie Fauset was helpful and hospitable to the young writers although she often disapproved of their subject matter and attitudes. She, with W. E. B. Du Bois, was dedicated to proving that there were no differences between black and white. They took the position that it was preferable to portray the lives of those well-traveled Negroes who discussed Shakespeare over tea than to dwell upon the problems of the poor, the mulatto or the very dark-skinned black. Fauset's home at 1947 Seventh Avenue, an attractive building with Ionic columns just north of the elegant Graham Court Apartments at 116th, was a center for what Langston Hughes called "cultural soirées." At her parties, he wrote, "there was always quite a different atmosphere from that at most other Harlem good-time gatherings. At Miss Fauset's, a good time was shared by talking literature and reading poetry aloud and perhaps enjoying some conversation in French . . . At her house one would usually meet editors and students, writers and social workers, and serious people who liked books and the British Museum, and had perhaps been to Florence. (Italy, not Alabama.)" Jessie Fauset and her husband, Herbert Harris, later moved to a cooperative in the Paul Laurence Dunbar Apartments.

Among the principal elder statesmen of the Renaissance was James Weldon Johnson, who lived in 1927 at 180 East 135th Street. Johnson, at various times in his life, was principal of a public school, member of the Florida bar, U.S. Consul to Venezuela and Nicaragua, professor at New York University and successful musical comedy writer. His 1912 novel, *Autobiography of an Ex-Coloured Man*, with its descriptions of

Negro life in New York, is considered by many to anticipate the Harlem Rennaissance school by more than a decade. It was in 1927, however, with *God's Own Trombones,* that he had his greatest literary success.

During the Renaissance years Johnson served as executive secretary of the NAACP and was in an ideal position to act as liaison between the Negro community and influential whites. His parties, at which he often introduced young writers to the publishing establishment, tended to be sedate. Blanche Ferguson wrote in *Countee Cullen and the Negro Renaissance* that "Mr. Johnson's appearance and background did not inspire levity. He was tall, lean and immaculate . . . But as a host he was modest and self-effacing, always focusing attention on others. And in the well-appointed home that exuded culture and comfort the Johnson's guests could generally count on meeting interesting personalities such as Van Vechten or Clarence Darrow." Johnson himself recalled a farewell party he gave for Claude McKay in a letter to him in 1930: "We often speak of that party back in '22 . . . Do you know that was the first getting together of the black and white literati on a purely social plane. Such parties are now common in New York, but I doubt if any has been more representative. You will remember there were present Heywood Broun, Ruth Hale, F. P. Adams, John Farrar, Carl Van Doren, Freda Kirchwey, Peggy Tucker, Roy Nash — on our side you, Du Bois, Walter White, Jessie Fauset, [Arthur] Schomburg, J. Rosamond Johnson — I think that party started something."

The phenomenon of the Negro Renaissance was very much a collaboration with the white world, and master collaborator of them all was Carl Van Vechten, author, photographer and master of ceremonies of the twenties. As a white writer, Van Vechten was able to introduce black writers to publishers and producers; also, he demonstrated with his novel *Nigger Heaven* that people might buy a book that went beyond stereotypes and described black people as they were. The success of *Nigger Heaven* in 1926 helped the other novelists of the Renaissance to find publishers.

Van Vechten's choice of a title was unfortunate, however, and earned him the undeserved scorn of some members of the black community. There were many who never understood that it was meant to be ironic: "Nigger Heaven!" moans the novel's protagonist, a tormented aspiring writer. "That's what Harlem is. We sit in our places in the gallery of this New York theater and watch the white world sitting down below in the good seats in the orchestra. Occasionally, they turn their faces up towards us, their hard, cruel faces, to laugh or sneer, but they never beckon . . . Harlem! The Mecca of the New Negro! My God!" Van Vechten, better than many of the black writers, understood that Harlem might be Mecca for the black elite but that there were many, like his protagonist, so mutilated by past oppression that they couldn't seize the opportunities opened up by the Renaissance.

Older than most of the writers associated with the Renaissance (Hurston, Bontemps, Hughes, Thurman and Cullen were all born in 1902 or 1903), Claude McKay was a precursor of the movement and a strong influence on those who came after him. Born in Jamaica in 1890, he came to the United States in 1912 and spent two years at Tuskegee Institute in Alabama and the University of Kansas before settling in Harlem in 1914 to become a writer. Until 1921, when he became associate editor of the *Liberator* under Max Eastman, he worked as porter, houseman, longshoreman, barman and dining car porter.

McKay's first novel, *Home to Harlem*, published in 1928 while he was abroad, was the first fictional work by a Negro to make the best-seller list. In rhapsodic prose, punctuated profusely with exclamation points, *Home to Harlem* romanticized the simple, instinctive life of an AWOL soldier turned dining car waiter named Jake. McKay's great facility with language— the novel is written primarily in a lyrical Harlem dialect — makes this one of the most beautiful of the Renaissance novels. Some years later McKay was to write, "Like a flock of luxuriant, large-lipped orchids spreading over the side of a towering rock, the color of African life has boldly splashed itself upon the north end of Manhattan." This was the way he saw Harlem and his first novel described its every exoticism — from the cabarets and speakeasies to "the Block Beautiful," an all-white enclave in the midst of black Manhattan on 130th Street between Lenox and Fifth avenues.

McKay was abroad from 1922 to 1934 and therefore absent during the honeyed days when black writers were pampered and courted. When he returned, he lived in an apartment, decorated with tapestries he had brought back from Africa, in a tenement building that stands at 147 West 142nd Street. Gradually, however, he became more and more isolated and impoverished.

Nella Larsen, too, belonged to a slightly older generation. Born in Chicago in 1893 of a West Indian father and Danish mother, she came to New York after attending Fisk University and the University of Copenhagen. She was at various times a nurse and a librarian and lived at 236 West 135th Street during her marriage to Dr. Elmer S. Imes. Her first novel, *Quicksand,* is generally conceded to be one of the best literary achievements of the Renaissance. Psychologically it is the most real, perhaps because unlike the other writers Larsen was describing a situation she knew intimately — the dilemma of the mulatto alienated from both the dominant culture and the black world because of her mixed blood. In 1930 she became the first black woman to win a Guggenheim Fellowship.

Of all the Renaissance writers, Countee Cullen was the only native New Yorker. Born Countee Porter in 1903, he was adopted by the Reverend Frederick Cullen when he was eleven years old and went to live with Cullen and his wife first at 234 West 131st Street and later in the parsonage that adjoined the Salem Methodist Episcopal Church at 2190 Seventh Avenue. Countee showed achievement from an early age. He won the Federation of Women's Clubs Prize for his poetry at DeWitt Clinton High School, the poetry prize established by poet, dramatist, translator and silk-manufacturing heir Witter Bynner at New York University, and received a master's degree from Harvard. His first volume of poetry, *Color,* appeared in 1925, and the following year he became assistant editor of *Opportunity* and started writing a column that he called "The Dark Tower." The most important social event of the twenties was undoubtedly Cullen's marriage in 1927 to W. E. B. Du Bois's daughter, Yolande. The ceremony took place before thirteen hundred people in Cullen's father's church. Du Bois directed the rehearsal himself, organizing the sixteen bridesmaids and the ushers, who included the poets Langston Hughes and Arna Bontemps. At the ceremony, canaries in gilded cages provided musical accompaniment. Shortly after the wedding Cullen went off to Paris on a Guggenheim Fellowship, leaving his bride behind. The marriage, less spectacular than the wedding, was dissolved in 1929.

Cullen returned to New York in the fall of 1930. His only novel, *One Way to Heaven,* published in 1932, presents a panorama of Harlem life, including a rather cynical view of the church. He juxtaposes the life of a Harlem maid with that of her Negro socialite mistress, whose chaotic parties bring together black intellectuals and celebrities and white curiosity-seekers.

Langston Hughes arrived in Harlem in 1921 and stayed at

From left, Langston Hughes, Charles S. Johnson, E. Franklin Frazier, Rudolph Fisher, Hubert Delaney on the roof of 580 St. Nicholas Avenue.

the 135th Street Y while making preparations to enter Columbia University. He had just graduated from high school in Cleveland, where he had lived with his mother. His father — lawyer, rancher, money-lender and manager of an electric company in Toluca, Mexico — provided the money for him to go to college. Hughes's grandmother was the widow of one of the five Negroes who attacked Harper's Ferry with John Brown, and the poet was also related to John Mercer Langston, a Reconstruction Congressman from Virginia and one-time dean of law at Howard University. After a year at Columbia, Hughes transferred to Lincoln University in Philadelphia, making frequent trips to New York to keep in touch with other young Harlem writers. He also corresponded with Claude McKay, then in Europe, who influenced him considerably.

While Hughes was a student at Columbia, Arna Bontemps came to New York from Los Angeles, where he had studied at Pacific Union College. Bontemps's first poetry appeared in the *Crisis* in 1924. From 1924 to 1931 he taught at the Harlem Academy, living during these years at various addresses; 305 Edgecombe Avenue and 75 St. Nicholas Avenue were two. Most of his work was published in the thirties, beginning with a novel, *God Sends Sunday,* in 1931. He and Cullen collaborated on a dramatization of it; it was renamed *St. Louis Woman* and was produced in 1946 with music and lyrics by Harold Arlen and Johnny Mercer. The production, introducing Pearl Bailey, ran 113 performances on Broadway.

Rudolph Fisher was one of the Renaissance's most versatile and intelligent figures. A brilliant student at Brown University, where he received his B.A. and M.A., he was Paul Robeson's accompanist and arranger on concert tours at the same time as he was earning his M.D. at Howard. He came to New York in 1924 to study bacteriology and pathology at Columbia's College of Physicians and Surgeons and went into the practice of radiology in 1927. From 1929 to 1932 he was superintendent of a hospital while living at 2816 Eighth Avenue at the Dunbar Apartments. He had begun writing when he was in medical school and published the first mystery to use all Negro characters, *The Conjure Man Dies,* in 1932. His later novel, *The Walls of Jericho,* describes the integration of white sections of Harlem.

In 1925 Zora Neale Hurston arrived in New York to attend Barnard. A desperately poor young woman from Eatonville, Florida, daughter of a tenant farmer, she made her way in the world on charm and determination as well as talent. At the age of fourteen, she left home employed as a maid with a traveling Gilbert and Sullivan company. Eighteen months later she quit the company in Baltimore, got a job as a waitress and started night school. She was soon convinced that literature was to be her world. Although she had no money, she immediately enrolled in the high school department of Morgan College. During the two years she spent there, she worked in the home of one of the trustees for room and board and two dollars a week. She then went to Howard but dropped out after a year and a half for lack of money. It was at this time that the letter from Charles Johnson inspired her to go to New York and try her luck there. She arrived the first week of January 1925 with "$1.50, no job, no friends, and a lot of hope." After she won a prize for a short story at an *Opportunity* dinner in May, Fannie Hurst offered her a job as secretary and one of Barnard's founders got her a scholarship there. She entered in the fall and graduated in 1928.

During her years at Barnard, she was very much present on the Harlem scene although she lived downtown at Fannie Hurst's 67th Street duplex (see Chapter VIII, The West Side). Langston Hughes remembered that "she went about Harlem with an anthropologist's ruler, measuring heads for Franz Boas." After graduation she was in New York intermittently, between trips to the South and the Caribbean to collect Negro folklore. In 1932 she was living at Graham Court, a white granite building at 116th Street and Seventh Avenue, then the most luxurious apartment house in Harlem.

Wallace Thurman also arrived in 1925 and set up housekeeping at what was probably the main gathering place of the younger writers of the Renaissance, a brick and brownstone building still standing at 267 West 137th Street. Langston Hughes had a room here one summer, and Zora Neale Hurston, Gwendolyn Bennett and the painter Aaron Douglas were frequent visitors.

Thurman, who had a biting sense of humor, called the Harlem literati the "niggerati" and immortalized his rooming house as Niggerati Manor in *Infants of the Spring,* a satirical roman à clef on the Renaissance. He took a pessimistic view of the future of Negro literature and alone seems to have understood the dimensions of the psychological obstacles Negroes faced. ". . . 99 and 99/100 per cent of the Negro race is patently possessed and motivated by an inferiority complex," says Raymond, the autobiographical protagonist of *Infants of the Spring.* "Being a slave race actuated by slave morality, what else could you expect?"

Thurman was managing editor of the *Messenger,* a radical weekly founded by A. Philip Randolph and Chandler Owen, and later worked as a reader at Macaulay's ("the only Negro reader, so far as I know, to be employed by any of the larger publishing firms," Langston Hughes wrote) and coauthored *Harlem,* the first successful play written by a Negro to appear on Broadway. And in 1926 Thurman edited the one and only issue of *Fire,* intended to be a Negro literary quarterly. Zora Neale Hurston, Aaron Douglas, Gwendolyn Bennett and Langston Hughes were on the staff. "The idea," said Hughes, was "that it would burn up a lot of the old, dead conventional Negro-white ideas of the past, *épater le bourgeois* into a realization of the existence of the younger Negro writers and artists, and provide us with an outlet for publication not available in the limited pages of the small Negro magazines then existing . . ." Although everyone else contributed fifty dollars, Thurman, the only steadily employed participant, bore most of the expenses. In the end, the first number cost almost a thousand dollars, and since nobody could afford to pay the bills there was no second issue.

The year 1926 stands out as the high point of the Negro Renaissance. It was the year of *Fire* and of Hughes's *The Weary Blues* and Van Vechten's *Nigger Heaven.* All the young writers were in New York, working on the books that would be published in the late twenties and early thirties. Even Jean Toomer, acknowledged by his contemporaries as well as most critics as the finest writer of the Renaissance, was in Harlem that year.

Toomer's *Cane,* the first novel of the Negro Renaissance, had been published in 1923. It sold only 500 copies, but was clearly a succès d'estime and had an importance to black writers far out of proportion to its sales figures. While most writers of the Renaissance, with the possible exception of Hughes, were stylistically way behind their times, Toomer was treated as an equal in the avant-garde magazines. *Cane,* portions of which originally appeared in *Broom,* the *Little Review* and the *Liberator,* was a formally experimental composite of portraits and stories, interspersed with poems, dealing with life in the South.

Although seldom present in Harlem, Toomer exercised a strong influence on the imaginations and aspirations of the younger Renaissance writers. "I know of only one Negro who has the elements of greatness, and that's Jean Toomer," says Wallace Thurman's Raymond in *Infants of the Spring.* "The rest of us are merely journeymen, planting seed for someone else to harvest." Unfortunately, Toomer's work appeared infrequently after the late twenties, and that fact has given rise to the notion that he stopped writing. In fact, unpublished novels and plays are among his papers at Fisk.

Soon after the publication of *Cane,* Toomer developed an interest in the mysticism of Gurdjieff, which culminated in a visit to the Gurdjieff Institute in Fontainebleau, France, during the summer of 1926. He returned to Harlem to spread his beliefs. Among those who became adherents were Wallace Thurman, Dorothy Peterson, Aaron Douglas and Nella Larsen. However, as Langston Hughes has observed, everyone in Harlem had to make a living and could not afford the amount of time required in study and meditation. Toomer's efforts were not very successful and he "shortly left his Harlem group and went downtown to drop the seeds of Gurdjieff in less dark and poverty-stricken fields."

In later years Toomer was to become a rather enigmatic figure. In 1922, in response to a request from the *Liberator* for some biographical information, he had written: "My family is from the South. My mother's father, P. B. S. Pinchback, born in Macon, Georgia, left home as a boy and worked on the Mississippi River steamers . . . Later, in the days of Reconstruction, he utilized the Negro's vote and won offices for himself, the highest being that of lieutenant, and then acting governor of Louisiana . . . Racially, I seem to have (who knows for sure) seven blood mixtures: French, Dutch, Welsh, Negro, German, Jewish, and Indian. Because of these, my position in America has been a curious one. I have lived equally amid the two race groups. Now white, now colored . . . I have strived for a Spiritual fusion analagous [sic] to the fact of racial intermingling . . . Within the last two or three years, however, my growing need for artistic expression has pulled me deeper and deeper into the Negro group. And as my powers of receptivity increased, I found myself loving it in a way that I could never love the other."

Later, Toomer married two women from socially distinguished white families. The first, whom he married in 1932, was Marjory Latimer, a descendant of Anne Bradstreet's. She died giving birth to their child the following year. The second was Marjorie Content, daughter of a member of the New York Stock Exchange and former wife of Harold Loeb, founder of *Broom*. (Her home at 3 East 9th Street was *Broom* headquarters; see Chapter II, Greenwich Village.) When asked at the time of his second marriage whether he was Negro or white, Toomer replied, ". . . I have not lived as [a Negro], nor do I really know whether there is any colored blood in me or not. My maternal grandfather, Pickney Benton Stewart Pinchback, was the 'carpet-bag' governor of Louisiana. In order to gain colored votes, he referred to himself as having colored blood. His two brothers never did so however; so the fact is, I do not know whether colored blood flows through my veins."

•

Negro Harlem in the twenties extended approximately from 130th to 145th streets, bounded on the east by Madison Avenue and on the west by Seventh, with its hub at 135th Street between Fifth and Seventh avenues. Seventh Avenue, "Harlem's Broadway during the week and its Fifth Avenue on Sunday," as Rudolph Fisher described it in *The Walls of Jericho,*

> remains for six days a walk for deliberate shoppers, a lane for tumultuous traffic, the avenue of a thousand enterprises and the scene of a thousand hairbreadth escapes; remains for six nights a carnival, bright with the lights of theaters and night clubs, alive with darting cabs, with couples moving from house party to cabaret, with loiterers idling and ogling on the curb, with music wafted from mysterious sources, with gay talk and loud Afric [sic] laughter. Then comes Sunday, and for a few hours Seventh Avenue becomes the highway to heaven; reflects that air of quiet, satisfied self-righteousness peculiar to chronic churchgoers. Indeed, even Fifth Avenue on Easter never quite attains to this; practice makes perfect, and Harlem's Seventh Avenue boasts fifty-two Easters a year."

Harlem, with its broad avenues, was as given to the promenade as any European city, and much of the action of the twenties' novels revolves around strolls and chance encounters on Seventh Avenue. Helga, the protagonist of Nella Larsen's *Quicksand,* remarks, "They say . . . that if one stands on the corner of 135th Street and 7th Avenue long enough, one will eventually see all the people one has ever known or met."

The fashionable district of the time is described in Wallace Thurman's *The Blacker the Berry* as the area between Seventh and Edgecombe avenues on 136th through 139th streets and the apartment buildings on Edgecombe, Bradhurst and St. Nicholas avenues. Most of the homes inhabited and visited by the Renaissance writers fall within these elegant precincts. The most popular social center of the twenties was the $90,000 mansion at 108 West 136th Street, built in 1913 of Indiana limestone by Madame C. J. Walker, a St. Louis laundress who had made a fortune with the discovery of a hair-straightening process. Mme. Walker's daughter, A'Lelia Walker Robinson, was Harlem's foremost hostess. Hughes says that the "big-hearted, night-dark, hair-straightening heiress, made no pretense at being intellectual or exclusive. At her 'at homes' Negro poets and Negro number bankers mingled with downtown poets and seat-on-the-stock-exchange racketeers. Countee Cullen would be there and Witter Bynner, Muriel Draper and Nora Holt . . . And a good time was had by all." She also helped writers with money; Pulitzer Prize-winning journalist Ted Poston has called her "a one-woman foundation." In 1928 A'Lelia Walker attempted to establish one floor of her house as a café for writers and artists. "She saw a real need for a place, a sufficiently sympathetic place in which they could meet and discuss their plans and arts, to which they could bring their friends, and at which they could eat for a price within their very limited means," wrote Roi Ottley and William J. Weatherby in *The Negro in New York*. "But the plans never jelled, because A'Lelia was always too busy with parties to find time to give approval, or the artists could not be found because of similarly important distractions." Finally, the café, its walls covered with lettered verses by Cullen and Hughes, opened. Named the Dark Tower after Cullen's column in

Opportunity, it served for a short time as a place where "the Negro Intelligentsia met influential white people, particularly publishers, critics, and potential 'sponsors.'" Less than two years after its opening, A'Lelia closed it and moved her social activities to her apartment at 80 Edgecombe Avenue.

Behind the site of the Walker mansion (now occupied by the Countee Cullen branch of the New York Public Library), stands a Harlem literary landmark of a different sort. The attractive, white, neoclassic building was the 135th Street branch of the New York Public Library during the twenties, when it served as a meeting place for all the people of the Renaissance. Today it houses the material on black history collected by Arthur A. Schomburg, a Puerto Rican Negro who dealt in rare books, and continues to function as one of the community's most influential literary centers. In addition to lending books, the library was the scene of innumerable meetings, debates and plays. In 1938, Langston Hughes's *Don't You Want to be Free?* played 135 performances here after its run at the Harlem Suitcase Theater. In later years, James Baldwin and Ralph Ellison have visited often, and today most black writers use the library at one time or another for researches into the Negro past.

Several blocks away is Striver's Row, made up of what were, during the twenties, Harlem's most fashionable homes. Actually four blocks of attached houses, the "Row" is mentioned in virtually every work of the Renaissance. At a time when working-class families paid between ten dollars and eighteen dollars a month for rent, these homes, which rented for about eighty dollars, symbolized affluence. Negroes, especially doctors and entertainers, first began to live in the houses in 1919. In 1933, Abram Hill, founder of the American Negro Theater, wrote a play, *On Striver's Row,* whose main characters were the Van Strivens.

Aaron Douglas, a painter closely associated with the Renais-

Aaron Douglas, whose book jackets were a hallmark of the Harlem
Renaissance.

sance, and his wife, Alta, lived on Striver's Row at 227 West 139th Street in 1927 but later moved up the Harlem Heights to 409 Edgecombe Avenue, in the exclusive area called Sugar Hill. The Douglases, who are portrayed in Thurman's *The Blacker the Berry* and *Infants of the Spring*, were frequent hosts to their friends. "Everybody dropped in; this was really a meeting place for all the artists and intellectuals in Harlem," remembered Arna Bontemps. "We talked about all of the literary subjects, historical subjects, about everything related to the black experience . . . Every night was memorable. The apartment was decorated with Douglas's own paintings. It almost became a hallmark of the Harlem period in literature to have a book jacket by him."

Upstairs in the same building lived Walter White, assistant and later successor to James Weldon Johnson at the NAACP. He was often present at the Douglases' and also had his own share of parties. Among the guests at what was sometimes called "the White House of Negro America" were such celebrities as Sinclair Lewis, Willa Cather, Heywood Broun and George Gershwin.

In addition to gathering at the homes of friends, Renaissance writers visited and wrote about Harlem's theaters, casinos and cabarets. One of the most famous of these institutions was the Lafayette Theater, at Seventh Avenue and 131st Street, which was originally a complete entertainment center with ballrooms, restaurant and tavern. In the early years of the century the Lafayette housed a repertory company that repeated downtown successes. By the twenties the program had changed to Negro sketches and musical shows. As a scene of entertainment for the common man, the Lafayette made its appearance in *The Blacker the Berry, Nigger Heaven* and other Harlem novels.

The casinos where Harlem went to dance the exuberant steps of the Charleston, the Lindy Hop and the Black Bottom included the Harlem Casino, at Seventh Avenue and 124th Street (now the Refuge Temple), and the Renaissance, at Seventh Avenue and 138th Street (now the New Lafayette Theatre). Harlem cabarets, each with its own clientele and personality, existed in great profusion. Some were known for catering to whites and many were owned by whites. Other clubs refused to admit whites at all. On one occasion Claude McKay took Max Eastman to Ned's Place, a cabaret mentioned in *Home to Harlem*. Despite McKay's intimacy with the owner, Ned told them, "Ride back! Ride back, or I'll sick mah bouncers on you-all!"

In the twenties Ed Smalls' Sugar Cane Club, a dimly lit cellar on 135th Street and Fifth Avenue, was Harlem's principal "jump joint." The minuscule dance floor, surrounded by a few dozen tables, necessitated the phenomenon known as "dancing on a dime." Arna Bontemps recalls the emcee admonishing, "Get off that dime!" Later the club moved to its present location at 136th Street and Seventh Avenue, and, as Smalls' Paradise, continued to figure importantly in black social life. W. E. B. Du Bois celebrated his eighty-third birthday there in 1950; Malcolm X worked there as a waiter when he first came to New York at the age of sixteen; and James Baldwin was honored at Smalls', his favorite restaurant, in 1960 with a publication party for *Another Country*. Today, owned by basketball star Wilt Chamberlain, Smalls' still thrives.

Best known among whites in the twenties was the Cotton Club, "the Aristocrat of Harlem," on Lenox Avenue and 143rd Street. It was here that Duke Ellington and Cab Calloway held court with a "high yaller" chorus line so famous that white girls tried to "pass" to join it. Lena Horne, a member of the chorus for a time, recalls that "the most galling thing was that

the club was owned by whites . . . who based their business
on giving their white brethren a thrilling peek at the 'exotic'
world of the Negro, but refused to allow Negroes into their
club as paying customers. There were bouncers at the door
to keep out Negroes."

.

The depression brought an abrupt end to the concept of a
"New Negro" and the image of Harlem as an exotic utopia,
and exposed the poverty and struggle that had underlaid it all
along. The literary output continued through the early
thirties — Bontemps and Hurston began to publish only after
the twenties had ended — but for most, the good days were
over. Rudolph Fisher and Wallace Thurman died the same
week in December of 1934; Thurman, after long bouts of
alcoholism, of tuberculosis in a charity ward at Bellevue. Cullen spent his last years as a teacher of French and English at
Frederick Douglass Junior High School at 301 West 149th
Street, and died of ulcers in 1946. McKay grew progressively
more cynical and isolated until his death in 1948. The same
year, Zora Neale Hurston was indicted on a charge of being a
party in sexual relationships with two mentally ill boys and an
older man. The charge, brought by the mother of the boys,
was totally unsubstantiated; Hurston was out of the country
when the incident was supposed to have occurred. Yet the
scandal dealt her a deathly psychological blow. In a letter to
Carl Van Vechten she wrote: "I care for nothing anymore.
My country has failed me utterly. My race has seen fit to destroy
me without reason, and with the vilest tools conceived of by
man so far . . . All that I have tried to do has proved useless.
All that I have believed in has failed me. I have resolved to
die." In the fifties she stopped writing and went to work as a
maid in Florida. Her employers were unaware of her former

career until they came upon a story of hers in the *Saturday Evening Post*. She died penniless in 1960. Nella Larsen never completed the novel she had planned to write on her Guggenheim Fellowship. She disappeared from public life, went back to nursing as a supervisor at Bethel Hospital in Brooklyn and died in obscurity in 1963. Clearly, most of the writers lacked the psychic strength to survive the terrible pressure of their positions and aspirations. The high optimism and promise of Alain Locke's New Negro was not fulfilled, but the work of the Renaissance laid the foundations for what was to come afterward. Thurman was right after all: the Renaissance writers planted the seed that was to be harvested by Richard Wright, James Baldwin, Ralph Ellison and a profusion of black writers in the sixties.

Langston Hughes was one of the few Renaissance writers to survive the era. He alone made some vital connection with the real life of Harlem, which enabled him to continue when the fad for black writers had passed. And he alone, drawing the rhythms of his poetry from blues, created a literature stylistically based on black culture. Hughes earned his familiarity and friendship with the common man of Harlem through long hours spent in the ginmills and barrooms between 125th and 128th streets on Lenox Avenue. In later years his favorite hangout was the Palm Café on 125th between Seventh and Eighth. Here, during the early years of World War II, he met a man who worked in a war plant making cranks but hadn't any idea what the cranks were for. "You know white folks don't tell colored folks what cranks crank," he told Hughes. It was this man who provided the model for Jess B. Semple (Just Be Simple), Hughes's prototype of the common man of Harlem.

"More than Paris, or the Shakespeare country, or Berlin, or the Alps, I wanted to see Harlem," Hughes had written of the time before he came to New York. It was a feeling he was

Langston Hughes.

never to lose. "Had I been a rich young man," he wrote of his early years, "I would have bought a house in Harlem and built musical steps up to the front door, and installed chimes that at the press of a button played Ellington tunes." But Hughes was not rich and instead lived in a series of rooming houses between his frequent travels until he was able to afford a studio apartment on 141st Street in 1942. He took his meals with an adopted uncle and aunt, Mr. and Mrs. Emerson Harper, who lived a short stroll down the hill at 634 St. Nicholas Avenue.

When the opportunity came for the Harpers to move into larger quarters, they asked Hughes what he thought of a place on 153rd Street and Riverside Drive. "It's a nice place, Aunt Toy, and I'll help you buy it. But I won't live in it with you. It is not Harlem; it never was Harlem, and it never will be Harlem — and I'll never leave Harlem for anywhere else." Instead, the Harpers moved to a three-story brownstone at 20 East 127th Street. Hughes had a workroom at the top of the house. Two long walls were covered with books, and a T-shaped desk stood between the windows. During the forties and fifties Hughes's many friends — musicians and actors as well as writers — visited the house on 127th Street; there were Canada Lee, Burl Ives, Robert Earl Jones, Ann Petry and Margaret Walker. In 1938 Hughes established the Harlem Suitcase Theater, in a loft on 125th Street, to present plays by black writers with black actors, directors and scene designers. His most enduring work, however, was his poetry. In the twenties he wrote about the blues and jazz scene in *The Weary Blues;* in *Shakespeare in Harlem,* published in 1942, he treated the effects of the depression on the community; and in *Montage of a Dream Deferred* he caught the underlying unrest and frustration that eventually surfaced in the protest of the sixties. Lorraine Hansberry's play *A Raisin in the Sun* takes its title from some lines in one of the poems, "Harlem":

> What happens to a dream deferred?
>
> > Does it dry up
> > like a raisin in the sun?
> > Or fester like a sore —
> > And then run?

During the thirties black literary output dwindled. Zora Neale Hurston published *Jonah's Gourd Vine* in 1934 and *Their Eyes Were Watching God* in 1937. Arna Bontemps, a late bloomer, started the decade with *God Sends Sunday* and published his best novel, *Black Thunder,* in 1936. Many black writers found work with the WPA Federal Writers' Project. A group that included Henry Lee Moon, Ellen Tarry, Richard Wright, Claude McKay, Ralph Ellison, Roi Ottley and Ted Poston worked on a project that was to be published years later as *The Negro in New York: An Informal Social History.*

The publication of Richard Wright's *Uncle Tom's Children* in 1936 foreshadowed the social realism of black writing in the forties. Although he lived in Harlem only briefly, Richard Wright dominated the decade. Most prominent among what has been called the Wright School was Ann Petry, a graduate of the University of Connecticut College of Pharmacy, who came to Harlem in 1938. Petry lived at 2 East 129th Street and worked for local newspapers, the *Amsterdam News* and the *People's Voice.* She sold her first short story to the *Crisis* and two years later won the 1945 Houghton Mifflin Fellowship Award for her first novel, *The Street.* The Harlem portrayed in *The Street* — 116th between Seventh and Eighth avenues — is radically different from the Harlem described just fifteen years earlier by James Weldon Johnson. The houses are no longer new; in fact, the dirt has become so deeply ingrained as to be ineradicable. "Layers and layers of paint won't fix that apartment," thinks Lutie Johnson, the book's heroine. "It would always smell; finger marks and old stains would come through the paint; the very smell of the wood itself would eventually win out over the paint. Scrubbing wouldn't help any." Petry later wrote two more novels, *Country Place* (1947) and *The Narrows* (1953), and a novella, "In Dark Confusion" (1947), set against the background of the Harlem riots of 1943.

The Harlem of the late thirties and early forties is the setting of the two great fifties' novels, Ellison's *Invisible Man* and Baldwin's *Go Tell It on the Mountain.* Both bring to it a new

perspective: Ellison is concerned with Harlem not in a natural-
istic or realistic sense, but as symbol. Baldwin is the first writer
born and bred in Harlem.

Ellison first came to New York in the summer of 1936, after
his junior year at Tuskegee, intending to earn money to return
to school that fall and study music and sculpture. He stayed
at the 135th Street YMCA and on his second day in the city
met Langston Hughes and Alain Locke on the steps of the
library across the street. He introduced himself and asked about
meeting Richard Wright. Hughes lent him Malraux's *Man's
Fate* and *Days of Wrath,* which were to affect him profoundly.
A short time later Hughes arranged the meeting with Wright.
"[He] had just come to New York and was editing a little
magazine," Ellison remembered. "I had read a poem of his
which I liked, and when we were introduced . . . he suggested
that I try to review a novel for his magazine. My review was
accepted and published and so I was hooked." Ellison later
wrote a short story for Wright's magazine, *New Challenge,*
but it was not published.

Like the narrator of *Invisible Man,* Ellison never got the
job that he anticipated would pay his school expenses and
therefore never went back to Tuskegee. He had very little
money and his living arrangements were improvised. Sometimes he slept on benches in St. Nicholas Park and for several
weeks he slept on the sofa at the home of Hughes's "aunt and
uncle," the Harpers. Wright continued to play a catalytic role
in Ellison's development as a writer. He gave him *Native Son*
to read as it came out of the typewriter and continued to advise
him. Ellison remembered his saying, " 'You must learn how
Conrad, Joyce, Dostoievsky get their effects . . .' He guided
me to Henry James and to Conrad's prefaces, that type of thing."

Between 1939 and 1945, Ellison lived at a series of addresses
on the western borders of Harlem. From 1945 to 1953, the

period covering the writing of *Invisible Man,* he lived at 749 St. Nicholas Avenue. Currently, he lives on upper Riverside Drive, in an apartment furnished with a Mies van der Rohe chair, which Ellison calls his equivalent of a Cadillac, and a collection of Hopi and Zuñi kachina dolls.

Ellison's attitude toward Harlem is a complex one. He seems always to have been somewhat aloof: "I did *not* come to New York to live in Harlem," he once explained. Instead, he sought "a wider world of opportunity. And, most of all, the excitement and impersonality of a great city. I wanted room in which to discover who I was." Although Ellison's experience in the most general sense is reflected in *Invisible Man* — its narrator leaves a college in the South, comes to stay in the "Men's House" and ends up living not in Harlem but "in a border area" — the novel is not a realistic one and Ellison has specifically denied that it is autobiographical. In it as well as in his essays, Ellison portrays Harlem in a symbolic way. At the same time, he has participated in its institutions and gloried in its pleasures, visiting the 135th Street library, Lewis Michaux's bookstore, then located at the corner of 125th Street and Seventh Avenue and, most of all, Minton's — the famous forties' jazz club in the Hotel Cecil on 118th Street, which Dizzy Gillespie, Charlie Christian, Charlie Parker, Thelonius Monk and many other musicians used as a jazz workshop. Ellison was one, as he wrote in an *Esquire* article, "who shared, night after night, the mysterious spell created by the talk, the laughter, grease paint, powder, perfume, sweat, alcohol and food — all blended and simmering, like a stew on the restaurant range, and brought to a sustained moment of elusive meaning by the timbres and accents of musical instruments locked in passionate recitative."

On the one hand, Ellison sees Harlem as a place where nightmares mingle with reality. "Harlem is a ruin — many of

its ordinary aspects (its crimes, its casual violence, its crumbling buildings with littered areaways, ill-smelling halls and
vermin-invaded rooms) are indistinguishable from the distorted
images that appear in dreams, and which, like muggers haunt-
ing a lonely hall, quiver in the waking mind with hidden and
threatening significance." On the other hand, Harlem is a
symbol of liberation and light. "In my novel," he has said,
"the narrator's development is one through blackness to light;
that is, from ignorance to enlightenment: invisibility to visibil-
ity. He leaves the South and goes North; this, as you will
notice in reading Negro folktales, is always the road to freedom — the movement upward." In the trip from the South
to Harlem, the century from slavery to postindustrial society
is radically telescoped. "Here," he writes,

> it is possible for talented youths to leap through the develop-
> ment of decades in a brief twenty years, while beside them
> white-haired adults crawl in the feudal darkness of their child-
> hood. Here a former cotton picker develops the sensitive
> hands of a surgeon, and men whose grandparents still believe
> in magic prepare optimistically to become atomic scientists.
> Here the grandchildren of those who possessed no written
> literature examine their lives through the eyes of Freud and
> Marx, Kierkegaard and Kafka, Malraux and Sartre . . .
> The real and the unreal merge, and the marvelous beckons from
> behind the same sordid reality that denies its existence.

James Baldwin was born in 1924 in Harlem Hospital. His
early years were spent in a house on upper Park Avenue, where
the New York Central trains rattled by. It was the typical
Harlem apartment: a railroad flat on the top floor, so thoroughly impregnated with dirt that it resisted all cleaning.
Later Baldwin moved to an apartment at 2171 Fifth Avenue,
since replaced by a housing project, where he spent his adolescence. His neighborhood, today called "Junkie's Hollow,"

was bounded by Lenox Avenue, the Harlem River, where "he and other children had waded into the water from the garbage-heavy bank or dived from occasional rotting promontories," 130th and 135th streets. In his short story "Sonny's Blues," a schoolteacher who has escaped Harlem revisits it with feelings that must have been Baldwin's own:

> These streets hadn't changed, though housing projects jutted up out of them now like rocks in the middle of a boiling sea. Most of the houses in which we had grown up had vanished . . . But houses exactly like the houses of the past yet dominated the landscape, boys exactly like the boys we once had been found themselves smothering in these houses, came down into the streets for light and air and found themselves encircled by disaster. Some escaped the trap, most didn't. Those who got out always left something of themselves behind, as some animals amputate a leg and leave it in the trap.

Baldwin went to Frederick Douglass Junior High School, where Countee Cullen was one of his teachers. A hill in the middle of Central Park near the reservoir was his refuge. From it, "cloudy, and far away, he saw the skyline of New York." Later, he went on to DeWitt Clinton High School, where he was editor-in-chief of the literary magazine, the *Magpie,* whose former editors included Paddy Chayefsky, Paul Gallico, Countee Cullen and the photographer Richard Avedon, who became Baldwin's close friend.

Baldwin's religious life, which he describes in *Go Tell It on the Mountain,* dominated his adolescence. He experienced a religious conversion at Mount Calvary of the Pentecostal Faith Church, known as Mother Horn's Church. (Mother Horn was the model for Sister Margaret in his play *The Amen Corner.*) There he came under the influence of Arthur Moore, a devoted communicant, who was also a fellow student at Frederick Douglass. The two boys often browsed on 125th

Street and picked up used books — one for a nickel and six for a quarter. Later, Baldwin followed Moore to the Fireside Pentecostal Assembly at 136th Street and Fifth Avenue. He went to church several nights a week from eight to midnight, and preached once a week on Young Ministers' Night.

In 1942, when he was eighteen, Baldwin left Harlem for Greenwich Village. Soon afterward he met Richard Wright, who seems to have functioned in his life as a spiritual father. (John Grimes's father in *Go Tell It on the Mountain* is named Richard.) By the time he was twenty-four, he told his biographer, Fern Marja Eckman, "since I was not stupid, I realized that there was no point in my staying in the country at all. If I'd been born in Mississippi, I might have come to New York. But, being born in New York, there's no place that you can go. You have to go *out. Out* of the country." Despite Baldwin's recognition and abhorrence of the destructive nature of Harlem, it still retains the meaning and emotional force of home for him. He has described it as "the only *human* part of New York" and in an interview in 1970 said that the only place outside Europe he felt at home in the world was Harlem, "where people know what I know, and we can talk and laugh, and it would never occur to anybody to say what we all know."

•

In 1945, the Harlem Writers' Workshop was founded at the YMCA by writer and historian John Henrik Clarke and others. James Baldwin dropped in and out at the Sunday evening meetings and Langston Hughes read his poetry at workshop meetings and acted as a critic for the group. In 1949 twelve members pooled their resources and founded a quarterly of their own because they were having trouble getting their work published. Parties, attended by such celebrities as Sidney Poitier, Harry Belafonte, Leon Bibb and Judy Holliday, were held to raise funds. The group often met at Clarke's apartment at 311 West

136th Street. Today his present home, an elegant brownstone on 137th Street, is still a meeting place for young writers and intellectuals.

In 1950 and 1951, writers Rosa Guy and John Oliver Killens got together to form the Harlem Writers' Guild, an institution completely unrelated to the Workshop of the late forties. The purpose was to train young black people in writing, for which a group also called the Harlem Writers' Workshop was set up, and to promote the writers' work by means of parties and publicity. Killens served as chairman of the Guild until 1960, and the Workshop met most often at his apartment in Brooklyn because he had the biggest place. Today it meets at the Countee Cullen branch of the New York Public Library.

Through the Harlem Writers' Workshop have passed a large percentage of the black writers who came to prominence during the fifties and sixties. It was there that Killens first read *Youngblood,* Guy read *A Bird at My Window* and Maya Angelou read *I Know Why the Caged Bird Sings.* Paule Marshall, Louis Meriwether, Lonne Elder III, Douglas Turner Ward and Julian Mayfield were also members of the Workshop. Its meetings featured open and intense criticism of structure, character building, style — every aspect of writing. A number of the novels by writers who came out of the Workshop were set in Harlem. Rosa Guy's *A Bird at My Window* is a story of ghetto life in the area around Lenox Avenue between 110th and 125th streets. Louise Meriwether's *Daddy Was a Number Runner* portrays the futility of Harlem life during the depression. Julian Mayfield also describes the numbers game in *The Hit,* and uses Harlem for the setting of *The Long Night.*

Two best sellers of the sixties were set in Harlem and portrayed its life vividly. *The Autobiography of Malcolm X* told the story of Malcolm Little from his childhood in Michigan and youth in Boston to his arrival in Harlem in 1941 as a sixteen-year-old sandwich hawker on the Yankee Clipper between Boston and New York. His first tour of Harlem included a stop at Smalls' Paradise, a show at the Apollo Theater on 125th Street and a few drinks at the Braddock Hotel on 126th Street. Malcolm, like so many of the literary figures who preceded him, first stayed at the 135th Street Y. In 1942 he took a job at Smalls' and roomed in the 800 block of St. Nicholas Avenue. With the loss of his job the following year, his descent into drug addiction and crime began, culminating in his imprisonment in Boston in 1946. He emerged in 1952 as Malcolm X. In 1954, he returned to Harlem to establish Temple 7 on the top floor of a four-story building at 116th Street and Lenox Avenue. Ten years later, he broke with the Muslims and established the Organization of Afro-American Unity at the Hotel Teresa. He was shot at a rally at the Audubon Ballroom on 166th Street between Broadway and St. Nicholas Avenue on February 21, 1965.

Claude Brown's *Manchild in the Promised Land* focuses on the block where he grew up — 145th Street between Seventh and Eighth avenues, particularly the concrete alley behind the tenements on his block, where much of its action takes place. After the publication of his book, he revisited it with journalist Tom Wolfe. "The strip is practically a block long but only 2-feet wide," wrote Wolfe. "It is like a six-story tar vat, with all that bright sky up above and this weird twilight at the bottom. The place is a garbage heap, all this junk piled up, beer cans, scraggly old gray cabbage heads, every damned thing, with nice great fluffy fumes of human urine rising up."

In the mid-sixties, LeRoi Jones changed his name to Amiri Baraka and moved up to Harlem for about seven months to found the Black Arts Repertory Theater School at 146 West 130th Street. The theater announced itself with a parade down Lenox Avenue led by jazz conductor Sun Rah. During 1965, the Black Arts Repertory Theater produced outdoor plays, poetry readings and concerts — "perhaps the first street theater of recent years," said poet Larry Neal. While in Harlem, Jones spent some time in Jock's Place, a bar at 2350 Seventh Avenue, which provides the setting for his story "Unfinished." Neal described Jock's, across the street from the New Lafayette Theatre, as the hangout of a "hip, bourgeois crowd, hip in a suave way, that included fast women, good-looking women."

Since the late sixties, a rebuilding of Harlem's cultural life has been taking place. Some of the old institutions — the Schomburg Collection, Lewis Michaux's National Memorial African Bookshop at its new location at 101 West 125th Street, the Harlem Writers' Guild — are still vital centers for black literary development, and now they are being joined by new ones, such as the New Lafayette Theatre and the Studio Museum at 2033 Fifth Avenue. "Folks are trying to settle down and build some institutions rather than use the place as a playground," said Neal. Like the members of the Harlem Writers' Workshop, who called their group by that name though few of them lived in Harlem and they seldom met there, many contemporary black writers, who also live elsewhere, use Harlem as a symbolic reference point. Neal called them "uptown folks" who are "in and around Harlem, and whose thinking is about Harlem." A few live there: Neal is on Jumel Terrace, which he regards as within the community's boundaries ("Harlem is where *we* are," he has said), and Albert Murray, Evan Walker and Frank Hercules are in a complex of buildings around 132nd Street and Fifth Avenue. Others — David Henderson, Rosa Guy and Maya Angelou — are among those who come to Harlem to see everything produced at the New Lafayette and attend every concert, poetry reading or exhibition at the Studio Museum. Although vastly different today from what it was during the twenties, when it was called Mecca, Harlem remains the center of the black literary world.

Harlem

W. 154th St.

(22)

(23) W. 149th St.

Convent Ave.

Edgecombe Ave.

W. 142nd St. (21)

HARLEM RIVER

Harlem River Drive

HUDSON RIVER

City Col.

of

N. Y.

(24)

W. 139th St.

(20)

(19) (15) W. 138th St.

(17) (18)

(16)

(14) W. 136th St.

W. 135th St.

(11)

(13)

(12)

W. 132nd St.

(10)

(9) W.130th St. (25) St.

Broadway

W. 125th St.

Eighth Ave.

W. 127th St.

(26)

EAST HARLEM

(6) (7)

(27) E. 125th St.

(8) W. 124th St.

Riverside Dr.

Barnard Col.

Columbia Univ.

Amsterdam Ave.

Morningside Dr.

St. Nicholas Ave.

Ave.

Seventh

Lenox Ave.

Mount Morris Park

Madison Ave.

Park Ave.

Lexington Ave.

Third Ave.

(5) W. 119th St.

(4)

(2) (3) W. 116th St.

Fifth Ave.

Henry Hudson Pkwy.

W. 110th St.

(1)

CENTRAL PARK

Harlem Tour

The playwright Arthur Miller lived as an infant in apartment 6B at 45 West 110th Street (1). This was one of many luxury apartment houses built in Harlem at the turn of the century. Most magnificent among them were the Graham Court Apartments on the northeast corner of Seventh Avenue and 116th Street (3). The white granite building surrounds an inner courtyard. Zora Neale Hurston lived here in 1932. Just north is the attractive building with Ionic columns where Jessie Fauset lived at 1947 Seventh Avenue (4). A fourth building, the De Peyster, on Seventh Avenue between 119th and 120th streets (5) was built by Nathanael West's father, Max Weinstein. West lived here in 1908. With its rundown tenements, the block of 116th between Seventh and Eighth avenues (2), which Ann Petry chose as the setting for her novel *The Street,* forms a sharp contrast.

Langston Hughes's favorite hangout in later years was the Palm Café on 125th Street between Seventh and Eighth avenues (6). Neon palm trees decorate the windows. It was here that he met the model for his character Jess B. Semple. At 101 West 125th Street (7) is Lewis Michaux's National Memorial African Bookshop, which houses a comprehensive collection of literature on black and African history and culture. The store has long been a gathering place for writers and a center of Harlem intellectual and political activity.

During Harlem's heyday, several large casinos provided space for dancing. One of these was the Harlem Casino on the northeast corner of 124th Street and Seventh Avenue (8). The building now houses the Refuge Temple. Several blocks farther up Seventh Avenue stands the Salem Methodist Episcopal Church, an attractive red brick building with a rose window and roman arches. Countee Cullen's father was the minister here and the Cullens lived in the parsonage that adjoins the church at 2190 Seventh Avenue (9). The Lafayette Theatre, once Harlem's entertainment center because of its ballroom, restaurant and public meeting rooms, is now the Williams Institutional Church. The building complex still stands on Seventh Avenue between 131st and 132nd streets (10). Two blocks north on the west side of the avenue is Smalls' Paradise (11), Harlem's most famous restaurant. A survivor from the mid-twenties, when it was founded by Edwin Smalls, it is now owned by Wilt Chamberlain and is called Big Wilt's Smalls' Paradise.

James Weldon Johnson once lived on the south side of 135th Street between Seventh and Lenox avenues. His house was replaced in 1931 by an annex (12) of the YMCA across the street (13). The Y has been an important Harlem cultural center. In 1945 the Harlem Writers' Workshop was founded there. Ralph Ellison and Langston Hughes both stayed at the Y at various times. A short distance east, at 103 West 135th Street (14), is the building that housed the 135th Street branch of the New York Public Library, a gathering place for the writers of the Renaissance during the twenties. Today it is the Schomburg Collection of Black History, Literature and Art. The white neoclassic building, dating from 1905, was designed by McKim, Mead and White. Directly behind the Schomburg Collection stands the Countee Cullen branch (15) of the New York Public Library, which was built on the site of A'Lelia Walker's famous mansion. Nella Larsen, who worked as a librarian at the 135th Street branch for a time, lived at 236 West 135th Street (16).

John Henrik Clarke's apartment in the brick house at 311 West 136th Street (17) was a meeting place for the Harlem Writers' Workshop during the forties. One block east at 267 West 136th Street (18) stands the brick and brownstone house

Striver's Row, Harlem's most fashionable houses during the 1920s.

where Wallace Thurman lived during the twenties. A rooming house then, it was an important meeting place for Renaissance figures, including Langston Hughes, Zora Neale Hurston, Gwendolyn Bennett and Aaron Douglas. Thurman portrayed it satirically as Niggerati Manor in his novel *Infants of the Spring*. At Seventh Avenue and 138th Street (19) is another surviving twenties' ballroom and theater complex, the Casino

Renaissance. The New Lafayette Theatre, which performs contemporary black plays, is housed there today.

Striver's Row is actually four rows of attached houses along 138th and 139th streets between Seventh and Eighth avenues (20). A designated landmark, the development represents a highly successful experiment in urban planning. David H. King, builder of the Times Building and the original Madison Square Garden, commissioned three of New York's most prominent architectural firms to build houses upon it. The red brick brownstone-trimmed houses on the south side of 138th Street were designed in the Georgian tradition by James Brown Lord. The buff-colored brick ones on the north side of 138th and the south side of 139th, which stand around a garden with flower beds and fountains, were done by Bruce Price and Clarence Luce. The third set, brown mottled brick in the Italian Renaissance style, were the creation of McKim, Mead and White.

Up the hill northwest of Striver's Row stands Harlem's most important architectural landmark, the house where Alexander Hamilton lived in the last years of his life. Designed by John McComb, Jr., Hamilton Grange, as the house was called, originally stood about a hundred yards from its present site on Convent Avenue between 141st and 142nd streets (21). It was moved here in 1889. Open to the public, the house is being restored and decorated with furnishings that either belonged to the Hamilton family or date from the period. It has charming octagonal rooms and room-high three-sash windows.

North, on top of the exclusive area called Sugar Hill, stands 409 Edgecombe Avenue (22), one of Harlem's most fashionable addresses. Aaron Douglas, the painter whose work adorned many book jackets during the Renaissance, lived here, as did Walter White, whose parties were attended by many celebrities. Another desirable address is the complex of buildings called the Paul Laurence Dunbar Apartments, which occupies the block from 149th to 150th streets and Seventh to Eighth avenues (23). Named after the early black writer (he was from Dayton, Ohio), the brick buildings have decorative friezes and portrait medallions of Dunbar. Financed by John D. Rockefeller, Jr., the apartments were originally cooperatives. Residents have included Jessie Fauset, W. E. B. Du Bois and Rudolph Fisher.

The tenement where Claude McKay lived when he came back after a decade abroad is still standing at 147 West 142nd Street (24). "The Block Beautiful," which he described in his first novel, *Home to Harlem,* survives on the south side of 130th Street between Lenox and Fifth avenues (25). The three-story brick houses, with their once white porches, are shabby now. The brownstone house where Langston Hughes lived with his good friends, the Emerson Harpers, is at 20 East 127th Street (26). One of Harlem's new cultural landmarks is the Studio Museum at 2033 Fifth Avenue (27).

X. The Bronx, Queens and Staten Island

The Bronx

THE BRONX has literary associations dating back to the Knickerbocker period. Joseph Rodman Drake, best known for his poem "The American Flag," lived here in the area around Hunts Point. His closest friend was Fitz-Greene Halleck and the two writers are commemorated in the names of adjacent Hunts Point streets. Drake died at the early age of twenty-five and is buried in a park named for him at Hunts Point and Oak Point avenues. Another Knickerbocker writer, James Fenimore Cooper, set his novel *Satanstoe* in the Bronx. "Satanstoe" was a name given to what is now Throgs Neck. Legend had it that when Satan was driven away by the Indians he used the rocky islets between Throgs Neck and City Island as stepping stones. Before jumping off, he left his toe print and that point of land became known as Satanstoe.

The Bronx's best-known literary resident was Edgar Allan Poe, who took a cottage in Fordham from 1846 to 1848 in the hope that it would improve the health of his wife, Virginia. He himself was none too well at the time. "I am living out of town about 13 miles, at a village called Fordham, on the railroad leading north," he wrote in a letter. "We are in a snug little cottage, keeping house, and would be very comfortable, but that I have been for a long time dreadfully ill." The house

Edgar Allan Poe's cottage in its original location on Kingsbridge Road near Fordham Road, where it stood until 1913.

was unheated and Virginia lay on a straw mattress with Poe's
West Point greatcoat wrapped around her and the cat hugged
close to her body for warmth. In 1847 Virginia died and was
buried in a nearby churchyard. (Her body was later moved
to Baltimore to be buried near Poe's.) Poe was found many
times at her tomb that winter in the middle of the night, having wandered there from his bed.

The Fordham cottage, moved a few hundred feet north of its
original location, now stands at 2460 Grand Concourse in Poe
Park. It is a simple, frame farmhouse, built around 1813.
During his time here, Poe wrote "Ulalume" and "The Bells"
and probably started "Annabel Lee."

The Bronx's next prominent literary resident lived in the
greatest possible contrast to the impoverished Poe. In 1901
Mark Twain, at the height of his success, moved to one of the

borough's most magnificent houses, Wave Hill. The fieldstone mansion stands overlooking the Hudson at 252nd Street and Sycamore Avenue. "We drifted from room to room on our tour of inspection," Clemens wrote, "always with a growing doubt as to whether we wanted that house or not; but at last, when we arrived in a dining room that was 60 feet long, 30 feet wide, and had two great fireplaces in it, that settled it." In 1902, Clemens's wife, like Poe's, became ill. He was permitted to see her two minutes a day by the clock. His bedroom was separated from hers by a bathroom and he left notes there for her every night; she answered as best she could on scraps of paper. This continued until her death two years later. The house, which had also been the home of Theodore Roosevelt, among others, has been given to the Parks Department and is now the Wave Hill Environmental Center.

Sholom Aleichem, known as the Jewish Mark Twain, also lived in the Bronx. Among the first to visit him was Clemens, who said, "Please tell him that I am the American Sholom Aleichem." Another Yiddish writer, Sholem Asch, guaranteed a loan to Leon Trotsky so that the revolutionary could buy furniture when he lived in the Bronx in 1917. Trotsky wrote, "We rented an apartment in a workers' district, and furnished it on the instalment plan." Trotsky stayed only two and a half months, working on the editorial board of *Novy Mir* on the Lower East Side, and returned to Russia when the revolution occurred. Asch had to complete the payments on the furniture.

The neighborhood in which Aleichem and Trotsky lived was a flourishing Jewish community in the period between the two World Wars. Herman Wouk was born in 1915 in a tenement here on 167th Street, just west of Southern Boulevard. He lived at several addresses in the neighborhood and attended Public School 48, the Joseph Rodman Drake School, in Hunts Point. The milieu of his novel *The City Boy: The Adventures of*

Herbie Bookbinder is the area around 1091 Longfellow Avenue, where he lived during his adolescence. In the novel he described his apartment building as "a brick cliff very much like the other brick cliffs that stood wall to wall for many blocks along the less rocky side of the street. It was gray, square, five stories high, punctured with windows, and saved from bleakness only by the entrance, which tried on a little matter of plaster gargoyles overhead and dead shrubs in cracked plaster urns on either side of the iron-grilled glass doors."

The playwright Clifford Odets spent his childhood in roughly the same neighborhood. *Awake and Sing* is set in an apartment on Longwood Avenue near Beck Street. Frank Gilroy wrote about another generation in another Bronx neighborhood in his play *The Subject Was Roses.* Gilroy grew up at 116 West 176th Street near University Avenue.

In 1931 Ogden Nash wrote:

> The Bronx? No thonx.

By 1964 he had revised his opinion:

> I wrote those lines, "The Bronx? No thonx."
> I shudder to confess them.
> Now I'm an older, wiser man I cry,
> "The Bronx? God bless them!"

Queens

Queens has had only the most fragmentary literary history. It is known as the home of Jupiter Hammon, said to be the first Negro poet. Hammon was a slave living in Queens Village and his first literary effort was a broadside called "An Evening Thought: Salvation by Christ, with Penitential Cries." His next known work was "A Poetical Address to Phyllis Wheatley,"

written in 1778. In the 1830s James Fenimore Cooper spent
the summers in the area of Queens known as Astoria, sailing
over to Manhattan daily on a sloop. Walt Whitman was working for the *Long Island Democrat* in 1839 and lived at the home
of the editor, James J. Brenton, in Jamaica. Jack Kerouac
lived with his mother in an apartment over a drugstore on
Cross Bay Boulevard in the late forties while writing *The
Town and the City*. In 1952 they took a two-story frame house
at 94–21 134th Street in Richmond Hill. He was writing *Dr.
Sax* and the following year would write *The Subterraneans*
there. Malcolm X lived in Queens in the late fifties.

The only major work in which Queens figures importantly
is F. Scott Fitzgerald's *The Great Gatsby*. In 1922 Fitzgerald
was living in Great Neck, outside the city limits. However, his
frequent trips into the city, either on the Long Island Railroad
or driving on Northern Boulevard and over the Queensboro
Bridge, gave him an opportunity to become familiar with
Queens. The climactic scene in *Gatsby*, the killing of Myrtle
Wilson in front of her husband's gas station, takes place near
Northern Boulevard in the area then known as the Corona
Dumps. "This is a valley of ashes," Fitzgerald wrote, " — a
fantastic farm where ashes grow like wheat into ridges and hills
and grotesque gardens; where ashes take the forms of houses
and chimneys and rising smoke and, finally, with a transcendent
effort, of men who move dimly and already crumbling through
the powdery air."

The most inspiring thing about Queens for Fitzgerald, however, was the view it gave of Manhattan from the Queensboro
Bridge. "Over the great bridge," he wrote, "with the sunlight
through the girders making a constant flicker upon the moving
cars, with the city rising up across the river in white heaps and
sugar lumps all built with a wish out of non-olfactory money.
The city seen from the Queensboro Bridge is always the city

seen for the first time, in its first wild promise of all the mystery and the beauty in the world."

Staten Island

In the nineteenth century Staten Island was a lovely rural paradise. As such it drew a number of distinguished visitors who have given it something of a literary history. In the 1840s, Dr. Samuel MacKenzie Elliott, who practiced in Manhattan and lived on Staten Island, had a reputation as an eye specialist among the literati. When writers outside the city came to consult him, they would often live at his house or nearby while undergoing treatment. James Russell Lowell stayed with him in 1843, and the historian Francis Parkman consulted him in 1846. Elliott had his patients lie on the floor and operated on their eyes with a knife, holding their heads between his knees. Although Parkman stayed under Elliott's care for two years, he later wrote that the doctor had "nearly blinded me, and for this and other reasons hated me to the extent of his capacity." Other writers who came to visit Elliott included Henry Wadsworth Longfellow and Richard Henry Dana. Elliott lived in thirty houses during the twenty-eight years he spent on Staten Island. One of them, a vine-covered stone house with aquamarine trim, still stands at 69 Delafield Place.

During the same period, the home of Ralph Waldo Emerson's brother William, on what is now known as Emerson Hill, had its share of visitors. Waldo, as the writer was known to his family and friends, spent several summers here and early in 1843 suggested that Henry David Thoreau come and serve as his nephew's tutor. He returned to Concord and from there wrote his brother: "I have to say that Henry Thoreau listens very willingly to your proposition he [sic] thinks it exactly fit

The "Snuggery," the Emerson house on Staten Island where Henry
David Thoreau served as tutor.

for him & he rarely finds offers that do fit him. He says that
it is such a relation as he wishes to sustain, to be the friend &
educator of a boy, & one not yet subdued by schoolmasters
. . . I have told him that you will give him board, lodging
(washing?) a room by himself to study in, when not engaged
with Willie, with fire when the season requires, and a hundred
dollars a year."

The arrangements were agreed to and Ralph Waldo Emerson
advanced Thoreau twenty dollars, which he used for clothes
and traveling expenses. On Staten Island he lived with the
Emersons (William was the county judge) in their house, a
low brown-shingled building with grapevines on the piazza,
called the Snuggery. This house burned down in 1855 but the
stone gate to the property remains on Douglas Road near
Richmond Road. Thoreau's schedule was to breakfast at six-

thirty, take his charge for long walks in the early morning, and tutor him from nine until two. Less than three weeks after his arrival, he was writing to Sophia Emerson in Concord:

> The cedar seems to be one of the most common trees here, and the fields are very fragrant with it. There are also gum and tulip trees . . . The woods are now full of a large honeysuckle in full bloom, which differs from ours in being red instead of white, so that at first I did not know its genus. The painted cup is very common in the meadows here. Peaches, and especially cherries, seem to grow by all the fences. Things are very forward here compared with Concord. The apricots growing out-of-doors are already as large as plums. The apple, pear, peach, cherry, and plum trees have shed their blossoms. The whole island is like a garden, and affords very fine scenery . . . Garlic, the original of the common onion, grows here all over the fields, and during its season spoils the cream and butter for the market, as the cows like it very much.

Thoreau was not impressed with Manhattan but was attracted by the sea. "I want a whole continent to breathe in," he wrote to his family in Concord, "and a good deal of solitude and silence, such as all Wall Street cannot buy — nor Broadway with its wooden pavement. I must live along the beach, on the Southern Shore, which looks directly out to sea, and see what that great parade of water means, that dashes and roars, and has not yet wet me, as long as I have lived."

William Emerson introduced Thoreau to several literary people. The writer reported to Waldo after a three-hour talk with Henry James, Sr., that "he has naturalized and humanized New York for me." But ultimately Thoreau found his situation uncongenial. His tuberculosis flared up; he suffered from chronic sleepiness; and he was homesick for Concord. Unlike Waldo, William Emerson was very conventional, and he and Thoreau agreed on nothing. Shortly before Thanksgiving, Thoreau returned to Concord.

The Pavilion, the Staten Island hotel where Henry James's family vacationed.

The Jameses spent summer vacations on Staten Island and the younger Henry recalled, "I seem more or less to have begun life with impressions of New Brighton." His family stayed at the Pavilion, a hotel on the north shore that had many famous visitors. James remembered that "to childish retrospect," its form "was that of a great Greek temple shining over blue waters in the splendour of a white colonnade and a great yellow pediment."

Another visitor was Herman Melville, who came frequently to see his brother Tom during the years between 1867 and 1884, when he was governor of Sailors' Snug Harbor. A home for old seamen, Sailors' Snug Harbor was established by a trust left by Captain Robert Richard Randall. The governor's mansion where Tom Melville lived has been torn down, but the remaining Greek Revival buildings are now the headquarters of the Staten Island Institute of Arts and Sciences and the Staten Island Council on the Arts.

Among the literary figures who actually lived on Staten Island was George William Curtis, editor of *Harper's Weekly*. Curtis said, "God might have made a more beautiful spot than Staten Island, but he never did." In 1856 Curtis was living in a gabled house at 234 Bard Avenue, which still stands today. During the draft riots of July 1863 Horace Greeley sought refuge here from mobs seeking to kill him for his abolitionist activities.

Later in the century, in the 1890s, the poet Alan Seeger was living with his family on top of Tompkins Hill in a gabled Victorian house surrounded by four acres of land. Seeger attended the Staten Island Academy before going to war.

In 1901 Edwin Markham came to Staten Island from Brooklyn. He lived first in a house at the corner of Waters and Livermore, then on the border of meadows extending toward Willowbrook Road. From 1909 until his death in 1940 he lived at 92 Waters Street, a brown-shingled house with yellow porches and a carved wood door. In addition to writing poetry (in 1910 he founded the Poetry Society of America), Markham frequently reviewed books. Virgil Markham, the poet's son, described their house: "It was evident to anyone setting foot inside the door that books were here the cornerstone and indeed the whole foundation of life. There were books on walls and floor and in every nook and cranny. There were books on every horizontal surface except the top of the piano, which had to be opened sometimes, and the seats of some often-sat-upon chairs." Since there were books and manuscripts on the dining room table where the Markhams did their literary work, eating was generally done in the kitchen. "When we had guests for meals, the debris was pushed to one end of the dining table and the vacant area set for places," Virgil recalled. "Unless, that is, there were several outsiders, when the cloth might be laid over a carefully leveled plateau of books."

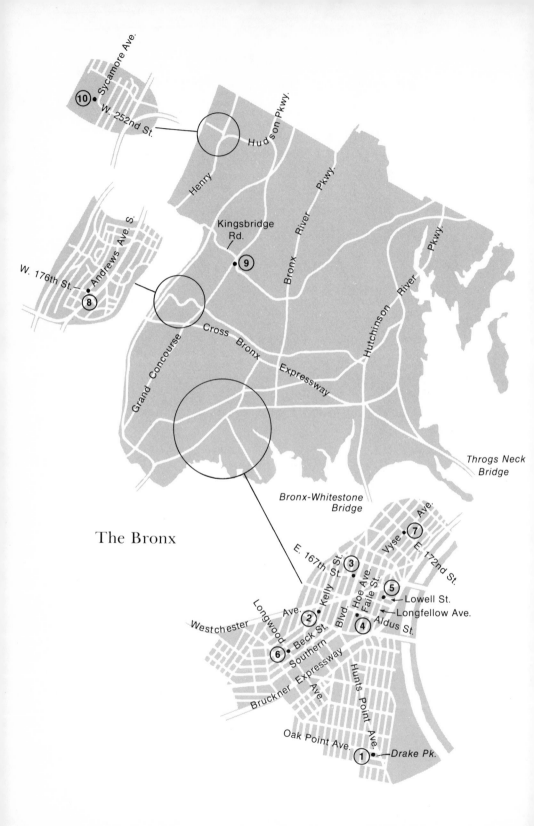

The Bronx

Sycamore Ave.
10 W. 252nd St.
Hudson Pkwy.
Henry
Bronx River Pkwy.
Kingsbridge Rd.
9
W. 176th St.
Andrews Ave. S.
8
Cross Bronx
Grand Concourse
Expressway
Hutchinson River Pkwy.
Throgs Neck Bridge
Bronx-Whitestone Bridge
E. 167th St.
Vyse Ave.
7
E. 172nd St.
St.
3
Hoe Ave.
5
Longwood Ave.
Kelly St.
Faile St.
Lowell St.
Longfellow Ave.
Westchester
2
Blvd.
4
Aldus St.
Beck St.
6
Southern
Bruckner Expressway
Ave.
Hunts Point Ave.
Oak Point Ave.
1
Drake Pk.

Other than Markham, twentieth-century literary figures have spent little time on Staten Island. Theodore Dreiser, who moved frequently and lived virtually everywhere in New York, stayed for a time at 109 St. Mark's Place. Maxim Gorky once spent a night in a house on Grymes Hill. In 1922, after Langston Hughes quit Columbia, he found a job on a Staten Island truck farm owned by a Greek family. He got bed and board — he slept in the hayloft — and fifty dollars a month. Jane and Paul Bowles once spent a summer on the island, an experience reflected in Jane's *Two Serious Ladies*. But throughout the nineteenth and twentieth centuries, Staten Island has been too remote from Manhattan and the literary mainstream for its associations with writing to be anything but incidental.

Bronx Tour

A literary tour of the Bronx encompasses the most radical extremes of New York City life. The area of the South Bronx that was a Jewish community between the wars and home to several writers is now a region of such desperate poverty and chaos that all who can have fled it. In contrast, the Riverdale where Mark Twain lived is still an area of mansions and lovely gardens.

The nineteenth-century graveyard in which Joseph Rodman Drake is buried is now the center of Drake Park (1) at Hunts Point and Oak Point avenues. Note that streets and avenues in the area — Bryant, Longfellow, Whittier, Drake and Halleck — are named for nineteenth-century writers.

The area north and slightly west of Hunts Point was a thriving Jewish neighborhood in the period between the two World Wars. Today, no vestiges of that community remain. The five- and six-story apartment houses that uniformly line the streets are often gutted and abandoned. Sholom Aleichem

was living at 968 Kelly Street (2) at the time of his death in
1916. His building, one in an attached row of four-story red
brick houses between Westchester Avenue and East 163rd
Street, was in the process of being demolished as of this writing.
Several blocks away, Herman Wouk was born in May 1915 in a
tenement on East 167th Street just west of Southern Boulevard
(3). That house is no longer standing. As a child he moved
first to 974 Aldus Street between Hoe Avenue and Faile
Street and then next door to 978 (4). The building is the typical five-story brick apartment house. He spent his adolescence
at 1091 Longfellow Avenue (5) at the corner of Lowell Street.
This was the setting for his novel *The City Boy: The Adventures of Herbie Bookbinder,* although his building is red brick
and he describes Herbie's as "gray."

Clifford Odets grew up on nearby Longwood Avenue near
Beck Street (6). His play *Awake and Sing* is set in an apartment on Longwood. In 1917 Leon Trotsky was somewhat
farther north, in a five-story brick apartment house called the
Mildred at 1522 Vyse Avenue (7).

Frank Gilroy lived in the area of the Bronx called Tremont.
His house was a six-story brick apartment at 116 West 176th
Street (8) on the corner of Andrews Avenue South. He wrote
about this neighborhood in his play *The Subject Was Roses.*

From 1846 to 1848 Edgar Allan Poe lived in a small farmhouse in Fordham. The cottage, which dates from about 1812,
is now the center of Poe Park at Kingsbridge Road and the
Grand Concourse (9). The house originally stood on Kingsbridge Road near Fordham Road but was moved to its present
location in 1913, when it was acquired by the city. The building is now maintained as a Poe museum.

In the early 1900s Mark Twain and his wife lived in Wave
Hill, one of the city's most magnificent mansions. Located at
West 252nd Street and Sycamore Avenue (10) in the River-
dale section of the Bronx, the house is built of fieldstone in the

Greek Revival style. Now owned by the Parks Department and called the Wave Hill Environmental Center, its grounds are open to the public.

Queens Tour

The house that Jack Kerouac took with his mother in 1952 is at 94–21 134th Street (1), in the Richmond Hill district of Queens. Here he wrote *Dr. Sax*.

Queens

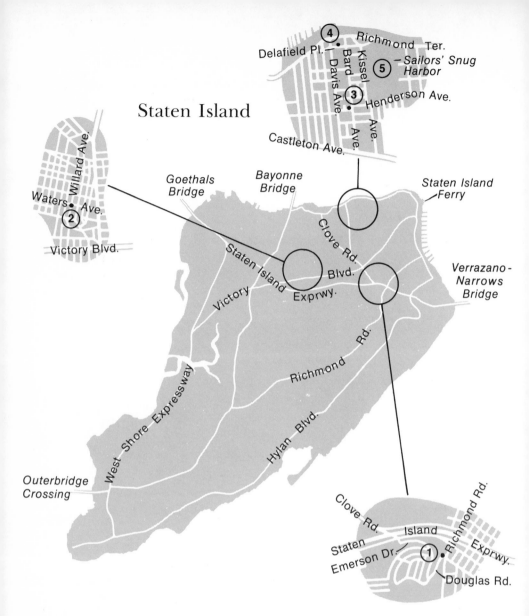

Staten Island

4   Richmond   Ter.

Delafield Pl.

Bard Ave.

Davis Ave.

Kissel Ave.

5   Sailors' Snug Harbor

3   Henderson Ave.

Ave.

Ave.

Castleton Ave.

Goethals Bridge

Bayonne Bridge

Staten Island Ferry

Clove Rd.

Staten Island Exprwy.

Blvd.

Waters Ave.

Willard Ave.

2

Victory Blvd.

Victory

Verrazano-Narrows Bridge

Richmond Rd.

West Shore Expressway

Richmond

Hylan Blvd.

Outerbridge Crossing

Clove Rd.

Staten Island Emerson Dr.

Island

1

Richmond Rd.

Richmond Rd.

Exprwy.

Douglas Rd.

Staten Island Tour

The stone gate that once led to the property of Judge William Emerson, Ralph Waldo Emerson's brother, still exists; it is off Richmond Road a short distance from the Staten Island Expressway (1). Henry David Thoreau lived here in Emerson's house, the Snuggery, while serving as tutor for the judge's son.

The house where Edwin Markham lived from 1910 to 1940 is still standing at 92 Waters Avenue (2) at the corner of Willard. A brown-shingled Victorian structure, the house has yellow porches and a carved wood door.

The nineteenth-century houses of George W. Curtis and Dr. Samuel MacKenzie Elliott are both of architectural interest. The Curtis house at 234 Bard Avenue (3), on the northwest corner of Bard and Henderson avenues, has a hipped roof with four bracketed gables. The Elliott house at 69 Delafield Place (4), between Davis and Bard avenues, was designed by the doctor himself. The house is constructed of fieldstone and has Gothic details.

Herman Melville often visited his brother Tom at Sailors' Snug Harbor on Richmond Terrace, between Tysen Street and Kissel Avenue (5). Five of the Greek Revival buildings remain, although the governor's house, where Tom Melville lived, has been torn down. The Pavilion, the hotel where Henry James stayed during the summer as a child, also stood on what is now Richmond Terrace. Just off the present Westervelt Avenue, it resembled the buildings of Sailors' Snug Harbor.

XI. Brooklyn and
Brooklyn Heights

Brooklyn

LIKE MANHATTAN, Brooklyn began as a series of villages, the first of which was settled near Red Hook in 1636. Some of the borough's many neighborhoods — Flatbush, New Utrecht, Gravesend and Bushwick — retain the names of these original towns. The village of Brooklyn itself originally centered on what are now Fulton and Smith streets, where downtown Brooklyn is today. Eventually all the villages joined to form the City of Brooklyn, which was incorporated into New York in 1898.

The borough's first and most significant writer, Walt Whitman, spent most of his life in the region north of downtown Brooklyn. In 1823, when Whitman was four years old, his family moved from Long Island to a house on Front Street, an area of taverns and grog shops near the waterfront. Whitman's father was a carpenter who built one house after another for his family, intending to sell them at a profit. In *Specimen Days* Whitman reminisced about these early years: "From 1824–'28 our family lived in Brooklyn in Front, Cranberry and Johnson streets. In the latter my father built a nice house for a home, and afterwards another in Tillary Street. We occupied them one after the other, but they were mortgaged, and we lost them." All of Whitman's houses are gone today, and housing projects and roadways to Manhattan have replaced most of the old neighborhood.

Whitman's father was never very successful at his house-building occupation, and in 1834 moved his family back to Long Island to earn his living at farming. Walt, only fifteen years old, stayed behind and found work in printing houses. In 1836, he rejoined his family and spent the next three years teaching and working on small Long Island papers. In the early 1840s he found work as a printer and newspaperman in Manhattan and then returned to Brooklyn in 1845. For the next five years he worked consecutively as a writer for the *Long Island Star,* editor of the *Brooklyn Daily Eagle* and editor of the *Brooklyn Freeman.* William Cullen Bryant came to visit him several times during this period. "We were both walkers," Whitman recalled at Bryant's death, "and when I work'd in Brooklyn he several times came over, middle of afternoons, and we took rambles, miles long, till dark, out towards Bedford or Flatbush, in company. On these occasions he gave me clear accounts of scenes in Europe — the cities, looks, architecture, art, especially Italy — where he had travel'd a good deal." During the next decade Whitman was variously occupied; for a while he was a real estate speculator, and from 1857 to 1859 he edited the *Brooklyn Times.* He was writing poetry throughout these years and in 1855 published the first edition of *Leaves of Grass* at the print shop of friends, setting some ten pages of type himself (see Brooklyn Heights in this chapter). In 1862 he went south to Fredericksburg, Virginia, to look for his brother George, who had been injured in battle, and began to visit the wounded in hospitals in Washington, D.C. He never came back to live in Brooklyn although he made several long visits.

Whitman, like most New Yorkers of the time, was enormously attached to the waterfront, and he especially enjoyed

Walt Whitman's house at 106 Myrtle Avenue, where he
lived when he was editor of the *Brooklyn Freeman*.

the ferry trips he made to Manhattan to attend the opera and
other entertainments or simply to walk the streets. "Living in
Brooklyn or New York City from this time forward," he wrote
of the period around 1840,

> my life . . . was curiously identified with Fulton ferry already
> becoming the greatest of its sort in the world for general im-
> portance, volume, variety, rapidity, and picturesqueness.
> Almost daily, later, . . . I cross'd on the boats, often up in
> the pilot houses where I could get a full sweep, absorbing
> shows, accompaniments, surroundings . . . The river and bay
> scenery . . . the hurrying, splashing sea-tides — the changing

panorama of steamers, all sizes, often a string of big ones out-
ward bound to distant ports — the myriads of white-sail'd
schooners, sloops, skiffs, and the marvelously beautiful yachts
— the majestic sound boats as they rounded the Battery and
came along toward five, afternoon, eastward bound — the
prospect off toward Staten island, or down the Narrows, or the
other way up the Hudson — what refreshment of spirit such
sights and experiences gave me . . ."

Brooklyn's next major writer was not to arrive until the end
of the century. In 1892 Henry Miller, then an infant, moved
with his family from Yorkville in Manhattan to the Williamsburg section of Brooklyn. "In my dreams I come back to the
Fourteenth Ward as a paranoiac returns to his obsessions,"
Miller wrote. "Where others remember of their youth a beautiful garden, a fond mother, a sojourn at the seashore, I remember, with a vividness as if it were etched in acid, the grim,
soot-covered walls and chimneys of the tin factory . . . and
the bright, circular pieces of tin that were strewn in the street,
some bright and gleaming, others rusted, dull, copperish, leaving a stain on the fingers . . ."

Opposite Miller's home, a three-story brick house still
standing at 662 Driggs Avenue, was the veterinary and on the
corner was a place where raw hides were stacked up in the
street. Like the tin factory, the place where the hides were
trimmed stank frightfully. But across from the factory was a
bakery, from which emanated the "sweet, irresistible odor of
bread and cake."

Miller's old neighborhood has undergone relatively little
renewal. In his time, the ground floor of his house was a barber shop and it remains a storefront today. Diagonally across
from the house was Miller's favorite street, Fillmore Place.
With the opening of the Williamsburg Bridge came the destruction of some of its houses. "Soon" he wrote, "the street

looked like a dirty mouth with all the prominent teeth missing, with ugly charred stumps gaping here and there, the lips rotting, the palate gone." By today's standards, the street, with its nineteenth-century houses renewed and repainted, is relatively intact.

When he was ten years old Miller moved to what he called "the street of early sorrows" — Decatur Street at number 1063. His new home was in Bushwick, a German-American neighborhood. Why he disliked it was unclear even to Miller, since his memories are not unhappy ones. "I recall some wonderful days in the autumn in empty lots in the neighborhood," he wrote. "We would dig caves in them. Some days we would shoot sparrows and roast them over a fire."

Growing up in Williamsburg, which gave Miller so much of his artistic material, was also the subject of Betty Smith's 1943 best seller, *A Tree Grows in Brooklyn*. The tree, *ailanthus glandulosa,* a variety of sumac imported from China, found great popularity in swampy areas like Williamsburg for its supposed power to dispel disease-producing vapors. Behind the house on Grand Street where Smith's heroine, Francie Nolan, lives, stood the tree. "It had pointed leaves which grew along green switches which radiated from the bough and made a tree which looked like a lot of opened green umbrellas," she wrote. ". . . No matter where its seed fell, it made a tree which struggled to reach the sky. It grew in boarded-up lots and out of neglected rubbish heaps and it was the only tree that grew out of cement."

With the opening of the Williamsburg Bridge in 1903, Jews from the Lower East Side began to cross over to Brooklyn. Around 1940 they were joined by Hassidic Jews fleeing persecution in Eastern Europe. The Hassidic community, which has only recently moved out of Williamsburg to Crown Heights, became the background of several books by Chaim Potok — *The Chosen, The Promise* and *My Name Is Asher Lev* — which deal with the conflict between Hassidic tradition and the development of the individual.

Although many Jews settled in Williamsburg and other parts of Brooklyn, the borough's pre-eminent Jewish community for many years was Brownsville. Jews, most of them in the needle trades, began to arrive in 1892. At first the community preserved the customs of an Eastern European *shtetl*, speaking Yiddish and reading Yiddish-language newspapers. But later generations, which included a number of writers — Matthew Josephson, Henry Roth, Alfred Kazin, Norman Podhoretz, Irving Shulman, Gerald Green and Murray Schisgal — broke away. Kazin, who grew up in the twenties at 256A Sutter Avenue, describes the neighborhood in *A Walker in the City:* "Every time I go back to Brownsville it is as if I had never been away. From the moment I step off the train at Rockaway Avenue and smell the leak out of the men's room, then the pickles from the stand just below the subway steps, an instant rage comes over me, mixed with dread and some unexpected tenderness . . . The early hopelessness burns at my face like fog . . . I can smell it in the air as soon as I walk down Rockaway Avenue." Growing up on Sutter Avenue, Kazin had a typical urban boyhood. "On the block itself everything rose up only to test me. We worked every inch of it, from the cellars and the backyards to the sickening space between the roofs. Any wall, any stoop, any curving metal edge on a billboard sign made a place against which to knock a ball; any bottom rung of a fire escape ladder a goal in basketball; any sewer cover a base; any crack in the pavement a 'net' for the tense sharp tennis that we played by beating a softball back and forth with our hands between the squares."

In *Making It,* Norman Podhoretz, who came a generation after Kazin, documents the social aspects of growing up in the forties in Brownsville at 2027 Pacific Street. "One of the longest journeys in the world," his book begins, "is the journey

Marianne Moore and her mother, Mary Warner Moore, at 260 Cumberland Street in the 1930s.

from Brooklyn to Manhattan — or at least from certain neighborhoods in Brooklyn to certain parts of Manhattan." *Making
It* documents the journey in speech, clothes, manners from
lower-class Brownsville, where Podhoretz was a member of the
red-satin-jacketed Cherokees, to the unaccented parlors of the
American literary elite.

•

Another old Brooklyn neighborhood, Fort Greene, was home
to two prominent writers, Marianne Moore and Richard
Wright. In 1931 Moore moved to an apartment building up
the street from the magnificent old mansions, now mostly rooming houses, facing Fort Greene Park. She told George Plimpton,
who came to interview her at 260 Cumberland Street in 1964,
"am on right, middle of the block, with what look like mothballs on iron stands flanking the entrance." She lived on the
fifth floor. "Piles of books were everywhere," Plimpton wrote.
"Tea-colored oils on the walls, and a fine clutter of memorabilia, of which she pointed out a marlinspike from Greely's
expedition to the Arctic." When Moore died (she had moved
to Greenwich Village), funeral services were held at the Lafayette Presbyterian Church half a block away, where she had
regularly attended Sunday morning and Wednesday evening
services during her years in Fort Greene.

Richard Wright lived several blocks from Marianne Moore
in 1938 when he moved in with his friends Jane and Herbert
Newton at 175 Carlton Avenue. Here he began *Native Son*.
As soon as the sun had taken the chill off the morning air,
around five-thirty during the summer, he went to write at the
top of the hill in Fort Greene Park. At 10:00 A.M. he would
return to the house for breakfast and type up what he had written. When the Newtons moved, he went with them because he
felt the atmosphere of their home helped him to write. They
were briefly at 522 Gates Avenue and then moved to 87 Lef-

ferts Place, a brownstone in an area near Bedford-Stuyvesant. When *Native Son* was finished, Wright and his friends read the whole book aloud here, accompanied sometimes by a Shostakovich prelude played at full volume. Wright later returned to this neighborhood after his marriage. From 1943 to 1945 he and his wife lived at 89 Lefferts Place, a brick apartment building. Here Wright organized a tenants' strike and had the rent lowered to the OPA level. He was writing *Black Boy* at the time.

Bedford-Stuyvesant itself was the home and subject of another black writer, Paule Marshall, who wrote about the area's West Indian community in *Brown Girl, Brownstones*. Black novelist John O. Killens now lives on Union Street near Kingston Avenue. When he first moved there fifteen years ago it was considered Crown Heights, but is now often referred to as part of Bedford-Stuyvesant. In the early years Killens's house was a meeting place for the Harlem Writers' Guild (see Chapter IX, Harlem). Among those who gathered to read and discuss their work were John Henrik Clarke, Rosa Guy, Paule Marshall, Louise Meriwether, Maya Angelou and Ossie Davis. The neighborhood was then mixed. Today, Killens writes, "my turf is mostly black. The houses, like most of the folk who live here, have a quiet grace and dignity. In the summer the front lawns are sparkling green and manicured. The proud majestic oak trees form a long green tunnel, as their leafy limbs reach over the streets and grasp each other in a fine display of brotherhood."

•

The newer area of Brooklyn south of Prospect Park was home to Arthur Miller when he was growing up. In 1929 he and his family moved from 110th Street in Manhattan to a two-story brick house at 1277 Ocean Avenue. Two or three years later they moved to a small house at 1350 East 3rd, "the version ten years later," Miller says, "of the kind of two-family house Willy Loman lived in. These were post-World War One, a little more jerry-built. They were square-front buildings, made of wood, with flat roofs. They were often built in sets of three and might be surrounded by tomato fields, beautiful elm trees, hickories, woods. The little guys used to go out there and hunt rabbits and snakes." To get there from New York, one rode an hour and a half on the Culver Line. Each car had a coal stove which the passengers fed and sat around for heat.

Miller recalls life in Brooklyn as being like that in a small town:

> My mother didn't go to Manhattan more than once or twice a year. The neighborhood was psychologically divorced from New York. There was a terrific autonomy in these neighborhoods. It was as if they were demarcated by an iron fence. One knew when he was passing into foreign territory. My neighborhood was bounded by Gravesend Avenue and Ocean Parkway, a matter of six blocks, and from Avenue M over to Avenue J. Once you got out of there you might as well have been taking a voyage to Kansas. You didn't know anyone. There were some blocks that you liked better than others. My block was a dead-end street with a great college track star and a Colgate University football star. It was great to live on because you never knew when they would be out playing touch football.

Growing up in a neighborhood like his, Miller said, "gives a sense of hierarchy — one belongs somewhere, a well-oriented, well-grounded sense of touch, a sense of history, people growing older, people getting married, careers. It was a stable, ongoing, articulated community in a sense that the suburb today is not . . . In my neighborhood there were always Swedes, Italians, black people, Jews, Irish. There was quite a mélange. I'm glad I grew up that way. You get a sense of

the *moyenne* man — God help us — the man who is the back-
bone of the country. It never leaves you; you get a good
sense of how he views the world."

Today many young writers live in Brooklyn. Paula Fox
lives in Cobble Hill, Sol Yurick in Park Slope, L. J. Davis in
Boerum Hill. Davis explained Brooklyn's appeal in an article
for the *New York Times:*

> Once one gets off the main commercial streets, one finds that
> the 19th century city is surprisingly intact and, in parts, it is
> unusually handsome, with its low skyline and big old trees
> and rows of sculptured houses in brick and brownstone . . .
> Compared to Manhattan, housing is relatively inexpensive and
> considerably more spacious; it is possible to achieve a measure
> of stability by purchasing one's own home . . . and it is
> easier to be alone. There is much to be said for the back parlor
> of the old house on Dean Street where I am writing this essay,
> with its generous proportions and shelves of books and high
> ornamental ceiling. The windows look out over trees and
> flower gardens. It is a good room to write in. Brooklyn is full
> of such rooms.

Brooklyn Heights

Brooklyn Heights has always had a greater affinity with Manhattan than with its own borough. While the rest of Brooklyn
was still farmland and small villages, the Heights became what
architectural historian Clay Lancaster called "America's first
suburb." In the early 1880s it was a bedroom community for
the merchants and businessmen who worked in Lower Manhattan. Since then, Brooklyn Heights has maintained its connection with Manhattan, and its literary history is more closely
allied with that of the sophisticated island across the river than
with that of the neighboring flatlands.

In a quiet, gentle way Brooklyn Heights has nurtured an impressive collection of major American writers, among them Hart Crane, Thomas Wolfe, W. H. Auden, Carson McCullers, Truman Capote, Arthur Miller and Norman Mailer. None was formed by the Heights — Wolfe, McCullers and Capote came from the South, Crane from small-town Ohio, Auden from England, and Mailer and Miller from yeastier areas of Brooklyn. But all found the Heights a good place to live when it came time to write.

First among the Heights' attractions was its physical beauty. In 1816, residents found it a great bluff, whose face and brow were covered with "a beautiful growth of cedar and locust." From its summit, the land stretched away in orchards, gardens and pasture. Today, a smaller population of locust trees still scents the air and geranium-filled window boxes are symbols of the larger gardens of the past. Unlike many of New York's neighborhoods, however, what the Heights has lost in natural beauty it has gained in the manmade achievements of the industrial age. Its view of the Manhattan skyline is unequaled, and the Brooklyn Bridge, a magnificent marriage of esthetics and engineering, is its link with the mainland. Great ships, looming up beside the promenade, compensate somewhat for the loss of the river's fishing and swimming.

The Heights is also one of the most architecturally distinguished areas of the city; over 700 of its houses predate the Civil War. A homogeneous, isolated enclave — only four of its streets connect with greater Brooklyn — it possesses a sense of history and community. Yet, paradoxically, its residents have always felt more of a connection with Manhattan than the rest of Brooklyn.

As early as 1870, the remark that "Brooklyn is only a large bedroom for the businessmen of New York" was a cliché. In fact, even a century earlier, when it was still farmland, it had

boasted three residents with businesses in the city. By 1819
land was specifically advertised for its suburban virtues: "Families who may desire to associate in forming *a select neighborhood and circle of society, for a summer's residence or a whole
year's,* cannot anywhere obtain more desirable situations,"
read an advertisement extolling the health of the location and,
especially, its proximity to the business center. The suburban
development of the Heights had been made possible by the
granting of a franchise to steamboat-inventor Robert Fulton
and his partner, William Cutting. In 1814 they began the operation of a steam ferry — it connected the present Fulton Street
in Manhattan with Fulton Street in Brooklyn (both, of course,
named after the owner of the ferry) — for a charge of four cents
a passenger. Later, in 1854, the Wall Street Ferry was established at the foot of Montague Street and further spurred the
suburban development of the Heights. It made access to the
financial and shipping district easy for bankers, brokers, law-
yers and export and import merchants. "Shipping men especially felt drawn to the Heights as from it they could view
their own gallant ships arriving and departing," wrote James
Callender in his history of the neighborhood. "The cargoes
from 'India and Cathay' were unloaded almost at their very
doors."

The Heights' earliest literary resident was Thomas Paine,
who spent some time in his last years "in a quiet and somewhat dreary existence" in the home of John Harmer at the
corner of Sands and Fulton streets. Next, almost half a century
later, came Henry Ward Beecher, Walt Whitman and John
Greenleaf Whittier. Brooklyn is known as "the city of churches"
and Beecher's Plymouth Congregation, still located on Orange
Street between Henry and Hicks, was the most renowned
church of its time, estimated to have the largest congregation
in the country. As the church was also the largest auditorium

in the city, it was here that all the famous readers and lecturers of the day spoke, among them Dickens, Thackeray and Emerson. Beecher, who was paid the then staggering salary of $20,000 a year, lived at 22 Willow Street in 1848 and at 176 Columbia Heights from 1851 to 1855.

During the same era, although with much less notice, the young Walt Whitman was supervising the typesetting of *Leaves of Grass* in a print shop on the southwest corner of Cranberry and what was then Fulton, now Cadman Plaza West. Unfortunately, this building, in recent years a little brick luncheonette, was torn down in 1964. Whitman was a long-time Brooklynite, but always lived on "the other side of Fulton," the boundary that separated the elite Heights from more common neighboring districts, except for a short time in 1824, when his family lived on Cranberry Street.

In 1867 a charter was granted for the construction of the Brooklyn Bridge, setting in motion a process that was to have great literary significance for the Heights. John A. Roebling, a native of Germany who had been a favorite pupil of Hegel's, conceived and designed the bridge. His foot was crushed by a ferry in 1869 when he was surveying to determine the exact location of the bridge's Brooklyn tower; he contracted tetanus and died within two weeks. His son Washington took charge, determined to fulfill his father's vision. Three years later Washington too met misfortune. He suffered an attack of caisson bends but, despite his illness, continued to press himself to the limit. Overwork, the residual effect of the bends and frustration at being unable to do more physical work resulted in what at the time was called "nervous prostration." From then on he directed construction of the bridge from a second-floor window at 110 Columbia Heights, using binoculars or a telescope to watch the work in progress.

Among those at work on the bridge down below was a sixteen-year-old Irish boy named Frank Harris, author in later years of *My Life and Loves*. Harris wrote of the disease that afflicted all who worked in the caissons:

> In a bare shed where we got ready, the men told me no one could do the work for long without getting the "bends" . . . When we went into the "air-lock" and they turned on one air-cock after another of compressed air, the men put their hands to their ears and I soon imitated them, for the pain was acute . . .
>
> When the air was fully compressed, the door of the air-lock opened at a touch and we all went down to work with pick and shovel on the gravelly bottom . . . The six of us were working naked to the waist in a small iron chamber with a temperature of about 80 degrees Fahrenheit: in five minutes the sweat was pouring from us, and all the while we were standing in icy water that was only kept from rising by the terrific pressure. No wonder the headaches were blinding. The men didn't work for more than ten minutes at a time, but I plugged on steadily, resolved to prove myself and get constant employment . . .

Had Harris been able to last, he would have earned enough in a month to live on for a year. But after the fifth or sixth day he was told he might be going deaf. A few days later, after seeing one of the men fall and writhe on the ground with blood spurting from his nose and mouth, he quit.

The bridge was completed at great human cost, but has perhaps repaid its debt better than other similar structures. In *The Brown Decades*, Lewis Mumford wrote: "A stunning act was necessary to demonstrate the aesthetic possibilities of the new materials . . . That act was the building of the Brooklyn Bridge — not merely one of the best pieces of engineering the 19th century can show anywhere but perhaps the most completely satisfactory structure of any kind that had appeared in America." In addition to being an immense architectural achievement, the bridge became an inspiration and a potent symbol to many.

One of the first to use its meaning in a work of art was Hart

Hart Crane on the roof of 110 Columbia Heights
with the Brooklyn Bridge in the background.

Crane, who in 1924 went to live in the very same house Washington Roebling had occupied. Crane previously had moved from one furnished room to another in the Village and was in constant search of more permanent inexpensive living quarters. A meeting with a young ship's steward named Emil Opffer seemed to offer a solution. Opffer's family had several rooms in a building that had been formed by connecting 110 Columbia Heights with the two adjoining houses at 106 and 108. An art school occupied the lower floors, and apartments and rooms were rented out upstairs. Opffer, who was to become Crane's intimate friend, suggested that the poet move to his building. Crane's room was on the fourth floor but he mistakenly fantasized that it was the very same one from which Roebling had directed the construction of the bridge. The view fascinated him. "Everytime one looks at the harbor and the New York skyline across the river it is quite different," he wrote, "and the range of atmospheric effects is almost endless. But at twilight on a foggy evening . . . it is beyond description. Gradually the lights in the enormously tall buildings begin to flicker through the mist . . . And up at the right Brooklyn Bridge, the most superb piece of construction in the modern world, I'm sure, with strings of light crossing it like glowing worms as the Ls and surface cars pass each other going and coming."

The bridge, finally, was the catalyst that caused the elements of the long poem he had been working on, eventually called *The Bridge,* to fall in place. The same perceptions found their way into the poem:

> O harp and altar, of the fury fused,
> (How could mere toil align thy choiring strings!)
> Terrific threshold of the prophet's pledge,
> Prayer of pariah, and the lover's cry, —
>
> Again the traffic lights that skim thy swift
> Unfractioned idiom, immaculate sigh of stars,

Beading thy path — condense eternity:
And we have seen night lifted in thine arms.

Emil, the bridge, Roebling's house together created for Crane a rare period of contentment and relative tranquility. Nevertheless, there were still drunken binges. John Dos Passos, who also had a room in 106–110 Columbia Heights, sometimes met Crane walking home across the bridge late at night after a round of Village parties. Appalled by the poet's generally disheveled, drunken state, Dos Passos would implore him to go home to bed. To avoid arguing, Crane would pretend to comply and then sneak back down the stairs to prowl among the bars along Sands Street near the navy yard.

Crane's stay in this room, interrupted by occasional travels, continued until 1929. He then took a trip to Europe, where Harry and Caresse Crosby encouraged him to complete *The Bridge* for publication by their Black Sun Press in France. When he returned, he moved to 130 Columbia Heights. On December 7, 1929, he gave a party attended by William Carlos Williams, Malcolm and Peggy Cowley, E. E. Cummings and the Crosbys to celebrate the near completion of the poem. On the day after Christmas he finished it.

Since Crane, the bridge has impressed its symbolism on many others. Marianne Moore, who lived near the Heights in Clinton Hill for many years, habitually took the Manhattan Bridge when crossing the East River to get a better view of the Roeblings' masterpiece. "Brooklyn Bridge," she wrote, recalling their sacrifices, "is synonymous with endurance . . . It was opened May 24, 1883 — a stern triumph, this feat — memorialized by the cables, towers, and centrally fixed arcs of filament united by stress, refined till diaphanous when seen from the Manhattan Bridge, silhouetted by the sun or the moon."

Arthur Miller, who used to walk home over the bridge from

Midtown when he lived in the Heights, has said that it was impossible not to respond to its symbolism. "It was so esthetically pleasing, such a wonderful model of how a utilitarian device could be done so beautifully. It seemed to hold a certain promise that we could build a society that would work and that would be inspiring at the same time. It is the most beautiful structure I know."

.

If Brooklyn Heights belonged to Hart Crane in the twenties, it was Thomas Wolfe's in the thirties. Where Crane had sought love, Wolfe fled it; he moved to the Heights to avoid Aline Bernstein, who for many years had encouraged and nurtured his writing. His first home was a few blocks away from the Heights at 40 Verandah Place. He described his apartment, which consisted of a high-ceilinged bedroom and, beneath it, a study opening onto a little garden, in *You Can't Go Home Again:* "The place may seem to you more like a dungeon than a room that a man would voluntarily elect to live in. It is long and narrow, running parallel to the hall from front to rear, and the only natural light that enters it comes through two small windows rather high up in the wall, facing each other at the opposite ends, and these are heavily guarded with iron bars . . ."

Wolfe left Verandah Place for the less miserable precincts of the Heights in October 1931. His first address was 111 Columbia Heights, one of a pair of Greek Revival row houses that have survived. He reported to his mother that he had "an entire floor — two big sunny rooms, a big fine kitchen, a good bath room." By August of 1932, he had moved again, this time a few doors away to 101 Columbia Heights. He wrote his mother that he had two "very nice rooms, a bath, and a kitchen, and although the place is not as big as the place I had

Thomas Wolfe with the manuscript of *Of Time and the River* in his Montague Terrace apartment.

before, it is cleaner and more modern and more private. The owners put in an electric icebox for me and the rent is $15 a month lower than it was at the other place. In addition, the place is cool and I have a very nice view of New York harbor and of the skyscrapers . . ."

Wolfe remained at 101 Columbia Heights until October of 1933, when he moved to 5 Montague Terrace, one of a row of seven brownstone houses. Here he did the final work on *Of Time and the River*. He lived on the fourth floor and had a large living room and moderate-sized bedroom. A visitor described the apartment:

> The chief piece of furniture was an old table, work worn and ancient but still sturdy. It was marked by many cigarette burns and its surface was dented like a shield after a hard battle . . . At the right, as one entered, and opposite the windows, was one alcove containing a gas range and another with an electric refrigerator which bumped and hummed as refrigerators did then. Tom claimed that this sound stimulated him by its rhythm. On the old table and on this refrigerator he did most of his writing . . . The adjoining bedroom contained a cot, an old battered bureau, and a straight chair.

In 1934, after an interview that mentioned his address, Wolfe was forced to give up this apartment. The day the article appeared fans began swarming to the building and Wolfe moved out of Brooklyn into a hotel.

•

Early in the 1940s, one address in Brooklyn Heights — 7 Middagh Street — became the gathering place for an extraordinary collection of people. George Davis, literary editor of *Harper's Bazaar*, claimed the house had appeared to him in a dream one night when he still lived in Manhattan. The next day he went to Brooklyn Heights and found it, exact in every detail.

Carson McCullers in Central Park, 1941.

By fortunate coincidence, it was for rent. He called his friend
Carson McCullers, who had just decided to leave her husband,
and asked if she wanted to take the house with him. She agreed,
and they soon found a third in W. H. Auden. In the beginning, the housekeeping chores fell to McCullers as the only
regular female occupant. Sometimes, with the assistance of
Auden (she always pronounced Wystan "Winston"), she cooked
dishes she had learned to make as a child in Columbus, Georgia.
Later their friend Gypsy Rose Lee found them a cook — a

former Cotton Club chorine. Auden collected the rents "as
George Davis was rather shy about money matters." He recalled that he "paid $25 a month for a floor, and I imagine
the others paid about the same." According to Auden, the
permanent residents included George Davis, Carson McCullers,
theatrical designer Oliver Smith, Golo Mann (Thomas Mann's
son), Jane and Paul Bowles and himself. "Then there were
those who came fairly often for a few days, Benjamin Britten,
Peter Pears, Louis MacNeice. And then there were those who
may have spent a night or two, like Christopher Isherwood.
Gypsy Rose Lee, who at that time was engaged to George Davis,
was a frequent visitor (as was Tchelitchev) but never, so far
as I can recall, stayed there. The 'permanents' had floors and
there was usually a room or two for transients." Others —
Anaïs Nin, Lincoln Kirstein, Leonard Bernstein, Salvador Dali,
Marc Blitzstein and Aaron Copland — came for an evening
or two.

Richard Wright, his wife and child, lived on the parlor floor
and in the basement for a time in 1940, but didn't stay long
enough to be considered permanent residents. The house
didn't suit them; as Anaïs Nin reported: "When he [George
Davis] invited them to live in his house, there were difficulties
with the neighbors. His superintendent, a faithful Negro who
had tended the furnace, resigned because he would not tend
a furnace for another Negro." In addition, the Wrights were
unhappy in what they considered an atmosphere of "general
overstimulation and excitement." Eventually Wright told his
wife, "This is not a proper environment in which to raise a
child," and they moved.

In her *Diary,* Anaïs Nin has recorded something of the physical character of 7 Middagh: "An amazing house, like some of
the houses in Belgium, the north of France, or Austria. He
[George Davis] filled it with old American furniture, oil lamps,

brass beds, little coffee tables, old drapes, copper lamps, old cupboards, heavy dining tables of oak, lace doilies, grandfather clocks. It is like a museum of Americana . . ." Though the name never took, Nin called it February House because she, Auden, George Davis and Carson McCullers were all born in February.

The best descriptions of 7 Middagh and its environs remain those of Carson McCullers: "The street where I now live has a quietness and sense of permanence that seem to belong to the nineteenth century. The street is very short. At one end, there are comfortable old houses, with gracious façades and pleasant back-yards in the rear." Like Hart Crane, McCullers was a habitué of Sands Street, where she frequently went at night with George Davis:

> At three o'clock in the morning, when the rest of the city is silent and dark, you can come suddenly on a little area as vivacious as a country fair. It is Sands [sic] Street, the place where sailors spend their evenings when they come here to port. At any hour of the night some excitement is going on in Sands street. The sunburned sailors swagger up and down the side-walks with their girls. The bars are crowded, and there are dancing, music, and straight liquor at cheap prices . . .
>
> In one bar, there is a little hunchback who struts in proudly every evening, and is petted by every one, given free drinks, and treated as a sort of mascot by the proprietor. There is a saying among sailors that when they die they want to go to Sands Street.

Unfortunately, were the sailors' souls to seek out Sands Street today, they would find no traces of it. The gaudy bars have been replaced by undifferentiated apartment-house projects. The hunchback, however, lives on in Carson McCullers's portrayal of Cousin Lyman in *The Ballad of the Sad Café*.

No one has immortalized 7 Middagh in prose or verse. Like

Brooklyn Heights, it provided the conditions rather than the material for creation. Paul Bowles has written: "It was just a nice old house with a comfortable atmosphere and rather uncomfortable furnishings. Each one did his work and minded his business; residents saw one another generally only at mealtimes. Auden sat at the head of the table and conducted the conversations." Jane and Paul Bowles lived on the second floor of the house during the winter of 1940–41. He recalled being in a room with a life-size cut-out photograph of Gypsy Rose Lee, "something from the lobby of a burlesque theatre, standing nearly six feet high."

With its heady assortment of creative people, it is a wonder that 7 Middagh functioned at all. There were arguments, of course, and Bowles's memory of one of them captures some of the spicier tones of the house's atmosphere:

> I remember having measles at Seven Middagh. It was midwinter, and I got grippe immediately after my recovery. I always kept a room to escape to, around the corner, on Columbia Heights, and it was to this room, I suppose, that Auden imagined I would go when he casually remarked to me one evening: "I shall be requiring your room over the weekend." However, I intended to stay in bed over the weekend, and not to stir out of Seven Middagh. I told him this, but he seemed not to want to understand. "I have a friend coming from Michigan, and he will go into your room." When I stated clearly that I was not giving up my room to anybody for any reason, Auden turned very white and went downstairs and out into the street, slamming the front door violently. I decided Auden disliked me because I was a Stalinist. (There was great feeling at the time between pro-Moscow Marxists and anti-Moscow Marxists.) From then on I would not let anything be said at the table without giving the Party's viewpoint on the subject; I knew this would annoy my antagonist rather more than anything else. It certainly made for unpleasant meals.

Bowles seems to have regarded himself as the stepchild of 7 Middagh. He recalled also that "Benjamin Britten used the big piano in the salon on the first floor, and I installed an upright in the coal room behind the furnace in the cellar, where it was both freezing and airless."

The household at 7 Middagh lasted for about five years. Following the death of her father, Carson McCullers took a house with her mother and sister in Nyack. Finally, in 1945, the entire block where the house stood was condemned for the construction of a wider access to the Brooklyn-Queens Expressway and the last residents moved out.

.

During the same period, unaware of the unusual ménage at Middagh Street, the young Arthur Miller had come to live in the Heights. His first home was an ornate apartment house crazily adorned with round rooms, towers and cupolas at 62 Montague Street. It was 1940 and Miller had just returned from the University of Michigan and gotten married to Mary Grace Slattery. He and his wife shared her seven-room apartment with her roommates. "We lived there because it was the cheapest place in New York," he recalled. "It was about eighty dollars a month for the whole apartment." The poet Willard Maas and his wife, filmmaker Marie Menken, were residents of a duplex in the same building; their home was the scene of frequent literary parties until their deaths in the early 1970s.

From Montague, the Millers moved to 18 Schermerhorn Street, one of the first Heights houses to be remodeled and converted into apartments. There the rent was thirty dollars a month, and Norman Rosten, a friend of Miller's from the University of Michigan, also lived in the building. Miller's window looked out on the backyard of a mosque. "I used to sit and watch the Moslems holding services," Miller wrote. "They had a real Moorish garden symmetrically planted with curving lines of white stones laid out in the earth, and they would sit in white robes — twenty or thirty of them, eating at a long table, and served by their women who wore the flowing purple and rose togas of the East."

In 1944 Miller moved to a duplex at 102 Pierrepont Street, which harbored another then unknown author. As Miller remembered it, "The rooms were very dark — wood-paneled. It had been a very elaborate home. We never could see anything. Norman Mailer lived upstairs, but much of the time he was away at war." Here, after the war, Mailer, who lived with his parents, wrote *The Naked and the Dead* and Miller wrote *All My Sons.*

In 1947 Miller bought 31 Grace Court and there wrote *Death of a Salesman.* In 1951 he bought one of the Heights' architectural prizes, a charming Federal brick row house at 155 Willow Street, and sold the Grace Court house to W. E. B. Du Bois. "We couldn't have rented here," Du Bois remarked at the time. "We had to buy. When we first came, the FBI swarmed around the neighborhood asking questions." Du Bois, who had joined the Communist party publicly, lived there until 1961.

During his time in Brooklyn Heights, Miller "never gravitated toward a society of writers." He was far more likely to explore the livelier neighborhoods just beyond the Heights. "I loved walking along the waterfront," he recalled. "When I got interested in the longshoremen, I spent a lot of time in Red Hook around Columbia Street. There was a movement at the time to rid the union of racketeers . . . I knew a newly graduated lawyer involved in that struggle. There were lots of murders, bodies dropping into the river in concrete slabs. He called me. He thought I could get some publicity in the papers. Then I became a supernumerary of that movement." Miller's experience in Red Hook gave him the background for *A View from the Bridge* and the young lawyer furnished part of the characterization of Alfieri.

In spite of his solitary habits, Miller did visit his old friend Norman Rosten, who had moved to 84 Remsen Street, where he still lives. Miller met Carl Sandburg at the Rostens' and went with Rosten to visit Louis Untermeyer, who had moved from Manhattan to the top floor of 88 Remsen Street next door. Robert Frost was there that evening and Rosten described the occasion: "Everybody tried to hold forth and Frost wouldn't let anybody have the floor. Frost was a very opinionated guy who knew that he was immortal. He was the only man I knew who could take the floor away from Untermeyer." Remsen Street had had another writer as resident when Henry Miller lived at 91 in 1924. He had quit his job and was writing full-time. In a letter to Anaïs Nin he reminisced about the apartment "where I refused to clutter the place with furniture, where I moved the bed or divan into the middle of the big open room and thought I was in Japan all the time, everything so clean, so polished, so decorative, so bare."

.

After Columbia Heights, Willow Street has probably housed more literary people than any other Brooklyn Heights thoroughfare. Down the block from Miller's former home is 128 Willow, one of the Heights' few apartment buildings, where Norman Mailer lived before moving to 142 Columbia Heights. Hart Crane stayed at 77 Willow for a short time in 1928, and 22 Willow was once the home of Henry Ward Beecher.

Marianne Moore, a frequent visitor to the Heights, wrote fondly of the street. "At No. 27 there is still one remaining willow, all curves and angles as though by Harunobu. Willow became official, it is *said,* when a Miss Middagh, undetected, substituted for the name 'Jones,' shingles on which she had painstakingly inscribed 'Willow' . . . On Willow Street the doors are black or green, their brass knobs complementing the old-style italic numeral in gold leaf on glass above the door. The numeral is usually repeated, one above the left and one above the right double door, with a gold dot between." One of the most impressive houses on Willow Street is number 70, the home of theatrical designer Oliver Smith and, for a time, his basement tenant, Truman Capote. Unlike the attached row houses that predominate on the Heights, this grand residence was originally surrounded by open space on all sides. Capote described how the house looked to him one night in 1957 when Smith invited him to visit:

> I was most impressed; exceedingly envious. There were twenty-eight rooms, high-ceilinged, well proportioned, and twenty-eight workable, marble-manteled fireplaces. There was a beautiful staircase floating upward in white, swan-simple curves to a skylight of sunny amber-gold glass. The floors were fine, the real thing, hard lustrous timber; and the walls! In 1820, when the house was built, men knew how to make walls — thick as a buffalo, immune to the mightiest cold, the meanest heat.
>
> French doors led to a spacious rear porch reminiscent of Louisiana. A porch canopied, completely submerged, as though under a lake of leaves, by an ancient but admirably vigorous vine weighty with grapelike bunches of wisteria. Beyond, a garden! a tulip tree, a blossoming pear, a perched black-and-red bird bending a feathery branch of forsythia.

Capote convinced Smith to let him live in part of the house and he set up housekeeping in the five-room basement apartment where he was to write *Breakfast at Tiffany's* and *In Cold Blood.* There was a bedroom that opened onto the garden, a kitchen with its floor painted lemon yellow and a Victorian parlor containing all Capote's personal treasures. Hanging over the sofa was a pair of gold mirrors in the shape of butterflies; on polished tables and bamboo bookcases were a golden Easter egg brought back from Russia, an iron dog, a Fabergé pillbox, blue ceramic fruit, a coquille bouquet, Battersea boxes, marbles, paperweights, old photographs — one of Capote with Jane and Paul Bowles in Africa — and, propped up in a corner, a Spanish saint.

Capote regularly took a walk that led past "a ghost hotel" down to the waterfront. "In aggravated moments," he wrote of the hotel, "I imagine retiring there, for it is as secluded as Mt. Athos, remoter than the Krak Chevalier in the mountains of wildest Syria. Daytimes the location, a dead-end Chiricoesque piazza facing the river, is little disturbed; at night, not at all; not a sound, except foghorns and a distant traffic whisper from the bridge which bulks above. Peace, and the shivering glow of gliding-by tugs and ferries." The hotel still stands at 1 Water Street. From here, Capote would walk along the waterfront past "silent miles of warehouses with shuttered wooden windows, docks resting on the water like sea spiders," past ships and the men who work on them. "Every kind of sailor is common enough here," he noted. "Even saronged East Indians, even the giant Senegalese, their onyx arms afire with blue, with yellow tattooed flowers, with saucy torsos and garish graffiti . . . Runty Russians, too — one sees them flapping in their pajama-like costumes."

Like Capote, many of the Heights residents of the fifties and sixties have departed. Alfred Kazin, who lived at 91 Pineapple Street in 1952, moved to the city; Louis Untermeyer to the country. But some have stayed, and there are always new, young writers to replace those who have left. Among the most loyal have been Norman Mailer and Norman Rosten. During

Norman Mailer standing beneath the gabled work area in
his Brooklyn Heights house.

the forties Rosten had a furnished room he used for writing in a house at 20 Remsen Street. Mailer took over the studio for a while when he came back from the war and then used a room in the Ovington Building at 246 Fulton Street. At that time he had already written *Barbary Shore,* which concerned a writer who became involved with a group of spies living in his rooming house. Later Mailer commented:

> . . . Writing about F.B.I. agents and Old Bolsheviks in *Barbary Shore,* the greatest single difficulty with the book was that my common sense thought it was impossible to have all these agents and impossible heroes congregating in a rooming house in Brooklyn Heights. Yet a couple of years later I was working in a studio on Fulton Street . . . On the floor below me, worked one Colonel Rudolph Abel, who was the most important spy for the Russians in this country for a period of about eight or ten years, and I am sure we used to be in the elevator together many times. I think he literally had the room beneath me.

Mailer now lives in the upper two floors of a brownstone at 142 Columbia Heights, where he has designed a unique work place: "Lofty, tenting, glass-and-wood gable that he pushed right through his roof like a small pyramid. Inside this structure, it is like a ship's forecastle. There are many different ways to reach many upper levels, but none of them is easy: climbing ropes, boarding nets, trapezes, deck ladders, catwalks and, for those who wish to rest halfway, a rope hammock slung between two beams over the dried-out skeletons of dead sea skates that roll like mobiles in the cross-ventilation below." Mailer's carrel "is tucked way up under the peak of the gable, its only ingress being a 6-inch-wide plank across the long drop down to the patrolling sea skates below. A lot of important people have bothered to inch their way across that plank for a visit, but what Norman really appreciates is any

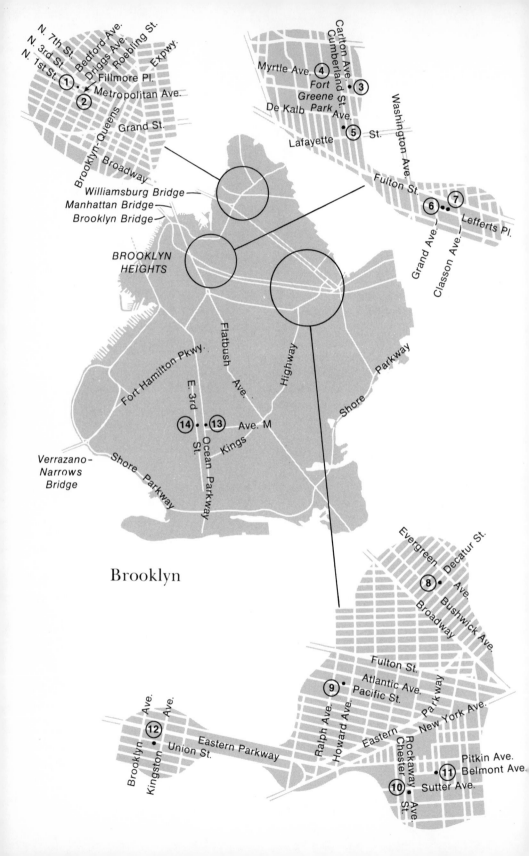

N. 7th St.
N. 3rd St.
N. 1st St.
Bedford Ave.
Driggs Ave.
Roebling St.
Expwy.
① ● Fillmore Pl.
② ↙ Metropolitan Ave.
Brooklyn-Queens
Grand St.
Broadway

Carlton Ave.
Cumberland St.
Myrtle Ave. ④
Fort ●
Greene ③
Park ⑦
De Kalb Ave. ●
⑤
Lafayette
Washington Ave.
St.
Fulton St.
⑥ ● ⑦
Lefferts Pl.
Grand Ave.
Classon Ave.

Williamsburg Bridge
Manhattan Bridge
Brooklyn Bridge

BROOKLYN
HEIGHTS

Fort Hamilton Pkwy.
Flatbush Ave.
Highway
Shore
Parkway

Verrazano-
Narrows
Bridge

Shore Parkway

E. 3rd St.
⑭ ● ⑬
Ocean Parkway
Kings
Ave. M

Brooklyn

Evergreen
Decatur St.
⑧ ●
Ave.
Bushwick Ave.
Broadway

Fulton St.
Atlantic Ave.
⑨ ●
Pacific St.
Parkway

Ave.
Ave.
⑫ ●
Brooklyn
Kingston
Union St.
Eastern Parkway
Ralph Ave.
Howard Ave.
Eastern
New York Ave.
Rockaway Ave.
Chester St.
Pitkin Ave.
⑪ Belmont Ave.
⑩ ● Sutter Ave.

cat sure-footed enough to cool it without using the handholds along the gable roof."

Today, in addition to Rosten and Mailer, writers James Purdy and Frank Conroy also live in the Heights. Undoubtedly, they will not be the last, for as Carson McCullers noted, "Comparing the Brooklyn that I know with Manhattan is like comparing a comfortable and complacent duenna to her more brilliant and neurotic sister." The Heights offers qualities writers have always valued — beauty, quiet, privacy, tradition and a sense of community.

Brooklyn Tour

Henry Miller spent his childhood at 662 Driggs Avenue (1) between North 1st Street and Metropolitan Avenue. The three-story brick house in which he lived is still standing. Diagonally across the way is Fillmore Place (2), Miller's favorite street. Most of the three-and-a-half-story brick row houses from Miller's time remain today, although one can see the gaps he compared to missing teeth.

Fort Greene has several literary landmarks. At 175 Carlton Avenue (3) is the house where Richard Wright began *Native Son*. The old three-and-a-half-story brick house is deserted and may not be standing long. Every morning Wright went to the top of the hill in Fort Greene Park (4) to write. A row of once magnificent brownstone mansions on Washington Street faces the park; most of the brownstones are now rooming houses. The apartment building where Marianne Moore lived for thirty-four years, the Cumberland, is up the street from the park at 260 Cumberland Street (5). The six-story building has bay windows and inlaid tile mosaics. The iron stands with the "mothballs" Moore described to George Plimpton are gone.

The Lafayette Presbyterian Church where she attended regularly twice a week is around the corner at Lafayette Avenue and South Oxford Street.

After living in Fort Greene, Richard Wright moved to 87 Lefferts Place (6), between Grand and Classon avenues. The house is a three-and-a-half-story brownstone with bay windows and an attractive iron fence. A short distance down the street at number 89 is the four-story brick apartment house (7) where Wright lived from 1943 to 1945.

At the age of ten Henry Miller moved to what he called "the street of early sorrows," 1063 Decatur Street (8) between Bushwick and Evergreen avenues. His house has been replaced by a school. The cobblestones he described can be seen in places where the asphalt has worn off the neighborhood streets.

Norman Podhoretz's Brownsville home is still standing at 2027 Pacific Street (9), a four-story brick apartment house between Howard Place and Ralph Avenue. Alfred Kazin's building on the southeast corner of Chester Street and Sutter Avenue has recently suffered a fire. Sheets of tin close up the entranceway where Kazin lived at 256A Sutter (10). The Belmont market on Belmont Avenue between Thatford and Stone avenues (11) is a reminder of the Jewish neighborhood that once flourished in Brownsville. Reminiscent of the Orchard Street market on the Lower East Side, with its push-carts and open stands, the Belmont market still has kosher butchers and Jewish-owned stores among those advertising *ropa para toda la familia* and *acceptamos cupones de comida*.

John Oliver Killens has lived for over fifteen years on Union Street near Kingston Avenue (12). He wrote, "Softly silent is our tree-lined block, save for the squealing laughter of children, the chirping of birds, the chattering of crazy crickets and the gentle rustling of wind in the trees that made the world around our house sound like continuous summer showers."

Arthur Miller grew up in the area bordered by Avenue J and Avenue M, Ocean Parkway and Gravesend Avenue (today McDonald Avenue). Miller's first Brooklyn address was a two-story brick house at 1277 Ocean Parkway (13). The second one, on which Willy Loman's house in *Death of a Salesman* was modeled, was a small house at 1350 East 3rd (14), a dead-end street.

Brooklyn Heights Tour

Brooklyn Heights' earliest literary resident was Thomas Paine, who stayed at the home of John Harmer at the corner of Sands and Fulton streets (1). *Leaves of Grass* was printed in 1855 in a shop on the southwest corner of Cranberry and what was then Fulton Street (2). This brick building, which housed a luncheonette in recent years, was torn down in 1964. At the same time Fulton Street, from the river to Court Street, was changed to Cadman Plaza West. Alfred Kazin was living at 91 Pineapple Street (3) in 1952. Henry Ward Beecher's church, today known as Plymouth Church of the Pilgrims, still stands on Orange Street off Hicks (4). 7 Middagh Street, where W. H. Auden, Carson McCullers and Jane and Paul Bowles lived in the early 1940s, was on the north side of Middagh between Willow and Columbia Heights (5), but the house was torn down during the war to make way for the Brooklyn-Queens Expressway.

Henry Ward Beecher lived at 22 Willow Street (6), a Greek Revival brick and brownstone house now painted gray, in 1848. In front of 27 Willow (7) stands the willow tree that was Marianne Moore's favorite. The wide yellow Greek Revival house at 70 Willow (8) is the home of theatrical designer

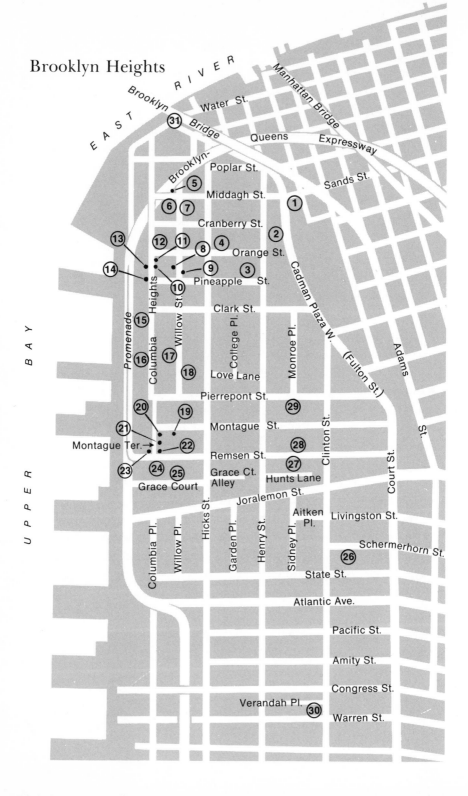

Brooklyn Heights

EAST RIVER

Brooklyn Bridge

Water St.

Manhattan Bridge

Queens Expressway

Sands St.

Poplar St.

Brooklyn-Bridge

(31)

(5)

Middagh St.

(6) (7)

(1)

Cranberry St.

(2)

(13)

(12) (11)

(8) (4)

Orange St.

(14)

(10)

(9) (3)

Pineapple St.

Heights

Willow St.

Clark St.

Cadman Plaza W.

(Fulton St.)

Adams St.

(15)

College Pl.

Monroe Pl.

Promenade

Columbia

(16) (17)

(18)

Love Lane

UPPER BAY

Pierrepont St.

(20)

(29)

(19)

Montague St.

(21)

Clinton St.

Montague Ter.→

(22)

(28)

(23)

(24) (25)

Remsen St.

(27)

Grace Ct. Alley

Hunts Lane

Grace Court

Joralemon St.

Court St.

Columbia Pl.

Willow Pl.

Hicks St.

Garden Pl.

Henry St.

Sidney Pl.

Aitken Pl.

Livingston St.

Schermerhorn St.

(26)

State St.

Atlantic Ave.

Pacific St.

Amity St.

Congress St.

Verandah Pl.

(30)

Warren St.

Oliver Smith. Truman Capote wrote *Breakfast at Tiffany's* and *In Cold Blood* in the basement apartment here. Hart Crane lived in the brownstone at 77 Willow (9) in 1928.

Most of the noteworthy houses on Columbia Heights are still standing and can be seen from the promenade. Thomas Wolfe lived at 111 Columbia Heights (10) in 1931. The following year he lived at number 101 (11), which has been replaced by high-rise buildings of the Jehovah's Witnesses. At various times the guests at the Hotel Margaret (12) have included H. G. Wells and Sigrid Undset. The home of Washington Roebling at 110 Columbia Heights (13) was also the residence of Hart Crane in 1924 and John Dos Passos in 1929. The house where Crane finished *The Bridge* at 130 Columbia Heights (14) has fallen to another of the Jehovah's Witnesses' buildings. Norman Mailer lives at 142 Columbia Heights (15), and 176 (16) was the home of Henry Ward Beecher from 1851 to 1855.

Back on Willow Street at number 128 (17) is the apartment house where Norman Mailer lived before moving to Columbia Heights. The landmark house Arthur Miller owned from 1951 to 1956 is at 155 Willow Street (18). A plaque designates the house and its attached neighbors at 157 and 159. The carriage house at 151 was once connected to Miller's house by an underground passage, and the glass panes of the passage's skylight can be seen near the gate to 157.

Another Arthur Miller address is the strange, ornate apartment house at 62 Montague Street (19), where the author lived in 1940. The east side of Montague Terrace is a "terrace" in the English sense, meaning a row of houses. W. H. Auden lived at number 1 (20), Thomas Wolfe at number 5 (21) and Jules Feiffer at number 11 (22). Maxwell Bodenheim lived directly across the street at number 10 (23), where he would work on the white balcony in his living room. The balcony can be seen from the street.

At the end of Montague Terrace stands 20 Remsen Street (24), where Norman Rosten and Norman Mailer consecutively used the same studio. Around on the other side of the block is 31 Grace Court (25), which was owned by Arthur Miller from 1947 to 1951 and by W. E. B. Du Bois from 1951 to 1961. Until it was covered with stucco and remodeled, the house was probably a mate to the Renaissance Revival building next door at number 29. In the early forties Miller had lived at 18 Schermerhorn Street (26), one of the first houses on the Heights to be remodeled and converted into apartments. In 1944 he moved to the brownstone at 102 Pierrepont Street (29), where Norman Mailer lived upstairs with his parents. Louis Untermeyer lived at 88 Remsen Street (27) in the early fifties, and Henry Miller lived at 91 Remsen Street (28) in 1924.

Beyond the strict limits of the Heights are two associated landmarks. Thomas Wolfe's first home in the area was 40 Verandah Place (30), an old three-story brick house on an alley running between Clinton and Henry streets about four blocks south of Atlantic Avenue. The hotel Truman Capote imagines retiring to is at 1 Water Street (31).

Notes
Index

Notes

I. Lower Manhattan (pages 1–34)

page

1 "After a hundred . . ." Lawrence C. Wroth, *The Voyages of Giovanni da Verrazzano: 1524–1528* (New Haven: Yale University Press, 1970), pp. 85–86.

2 "Safe from the fury . . ." Rodman Gilder, *The Battery* (Boston: Houghton Mifflin Co., 1936), p. 3.

3 "See, two streams . . ." Meyer Berger, *Meyer Berger's New York* (New York: Random House, 1960), pp. 37–38.

6 "What a contrast . . ." William Smith, quoted in Moses Coit Tyler, *A History of American Literature, 1607–1783,* abridged and edited by Archie H. Jones (Chicago: University of Chicago Press), p. 116.

"I offered my services . . ." Benjamin Franklin, *The Autobiography of Benjamin Franklin and Selections from His Other Writings* (New York: Random House, Modern Library, 1950), p. 26.

"a monkey of the . . ." Edward Ellis, *The Epic of New York City* (New York: Coward McCann, 1966), p. 120.

8 "all you have to do . . ." reprinted in *The American Literary Revolution: 1783–1837,* edited by Robert E. Spiller (New York: Doubleday & Co., 1967), p. 6.

9 "a free newspaper . . ." Lewis Leary, *That Rascal Freneau* (New Brunswick: Rutgers University Press, 1941), p. 14.

"He was regarded . . ." Vernon Louis Parrington, *Main Currents in American Thought* (New York: Harcourt, Brace & Co., 1958), p. 328.

11 "Both were staunch . . ." Alfred Owen Aldridge, *Man of Reason: The Life of Thomas Paine* (Philadelphia: Lippincott Co., 1959), p. 295.

12 "It was exceedingly pleasant . . ." Spiller, *American Literary Revolution,* p. 225.

page

13   "DISTRESSING" and all subsequent quotations from the hoax, Washington Irving, *Diedrich Knickerbocker's History of New York* (New York: The Heritage Press, 1940), pp. xv–xvi.

17   "one of two recently . . ." Susan Cooper, "Small Family Memories" (1883), in *Correspondence of James Fenimore Cooper,* edited by his grandson James Fenimore Cooper (New Haven: Yale University Press, 1922), p. 48.

"The number of rats . . ." Cooper, *Correspondence,* p. 53.

"the bark of the cinnamon . . ." William Cullen Bryant, "Discourse on the Life, Genius, and Writings of J. Fenimore Cooper," in James Fenimore Cooper's *Precaution and Ways of the Hour* (Boston: C. T. Brainard Publishing Co., n.d.), pp. 32–33.

19   "the disagreeable, disgusting drudgery . . ." John Bigelow, *William Cullen Bryant* (New York: Arno and the *New York Times,* 1970), p. 62.

20   "is the strong temptation . . ." Allan Nevins, *The Evening Post: A Century of Journalism* (New York: Russell & Russell, 1968), p. 350.

21   "he believed that . . ." John Bigelow, quoted in Charles Brown, *William Cullen Bryant* (New York: Charles Scribner's Sons, 1971), note p. 250.

"I do not know . . ." Bigelow in Brown, *Bryant,* p. 292.

"Cooper, burly, brusque . . ." Nevins, *The Evening Post,* p. 191.

"As Audubon . . ." Van Wyck Brooks and Otto L. Bettmann, *Our Literary Heritage: A Pictorial History of the Writer in America* (New York: E. P. Dutton & Co., 1965), p. 40.

22   "The face of the island . . ." Asa Greene, *A Glance at New York* (New York: A. Greene, 1837), pp. 1–2.

"As certain kings . . ." Greene, *A Glance at New York,* p. 152.

23   "To the Readers . . ." Nevins, *The Evening Post,* p. 159.

24   "Coming up Broadway . . ." Joseph Jay Rubin and Charles H. Brown, *Walt Whitman of the New York Aurora* (State College, Pa.: Bald Eagle Press, 1950), p. 18.

25   "a strange, natural . . ." Walt Whitman, *Specimen Days* (New York: E. P. Dutton & Co., n.d.), p. 19.

"Mannahatta," Walt Whitman, *Leaves of Grass and Selected Prose,* edited by Sculley Bradley (New York: Rinehart & Co., 1949), p. 413.

"Leading traits . . ." Gay Wilson Allen, *The Solitary Singer: A Critical Biography of Walt Whitman* (New York: Macmillan, 1955), p. 103.

page

26 "very kindly and human . . ." Perry Miller, *The Raven and the Whale* (New York: Harcourt, Brace & Co., 1956), p. 148.

27 "I have been roaming . . ." Edgar Allan Poe, *Doings of Gotham,* collected by Jacob E. Spannuth, with preface, introduction and comments by Thomas O. Mabbott (Pottsville, Pa.: J. E. Spannuth, 1929), Letter I, p. 25.

28 "In a week . . ." Jay Leyda, *The Melville Log, A Documentary Life of Herman Melville, 1819–1891,* Vol. 1 (New York: Harcourt, Brace & Co., 1951), p. 414.

29 Murray speculates . . . Herman Melville, *Pierre; or, the Ambiguities,* edited by Henry A. Murray (New York: Hendricks House, 1962), p. 484.

"Another scholar . . . Correspondence with Hans Bergmann.

30 "the multitudinous . . ." Henry James, *The American Scene* (New York: Charles Scribner's Sons, 1946), p. 76.

"the new landmarks . . ." James, *The American Scene,* p. 81.

"the special skyscraper . . ." James, *The American Scene,* p. 83.

"'Jimmy the Priest's' . . ." Louis Sheaffer, *O'Neill, Son and Playwright* (Boston: Little, Brown & Co., 1968), p. 190.

32 "a receptacle of all the . . ." Gilder, *The Battery,* p. 75.

"a small country jail . . ." Poe, *Doings of Gotham,* p. 26.

II. Greenwich Village (pages 35–110)

The Nineteenth-Century Village: Washington Square

35 "It has a kind . . ." Henry James, *Washington Square* (New York: Random House, Modern Library, 1950), p. 22.

37 "too magnificent . . ." James Fenimore Cooper, *The Letters and Journals of James Fenimore Cooper,* edited by James Franklin Beard (Cambridge: Harvard University Press, 1964), p. 4.

39 "I suppose the Knights . . ." Letter of Melville to Duyckinck, November 7, 1851, Duyckinck Collection, New York Public Library.

40 "The grey and . . ." Henry James, *The American Scene* (New York: Charles Scribner's Sons, 1946), p. 91.

"a stout red-faced . . ." Henry James, *A Small Boy and Others* (New York: Charles Scribner's Sons, 1913), p. 17.

41 "in 'grounds' peopled . . ." James, *A Small Boy and Others,* p. 24.

"the ideal of quiet . . ." James, *Washington Square,* p. 21.

page

42 "was as if the wine . . ." James, *The American Scene*, p. 88.

43 "I was a failure . . ." Edith Wharton, *A Backward Glance: The Autobiography of Edith Wharton* (New York: Charles Scribner's Sons, 1962), p. 119.

"The Jameses were . . ." Louis Auchincloss, *Edith Wharton, A Woman In Her Time* (New York: Viking Press, 1971), p. 12.

"then just within . . ." Wharton, *A Backward Glance*, p. 18.

45 " 'purest 1830,' with . . ." Edith Wharton, *The Age of Innocence* (New York: Random House, Modern Library, [c.] 1920), p. 24.

47 "One could never begin . . ." Clara Clemens, *My Father, Mark Twain* (New York: Harper & Brothers, 1931), p. 217.

"his efflorescence . . ." and "Until he imagined . . ." William Dean Howells, *My Mark Twain* (New York: Harper & Brothers, 1910), p. 96.

48 "But all I remember . . ." John Dos Passos, *The Best Times: An Informal Memoir* (New York: New American Library, 1966), p. 14.

"with his white hair . . ." Van Wyck Brooks, *An Autobiography* (New York: E. P. Dutton & Co., 1965), p. 158.

"a self-conscious entity . . ." Max Eastman, *Enjoyment of Living* (New York: Harper & Brothers, 1948), p. 416.

The Birth of Bohemia

49 "do not know how . . ." Roi Ottley and William J. Weatherby, editors, *The Negro in New York* (New York: The New York Public Library, 1967), p. 73.

"Of all the ambitions . . ." Van Wyck Brooks, *The Confident Years: 1885–1915* (New York: E. P. Dutton & Co., 1955), p. 265.

50 "In 1906 . . ." Edith Lewis, *Willa Cather Living* (New York: Alfred A. Knopf, 1953), p. xv.

51 "Forty-Two Washington Square," in Allen Churchill, *The Improper Bohemians* (New York: E. P. Dutton & Co., 1959), p. 37.

"I used to go . . ." Steffens, *Autobiography*, p. 654.

52 "Why don't you . . ." Richard O'Connor and Dale L. Walker, *The Lost Revolutionary: A Biography of John Reed* (New York: Harcourt, Brace & World, 1967), p. 75.

53 "she sat quietly . . ." Steffens, *Autobiography*, p. 655.

56 "You are elected . . ." Churchill, *The Improper Bohemians*, p. 93.

"Voting! . . . Poetry is something . . ." Churchill, *The Improper Bohemians*, p. 108.

page

57 "We had a custom . . ." Eastman, *Enjoyment*, p. 439.

58 "Before O'Neill . . ." Louis Sheaffer, *O'Neill, Son and Playwright* (Boston: Little, Brown & Co., 1968), p. 481.

"that there is always . . ." Interview with Karl Schriftgiesser for the *New York Times* quoted in Crosswell Bowen, *The Curse of the Misbegotten, A Tale of the House of O'Neill* (New York: McGraw-Hill, 1959), p. 310.

61 "It was wonderful . . ." John Dos Passos, *The Fourteenth Chronicle: Letters and Diaries of John Dos Passos*, edited and with a biographical narrative by Townsend Ludington (Boston: Gambit, 1973), p. 75.

62 "We bought gold . . ." Margaret Anderson, *My Thirty Years' War* (New York: Horizon Press, 1969), p. 152.

63 "At auction rooms . . ." Lewis, *Willa Cather*, p. 89.

"so popular, in fact . . ." Lewis, *Willa Cather*, p. 134.

64 "the sounds the leopards . . ." Lewis, *Willa Cather*, p. 139.

66 "The thing that interested me . . ." Theodore Dreiser, *Color of a Great City* (New York: Boni and Liveright, 1923), pp. 1-2.

"the ponderous battering ram . . ." Allen Churchill, *The Literary Decade* (Englewood Cliffs: Prentice-Hall, 1971), p. 18.

67 "with a large eraser . . ." Floyd Dell, *Homecoming, An Autobiography* (New York: Farrar & Rinehart, 1933), p. 269.

68 "I decided I would go . . ." *Sherwood Anderson's Memoirs*, edited by Ray Lewis White (Chapel Hill: University of North Carolina Press, 1942), p. 452.

The Lost Generation

69 "After college and the war . . ." Malcolm Cowley, *Exile's Return: A Literary Saga of the 1920's* (New York: Viking Press, 1951), p. 48.

70 "Marianne had two cords . . ." quoted in Donald Hall, *Marianne Moore, The Cage and the Animal* (New York: Pegasus, 1970), p. 25.

"an astonishing person . . ." Hall, *Marianne Moore*, p. 24.

71 "Lola Ridge had a party . . ." Hall, *Marianne Moore*, p. 57.

"She lived in that . . ." Floyd Dell, *Love in Greenwich Village* (New York: George H. Doran Co., 1926), p. 33.

72 "One cannot really . . ." Edmund Wilson, *The Shores of Light* (New York: Farrar, Straus & Young, Inc., 1952), p. 751.

73 "never a great fan . . ." John Unterecker, *Voyager: A Life of Hart Crane* (New York: Farrar, Straus & Giroux, 1969), p. 89.

page

73 "inquisitive landlady . . ." Hart Crane, *The Letters of Hart Crane, 1916–1932,* edited by Brom Weber (New York: Hermitage House, 1952), pp. 134–35.

74 "Italian speakeasy of the moment . . ." Dos Passos, *The Best Times,* p. 83.

"'4' signifies a delapidated . . ." E. E. Cummings, *Selected Letters of E. E. Cummings,* edited by F. W. Dupee and George Stade (New York: Harcourt, Brace & World, 1969), p. 184.

77 "About nine o'clock . . ." Burton Rascoe, *A Bookman's Daybook,* edited with an introduction by C. Hartley Grattan (New York: Horace Liveright, 1929), p. 28.

"There appeared a slight . . ." Dos Passos, *The Best Times,* p. 139.

78 "accompanied by a wispy . . ." Matthew Josephson, *Life Among the Surrealists* (New York: Holt, Rinehart & Winston, 1962), p. 252.

"disenchanted with the . . ." John L. Stewart, *The Burden of Time: The Fugitives and Agrarians* (Princeton: Princeton University Press, 1965), p. 85.

"We were all writing . . ." Cowley, *Exile's Return,* p. 222.

79 "a foot on the loud . . ." Susan Jenkins Brown, *Robber Rocks* (Middletown: Wesleyan University Press, 1969), p. 26.

80 "If there is a loonier . . ." *A Dial Miscellany,* edited with an introduction by William Wasserstrom (Syracuse: Syracuse University Press, 1963), p. xiv.

"there is far too much . . ." B. L. Reid, *The Man From New York: John Quinn and His Friends* (New York: Oxford University Press, 1968), p. 434.

"it was the best . . ." Wasserstrom, *A Dial Miscellany,* p. xv.

81 "I think of the . . ." Marianne Moore, "The Dial: Part I," *Life and Letters Today,* December 1940, quoted in Frederick J. Hoffman et al., *The Little Magazine: A History and Bibliography* (Princeton: Princeton University Press, 1947), p. 201.

"at the slightest excuse . . ." Dos Passos, *The Best Times,* p. 132.

"small square bleak . . ." John Dos Passos, *Manhattan Transfer* (Boston: Houghton Mifflin Co., 1925), p. 344.

82 "I am living . . ." *Thomas Wolfe's Letters to His Mother Julia Elizabeth Wolfe,* edited by John Skally Terry (New York: Charles Scribner's Sons, 1943), p. 138.

"the sag and lean . . ." Thomas Wolfe, *The Web and the Rock* (New York: Harper & Brothers, 1939), p. 387.

"It is a magnificent . . ." *Wolfe's Letters to His Mother,* pp. 150–51.

page

83 "He loved this old house . . ." Thomas Wolfe, *You Can't Go Home Again* (New York: Grosset & Dunlap, 1940) , p. 26.

"The life of the great . . ." Thomas Wolfe, *The Story of a Novel* (New York: Charles Scribner's Sons, 1949) , p. 28.

84 "About the year 1924 . . ." Cowley, *Exile's Return,* p. 210.

"Greenwich Village Too Costly . . ." Carolyn F. Ware, *Greenwich Village: 1920–1930* (New York: Harper & Row, 1965), p. 21.

"What in Washington . . ." Carl Van Doren, "Elinor Wylie," *Harper's Magazine,* September 1936, p. 360.

85 "the same imperious brows . . ." Louis Untermeyer, *From Another World* (New York: Harcourt, Brace & Co., 1939) , p. 241.

"White faced . . . she . . ." Carl Van Doren, "Elinor Wylie," p. 360.

"then still one . . ." Nancy Hoyt, *Elinor Wylie: The Portrait of An Unknown Lady* (New York: Bobbs-Merrill, 1935) , p. 69.

"That one room . . ." Hoyt, *Elinor Wylie,* p. 69.

86 "a tiny, cheerful apartment . . ." Hoyt, *Elinor Wylie,* p. 90.

"an enormous deal table . . ." Hoyt, *Elinor Wylie,* p. 90.

"in the largest of American . . ." Vincent Sheean, *Dorothy and Red* (Boston: Houghton Mifflin, 1963) , p. 146.

"Red's hospitality was incorrigible . . ." Sheean, *Dorothy and Red,* p. 145.

87 "the most exclusive . . ." Churchill, *The Literary Decade,* p. 272.

"demolished back fences . . ." Mark Van Doren, *The Autobiography of Mark Van Doren* (New York: Harcourt, Brace & Co., 1958), p. 173.

"What first made me . . ." Carl Van Doren, *Three Worlds* (New York: Harper & Brothers, 1936) , p. 208.

88 "I used to walk . . ." E. B. White, *Here Is New York* (New York: Harper & Brothers, 1949) , p. 32.

"I signalized my solidarity . . ." Lionel Trilling, *A Gathering of Fugitives* (Boston: Beacon Press, 1956) , p. 49.

After the Twenties

89 "There is too much . . ." Sherwood Anderson, *Letters of Sherwood Anderson,* selected and edited with an introduction and notes by Howard Mumford Jones in association with Walter B. Rideout (Boston: Little, Brown & Co., 1953) , Letter to Roger Sergel, Dec. 21, 1937.

page

91 "a nice and unusually . . ." *Letters of James Agee to Father Flye* (New York: George Braziller, 1962), p. 65.

92 "so good a novel . . ." Djuna Barnes, *Nightwood* (Norfolk: New Directions, 1961), p. xii.

"I bought the simplest . . ." Anaïs Nin, *The Diary of Anaïs Nin, 1939–1944*, edited and with a preface by Gunther Stuhlmann, (New York: Harcourt Brace & World, 1969), p. 46.

93 "would tolerate no ill . . ." Constance Webb, *Richard Wright: A Biography* (New York: G. P. Putnam's Sons, 1968), p. 236.

"By the time . . ." Fern Marja Eckman, *The Furious Passage of James Baldwin* (New York: M. Evans & Co., 1966), p. 113.

94 "It was a period . . ." Doris Grumbach, *The Company She Kept* (New York: Coward McCann, 1967), p. 73.

"For some of us . . ." William Barrett, "The Truants: 'Partisan Review' in the 40's," *Commentary*, Vol. 57, No. 6, June 1974, p. 49.

"There was a ceaseless flow . . ." Interview with Elizabeth Hardwick, June 13, 1974.

95 "I found myself surrounded . . ." Simone de Beauvoir, *America Day by Day* (New York: Grove Press, 1953), p. 41.

"bad, yellowed paintings . . ." Michael Harrington, "We Few, We Happy Few, We Bohemians," *Esquire*, August 1972, p. 101.

"heterosexuals on the make . . ." Harrington, "We Few," p. 101.

"all it was was . . ." Interview with Gregory Corso, April 1971.

96 "I want you to . . ." Interview with Gregory Corso.

97 "Before the incident . . ." Interview with Ed Fancher, Spring 1971.

"a horrible single room . . ." Letter from William Styron, November 28, 1972.

"took your heart . . ." *Writers at Work: The Paris Review Interviews*, edited by Malcolm Cowley (New York: Viking Press, 1958), p. 78.

98 "a tiny but rather . . ." Letter from William Styron.

"on a wobbly table . . ." "The Talk of the Town," *New Yorker*, March 25, 1961, p. 31.

"I did a draft . . ." *New Yorker*, p. 31.

99 "There was a saloon . . ." *Writers at Work: The Paris Review Interviews*, Third Series, introduced by Alfred Kazin (New York: Viking Press, 1967), p. 333.

"Norman found that . . ." Interview with Dan Wolf, Spring 1971.

page
100 "every English major . . ." Harrington, "We Few," p. 103.

"As the people . . ." Harrington, "We Few," p. 162.

"they decided then . . ." Letter from Vance Bourjaily, December 14, 1972.

III. Lower East Side (pages 111–146)

The Immigrants' City

111 "the foul core . . ." Jacob Riis, *How the Other Half Lives* (New York: Charles Scribner's Sons, 1922), p. 55.

"with these hapless . . ." Riis, *How the Other Half Lives*, pp. 95–96.

"all that is loathsome . . ." Roi Ottley and William J. Weatherby, editors, *The Negro in New York: An Informal Social History* (New York: The New York Public Library, 1967), p. 77.

"picketed from end to end . . ." Riis, *How the Other Half Lives*, p. 58.

113 "We stand upon . . ." Riis, *How the Other Half Lives*, pp. 28–29.

"the region of Jews . . ." Joseph Jay Rubin and Charles H. Brown, *Walt Whitman of the New York Aurora* (State College, Pa.: Bald Eagle Press, 1950), p. 18.

114 "the wiping out . . ." Lincoln Steffens, *The Autobiography of Lincoln Steffens* (New York: Harcourt, Brace & Co., 1931), p. 203.

"It was on the Bowery . . ." Van Wyck Brooks and Otto L. Bettmann, *Our Literary Heritage: A Pictorial History of the Writer in America* (New York: E. P. Dutton & Co., 1956), p. 15.

115 "It is inevitable . . ." Stephen Crane, *The Red Badge of Courage and Selected Prose and Poetry*, edited with an introduction by William M. Gibson (New York: Rinehart & Co., 1958), p. vii.

"Eventually they entered . . ." Crane, *Maggie* in *The Red Badge of Courage*, pp. 4–5.

"the only interesting . . ." Van Wyck Brooks, *An Autobiography* (New York: E. P. Dutton & Co., 1965), p. 128.

116 "the best years . . ." Abraham Cahan, *The Education of Abraham Cahan* (Philadelphia: Jewish Publication Society of America, 1969), p. 264.

117 "In other languages . . ." Samuel Niger, "Yiddish Culture in the United States," *The Jewish People, Past and Present*, Vol. 4 (New York: Jewish Encyclopedic Handbooks, 1955), p. 288.

118 "before you have . . ." Riis, *How the Other Half Lives*, p. 108.

page
119 "Over steaming Russian . . ." Moses Rischin, *The Promised City: New York's Jews, 1870–1914* (Cambridge: Harvard University Press, 1962), pp. 141–42.

120 "the only Gentile . . ." Hutchins Hapgood, *The Spirit of the Ghetto,* edited by Moses Rischin (Cambridge: Belknap Press of Harvard University Press, 1967), p. xxviii.

"When my parents . . ." Jacob Epstein, *Let There Be Sculpture* (New York: G. P. Putnam's Sons, 1940), p. 4.

"The name was . . ." Riis, *How the Other Half Lives,* p. 115.

122 "I at that time . . ." Steffens, *The Autobiography of Lincoln Steffens,* p. 244.

"spent the whole . . ." Brooks, *An Autobiography,* p. 156.

"My eyes are fond . . ." E. E. Cummings, *Poems 1923–1954* (New York: Harcourt, Brace & Co., 1954), p. 81.

123 "a tenement canyon . . ." Michael Gold, *Jews Without Money* (New York: Horace Liveright, 1930), p. 13.

"Continuity was destroyed . . ." Henry Roth, "Henry Roth: No Longer At Home," *New York Times,* April 15, 1971.

The East Village

127 "New York was Charlie . . ." Interview with Allen Ginsberg, December 21, 1971.

"John Clellon Holmes . . ." Jack Kerouac, "The Origins of the Beat Generation," *Playboy,* June 1959, reprinted in *A Casebook on the Beat,* edited by Thomas Parkinson (New York: Thomas Y. Crowell Co., 1961), p. 70.

"being right down to it . . ." John Clellon Holmes, "The Philosophy of the Beat Generation" in *The Beats,* edited by Seymour Krim (Greenwich: Gold Medal Books, Fawcett Publications, 1960), p. 15.

128 "three full moon nights . . ." Bruce Cook, *The Beat Generation* (New York: Charles Scribner's Sons, 1971), p. 79.

"the Pierre-of Melville goof . . ." Jack Kerouac, *The Subterraneans* (New York: Grove Press, 1958), p. 15.

129 "Melville, armed with the manuscript . . ." quoted in Cook, *The Beat Generation,* p. 45.

"Like *The Subterraneans* . . ." Interview with Ginsberg, Winter 1971.

130 "the real thing to remember . . ." Cook, *The Beat Generation,* p. 51.

"Williams' precise real images . . ." Jane Kramer, *Allen Ginsberg in America* (New York: Random House, 1969), p. 174.

page
130 "transcribe the thought . . ." Kramer, *Allen Ginsberg in America,* p. 171.

"If I had a Green Automobile . . ." Allen Ginsberg, *Reality Sandwiches* (San Francisco: City Lights Books, 1963), p. 11.

131 "Who ate fire . . ." Allen Ginsberg, *Howl* (San Francisco: City Lights Books, 1965), p. 9.

"Way over on the lower . . ." Norman Mailer, *Advertisements for Myself* (New York: New American Library, A Signet Book, 1960), p. 139.

"hole in New York . . ." Norman Mailer, *The Deer Park* (New York: Berkley Publishing Corporation, A Berkley Medallion Book, December 1970), p. 300.

"There was a kosher brewery . . ." and subsequent quotations this paragraph, interview with Dan Wolf, Spring 1971.

132 "It was a very rough neighborhood . . ." Interview with Dan Wolf.

"The Beat Generation . . ." Mailer, *Advertisements for Myself*, p. 334.

133 "Tonite I got hi . . ." Ginsberg, *Reality Sandwiches,* p. 77.

134 "Who was there? . . ." Cook, *The Beat Generation,* p. 51.

"John Ashbery, Barbara Guest . . ." Frank O'Hara, "Larry Rivers: A Memoir," in *The Collected Poems of Frank O'Hara,* edited by Donald Allen, with an introduction by John Ashbery (New York: Alfred A. Knopf, 1971), p. 512.

"I live above a dyke bar . . ." Allen, *The Collected Poems of Frank O'Hara,* p. 286.

136 "a tenement dump . . ." and subsequent quotations this paragraph, interview with Patsy Southgate, April 29, 1971.

"The apartment was . . ." Interview with Patsy Southgate.

"LeRoi turned up . . ." Interview with Patsy Southgate.

137 "The people in San Francisco . . ." Interview with Hettie Jones, May 17, 1971.

"You just go on your nerve . . ." Allen, *The Collected Poems of Frank O'Hara,* p. 498.

"A poem is energy . . ." Cook, *The Beat Generation,* p. 121.

138 "It was huge, baronial . . ." Interview with Hettie Jones.

"then I go back . . ." Allen, *The Collected Poems of Frank O'Hara,* p. 325.

"cold-water flophouse . . ." Interview with Hettie Jones.

page

139 "Auden writes on a new . . ." Judson Hand, *The New York Daily News,* January 13, 1971.

141 "rundown smelly . . ." Interview with Jack Gelber, September 18, 1974.

"right in the heart . . ." Interview with Gregory Corso, April 1971.

IV.   Gramercy Park (pages 147-164)

147 "the pioneers of the younger set . . ." Edith Wharton, *Old New York* (New York: Charles Scribner's Sons, 1924) , p. 80.

148 "If I wrote the Gospels . . ." quoted in Alfred Kazin, "Melville the New Yorker," *New York Review of Books,* April 5, 1973, p. 5.

"a most inglorious one . . ." Lewis Mumford, *Herman Melville* (New York: The Literary Guild of America, 1929) , p. 307.

"Our home . . ." Frances Thomas Osborne, *Bulletin of the New York Public Library,* Vol. 69, No. 10, December 1965, p. 656.

149 "a quiet interior of its own . . ." Mumford, *Herman Melville,* p. 326.

"Grandpa would walk . . ." Osborne, *Bulletin,* p. 660.

150 "the variety . . ." William Dean Howells, *A Hazard of New Fortunes* (New York: New American Library, Signet edition, 1965) , p. 158.

"New York is still . . ." Howells, *A Hazard of New Fortunes,* p. 159.

151 "There's only one city . . ." Howells, *A Hazard of New Fortunes,* p. 12.

"If a novel flatters the passions . . ." Clara M. Kirk and Rudolph Kirk, *William Dean Howells* (New York: Twayne Publishers, 1962) , p. 124.

"We must ask ourselves . . ." William Dean Howells, *The Rise of Silas Lapham* (New York: Bantam Books, 1971) , p. ix.

153 "Occasionally one could hear . . ." Stephen Crane, *The Complete Novels of Stephen Crane,* edited with an introduction by Thomas A. Gullason (New York: Doubleday & Co., 1967) , p. 394.

"The flood of orange light . . ." Crane, *The Complete Novels,* p. 394.

"Every incident and phase . . ." John Berryman, *Stephen Crane* (New York: William Sloane Associates, 1950) , p. 73.

154 "The big hall . . ." William S. Porter, *The Complete Works of O. Henry* (New York: Doubleday & Co., 1953) , p. 529.

page
154 "three doors from . . ." William Wash Williams, *The Quiet Lodger of Irving Place* (New York: E. P. Dutton & Co., 1936), p. 49.

155 When Washington Irving visited . . . This is well documented in Stanley T. Williams's biography of Irving. Williams quotes a letter from the writer's grandnephew John Irving: "The third-story front room in my father's house was set apart for my uncle, who had his books and papers there and could work undisturbed. He came and went as he pleased, sometimes staying a week or a month; and once he stayed nearly all winter . . . I can say positively that he never lived at the corner of Irving Place and Seventeenth Street . . . We lived in East Twenty-first Street when my uncle stayed with us."

"Fourth Avenue — born and bred . . ." Porter, *Complete Works of O. Henry*, pp. 1569–70.

156 "an interior that might . . ." *Paul Rosenfeld: Voyage in the Arts*, edited by Jerome Mellquist and Lucie Wiese (New York: Creative Age Press, 1948), p. 20.

"poets read their poetry . . ." Mellquist and Wiese, *Paul Rosenfeld*, p. 9.

"beneath his little collection . . ." Mellquist and Wiese, *Paul Rosenfeld*, p. 11.

157 "The really important thing . . ." Mellquist and Wiese, *Paul Rosenfeld*, p. 95.

158 "Someone gathered Zelda up . . ." Van Wyck Brooks, *An Autobiography* (New York, E. P. Dutton & Co., 1965), p. 361.

"Badly designed, with small rooms . . ." Jay Martin, *Nathanael West: The Art of His Life* (New York: Farrar, Straus & Giroux, 1970), pp. 121–22.

" 'Register him under . . .' " James F. Light, *Nathanael West: An Interpretive Study* (Evanston: Northwestern University Press, 1971), p. 70.

V. Chelsea (pages 165–183)

165 "One of the most depressing . . ." Edith Wharton, *A Backward Glance: The Autobiography of Edith Wharton* (New York: Charles Scribner's Sons, 1962), p. 54.

166 "cultivated ferns . . ." Edith Wharton, *The Age of Innocence* (New York: Random House, Modern Library, 1948), p. 31.

167 "one of those ancient . . ." Stephen Crane, *The Complete Short Stories and Sketches of Stephen Crane,* edited by Thomas A. Gullason (New York: Doubleday & Co., 1963), p. 197.

page

167 "where from the streams . . ." Crane, *Complete Short Stories*, p. 311.

"He was my father's . . ." *Writers at Work: The Paris Review Interviews*, Second Series, edited by Malcolm Cowley (New York: Viking Press, 1963), p. 142.

168 "Silent, grim, colossal . . ." William S. Porter, *The Complete Works of O. Henry* (New York: Doubleday & Co., 1953), p. 17.

"Invoke your consideration . . ." Porter, *Complete Works of O. Henry*, p. 11.

169 "New York City is . . ." James Weldon Johnson, *Autobiography of an Ex-Coloured Man* (New York: Alfred A. Knopf, 1970), p. 89.

170 "This is not a bourgeois . . ." Interview with Virgil Thomson, June 24, 1974.

171 "Then who will know . . ." Edgar Lee Masters, "The Hotel Chelsea," *The Chelsean*, Vol. 1., No. 6, April 1940, p. 1.

"The rooms were dark . . ." Elizabeth Nowell, *Thomas Wolfe: A Biography* (New York: Doubleday & Co., 1960), p. 400.

172 "I would hope . . ." Brendan Behan, *Brendan Behan's New York* (New York: Bernard Geis, 1964), p. 78.

"It is the only hotel . . ." Arthur Miller, quoted in Marshall Smith, "A Room With Ghost $4 and Up," *Life*, September 18, 1964.

174 "he had been no more . . ." Samuel French Morse, *Wallace Stevens: Poetry As Life* (New York: Pegasus, 1970), p. 65.

"I got a cheap . . ." Sherwood Anderson, *Sherwood Anderson's Memoirs*, edited by Ray Lewis White (Chapel Hill: University of North Carolina Press, 1942), p. 407.

175 "And so there . . ." Sherwood Anderson, *A Story Teller's Story*, edited by Ray Lewis White (Cleveland: The Press of Case Western Reserve University, 1968), p. 286.

"There were three big trees . . ." Van Wyck Brooks, *An Autobiography* (New York: E. P. Dutton & Co., 1965), p. 153.

176 "who invariably, when asked . . ." Conrad Aiken, *Ushant: An Essay* (New York: Oxford University Press, 1971), p. 71.

177 "abounded in recollections . . ." Brooks, *An Autobiography*, pp. 176–77.

"The lead review . . ." Alfred Kazin, *Starting out in the Thirties* (Boston: Atlantic Monthly Press, Little, Brown & Co., 1965), p. 18.

VI. Midtown (pages 184–221)

page
184 "While New York . . ." Van Wyck Brooks, *The Times of Melville and Whitman* (New York, E. P. Dutton & Co., 1947), p. 324.

186 "put the crowning . . ." Edith Wharton, *The Age of Innocence* (New York: Random House, Modern Library, 1948), p. 10.

"He goes into . . ." Van Wyck Brooks, "Mr. Howells at Work at Seventy-Two," *The World's Work*, May 1909, p. 11548.

"He was a short . . ." Franklin Walker, *Frank Norris, A Biography* (New York: Russell & Russell, 1963), p. 170.

188 "About eleven o'clock . . ." Vachel Lindsay in Edgar Lee Masters, *Vachel Lindsay: A Poet in America* (New York: Charles Scribner's Sons, 1935), pp. 124, 126, 127–28.

"New York society . . ." William Dean Howells, *Literature and Life* (New York: Harper & Brothers, 1902), p. 179.

189 "I thoroughly detest . . ." H. L. Mencken, *Letters of H. L. Mencken,* selected and annotated by Guy J. Forgue (New York: Alfred A. Knopf, 1961), p. 134.

190 "Don't ever if . . ." Allen Churchill, *The Literary Decade* (Englewood Cliffs: Prentice-Hall, 1971), p. 157.

191 "*The Smart Set* . . ." Mencken, *Letters,* p. 269.

"Under you and Nathan . . ." Mencken, *Letters,* p. 65.

193 "one cubic foot . . ." Nathaniel Benchley, *Robert Benchley, A Biography* (New York: McGraw-Hill, 1955), p. 70.

194 "a cheaply furnished . . ." John Keats, *You Might As Well Live: The Life and Times of Dorothy Parker* (New York: Simon & Schuster, 1970), p. 70.

"Oh, so they . . ." Benchley, *Robert Benchley,* p. 183.

195 "As a result . . ." Benchley, *Robert Benchley,* p. 135.

"leadership in the group . . ." Samuel Hopkins Adams, *A. Woollcott, His Life and His World* (New York: Reynal & Hitchcock, 1945), p. 120.

196 "Their standards were . . ." quoted in Adams, *A. Woollcott,* p. 123.

"People romanticize . . ." Keats, *You Might As Well Live,* p. 295.

197 "It had been made . . ." "*The New Yorker*," *Fortune*, August 1934, p. 82.

198 "No restaurant keeps . . ." Brendan Gill, *Here at the New Yorker* (New York: Random House, 1975), p. 193.

page

199 "The new magazine . . ." James Thurber, *Credos and Curios* (New York, Harper & Row, 1962), p. 27.

"The *New Yorker* . . ." Dwight Macdonald, "Lie Down and Laugh," *Partisan Review,* December 1937, p. 46.

200 "The different temperaments . . ." Dwight Macdonald, "Parajournalism II: Wolfe and the New Yorker," *New York Review of Books,* February 3, 1966, p. 23.

"At her untidy . . ." Edna Ferber, *A Peculiar Treasure* (New York: Doubleday, Doran & Co., 1939), p. 293.

201 "The population is . . ." Edwin P. Hoyt, *Alexander Woollcott: The Man Who Came to Dinner* (New York: Abelard-Schuman, 1968), p. 160.

202 "a small and disordered . . ." Adams, *A. Woollcott,* p. 110.

"a large room . . ." Carl Van Vechten, *Sacred and Profane Memories* (New York: Alfred A. Knopf, 1932), p. 226.

203 "as exotic as pomegranates," Bruce Kellner, *Carl Van Vechten and the Irreverent Decades* (Norman: University of Oklahoma Press, 1968), p. 45.

"full of silver . . ." Langston Hughes, *The Big Sea* (New York: Alfred A. Knopf, 1940), p. 251.

"with George Gershwin . . ." Emily Clark, *Innocence Abroad* (New York: Alfred A. Knopf, 1931), pp. 144-45.

204 "In the fifty . . ." Edward Lueders, "Mr. Van Vechten of New York City," *New Republic,* May 16, 1955, p. 36.

205 "the marble and gold . . ." Virgil Thomson, *Virgil Thomson* (New York: Alfred A. Knopf, 1966), p. 135.

207 "I loved being . . ." William Saroyan, *Places Where I've Done Time* (New York: Praeger Publishers, 1972), pp. 80-81.

208 "To this day . . ." Alfred Kazin, "The Writer and the City," *Harper's,* December 1968, p. 122.

"New York burst . . ." F. Scott Fitzgerald, *This Side of Paradise* (New York: Charles Scribner's Sons, Scribner Library Edition, n.d.), pp. 29-30.

210 "When I went . . ." Walker Gilmer, *Horace Liveright, Publisher of the Twenties* (New York: David Lewis, 1970), p. 235.

211 "a job with any . . ." Lillian Hellman, *An Unfinished Woman — A Memoir* (Boston: Little, Brown & Co., 1969), p. 33.

VII.   East Side (pages 222–245)

page
222   "A day or two since . . ." Edgar Allan Poe, *Doings of Gotham,* collected by Jacob E. Spannuth, with preface, introduction and comments by Thomas O. Mabbott (Pottsville, Pa.: J. E. Spannuth, 1929), Letter III, p. 40.

223   "was located on eight . . ." Margaret Fuller, *The Love Letters of Margaret Fuller,* introduction by Julia Ward Howe (New York: D. Appleton and Co., 1903), p. 209.

"I now know all . . ." Mason Wade, *Margaret Fuller, Whetstone of Genius* (New York: Viking Press, 1940), p. 72.

224   "Stopping on the Harlem . . ." Wade, *Margaret Fuller,* p. 141.

"New York is the focus . . ." Margaret Fuller, in *Margaret Fuller, American Romantic,* edited by Perry Miller (New York: Cornell University Press, 1963), p. 251.

225   "We rented a furnished . . ." Mary Colum, *Life and the Dream* (New York: Doubleday & Co., 1947), p. 208.

226   "We heard Amy's voice . . ." Colum, *Life and Dream,* p. 216.

227   "bare as a bald . . ." *Dear Scott/Dear Max, The Fitzgerald-Perkins Correspondence,* edited by John Kuehl and Jackson Bryer (New York: Charles Scribner's Sons, 1971), p. 239.

"I am sitting at the moment . . ." E. B. White, *Here Is New York* (New York: Harper & Brothers, 1949), pp. 10–11.

228   "circle of lemon-colored . . ." Louise Bogan, *What the Woman Lived: Selected Letters of Louise Bogan 1920–1970,* edited and with an introduction by Ruth Limmer (New York: Harcourt Brace Jovanovich, 1973), p. 258.

"In Turtle Bay . . ." White, *Here Is New York,* p. 53.

"Walls papered with maps . . ." Marion K. Sanders, *Dorothy Thompson: A Legend In Her Time* (Boston: Houghton Mifflin Co., 1973), p. 289.

230   "It did not matter . . ." John P. Marquand, *Point of No Return* (Boston: Little Brown & Co., 1949), p. 24.

"Tawny wall-to-wall . . ." Curtis Cate, *Antoine de Saint-Exupéry* (New York: G. P. Putnam's Sons, 1970), p. 483.

231   "a dusty-plush . . ." Gloria Steinem, "A Visit with Truman Capote," *Glamour,* April 1966, p. 239.

"As long as I live . . ." Edith Wharton, *A Backward Glance* (New York: Charles Scribner's Sons, 1964), p. 109.

page

231 "a bonbonnière of the last . . ." Leon Edel, *Henry James*, Vol. 5, *The Master: 1901–1916* (Philadelphia: Lippincott Co., 1972), p. 262.

". . . She was charming . . ." Edel, *Henry James*, p. 262.

232 "I would go to . . ." Quentin Reynolds, *By Quentin Reynolds* (New York: McGraw-Hill, 1963), p. 67.

"West's Disease" W. H. Auden, *The Dyer's Hand and Other Essays* (New York: Random House, 1962), p. 241.

233 "a continuing, well-organized . . ." John Houseman, *Run-Through: A Memoir* (New York: Simon & Schuster, 1972), p. 97.

"looks like something . . ." Charles A. Fenton, *Stephen Vincent Benét: The Life and Times of an American Man of Letters, 1898–1943* (New Haven: Yale University Press, 1958), p. 247.

234 "I shall miss this tiny . . ." André Maurois, *From My Journal* (New York: Harper & Brothers, 1948), pp. 3–4.

235 "the city had beaten . . ." John Steinbeck, "Making of a New Yorker," *New York Times Magazine,* February 1, 1953, p. 27.

"My new home consisted . . ." Steinbeck, "Making of a New Yorker," p. 66.

"New York is an ugly . . ." Steinbeck, "Making of a New Yorker," p. 66.

237 "There's the whole story . . ." Eugene O'Neill in Hamilton Basso, "Profile," *New Yorker,* February 28, 1948, p. 34.

"A street lined . . ." Anaïs Nin, *The Diary of Anaïs Nin, 1944–1947,* edited and with a preface by Gunther Stuhlmann (New York: Harcourt Brace Jovanovich, 1971), p. 83.

". . . It reminded me . . ." Sylvia Plath, *The Bell Jar* (New York: Bantam, 1972), p. 3.

238 "stark, bare, colorless . . ." John Keats, *You Might As Well Live: The Life and Times of Dorothy Parker* (New York: Simon & Schuster, 1970), p. 274.

239 "He brought writers . . ." Norman Podhoretz, *Making It* (New York: Random House, 1967), p. 237.

240 "It was one room . . ." Truman Capote, *Breakfast at Tiffany's: A Short Novel and Three Stories* (New York: Random House, 1958), p. 3.

"God, to think . . ." Finis Farr, *O'Hara, A Biography* (Boston: Little, Brown & Co., 1973), p. 150.

241 "No writer today . . ." Interview with Louis Auchincloss, April 11, 1973.

VIII. The West Side (pages 246–268)

page
246 "signalized [his] solidarity with . . ." Lionel Trilling, *A Gathering of Fugitives* (Boston: Beacon Press, 1956), p. 49.

247 "a sweet rural valley . . ." quoted in Harmon H. Goldstone and Martha Dalrymple, *History Preserved: A Guide to New York City Landmarks and Historic Districts* (New York: Simon & Schuster, 1974), p. 294.

249 John Hall Wheelock recalls . . . Interview with John Hall Wheelock, January 21, 1974.

250 "I have taken . . ." Mark Schorer, *Sinclair Lewis, An American Life* (New York: McGraw-Hill, 1961), p. 699.

"Baronial living room . . ." Fannie Hurst, *Anatomy of Me* (New York: Doubleday & Co., 1958), p. 287.

251 "2 boston . . ." E. E. Cummings, *Poems 1923–1954* (New York: Harcourt, Brace & Co., 1954), p. 229.

"I simply rejoiced . . ." Gertrude Stein, *Fernhurst, Q. E. D., and Other Early Writings* (New York: Liveright, 1971), p. 101.

252 "two separate lives" Interview with Louis Untermeyer, November 11, 1970.

"the upper-class . . ." Interview with Louis Untermeyer.

"Frost read with just . . ." Interview with Louis Untermeyer.

"one hundred and twenty-two rejection slips . . ." Arthur Mizener, *The Far Side of Paradise* (Boston: Houghton Mifflin Co., 1965), p. 86.

253 "one slice in a long . . ." F. Scott Fitzgerald, *The Great Gatsby* (New York: Charles Scribner's Sons, 1953), p. 28.

"The Newhouse apartment . . ." Lillian Hellman, *An Unfinished Woman — A Memoir* (Boston: Little, Brown & Co., 1969), pp. 3–4.

254 "As we played . . ." J. D. Salinger, *Raise High the Roof Beam, Carpenters and Seymour, An Introduction* (New York: Bantam, 1971), p. 198.

"at 108th and Broadway . . ." Salinger, *Raise High the Roof Beam*, p. 162.

"luxurious Manhattan apartment . . ." Letter from Herman Wouk, October 29, 1974.

"furnished the milieu . . ." Letter from Herman Wouk.

255 "The Village was . . ." Interview with Elizabeth Hardwick, June 13, 1974.

page

255 "I was rehabilitating . . ." Meyer Levin in Frederic Morton, "Bohemia, Such As It Is, On the West Side," *New York Times Magazine,* May 9, 1971, p. 72.

"the mass migration . . ." Morton, "Bohemia, Such As It Is, On the West Side," p. 92.

"If you're interested . . ." Interview with Alfred Kazin, September 6, 1974.

"They are, or until . . ." Irving Howe, "The New York Intellectuals, A Chronicle and A Critique," *Commentary,* October 1968, p. 29.

257 "but its characteristic . . ." Norman Podhoretz, *Making It* (New York: Bantam, 1969), p. 197.

"the last gasp . . ." Robert Lowell, *Notebook 1967–68* (New York: Farrar, Straus & Giroux, 1969), p. 155.

258 "The reason there are no . . ." Victor Navasky, "Notes on Cult; or, How to Join the Intellectual Establishment," *New York Times Magazine,* March 27, 1966, p. 128.

"until recently . . ." Alfred Kazin, "The Writer and the City," *Harper's,* December 1968, p. 111.

"On some nights . . ." Saul Bellow, *The Victim* (New York: Viking Press, Compass Books edition, 1961), p. 3.

259 "like a baroque . . ." Saul Bellow, *Seize the Day* (New York: Viking Press, 1961), p. 5.

"Unless the weather . . ." Bellow, *Seize the Day,* p. 4.

"Brownstones, balustrades, bay windows . . ." Saul Bellow, *Mr. Sammler's Planet* (New York: Fawcett, 1970), p. 12.

"It was aware . . ." Bellow, *Mr. Sammler's Planet,* p. 134.

"New York makes . . ." Bellow, *Mr. Sammler's Planet,* p. 277.

"By a convergence . . ." Bellow, *Mr. Sammler's Planet,* p. 255.

260 "Most of the interaction . . ." Interview with Jack Gelber, September 18, 1974.

"as long as I lived . . ." Isaac Bashevis Singer, *A Friend of Kafka, and Other Stories* (New York: Farrar, Straus & Giroux, 1970), p. 78.

262 "Carl Van Doren . . ." Interview with Alfred Kazin.

"taught Kerouac Shakespeare . . ." Obituary in *New York Times,* December 12, 1972.

264 "This," said Ginsberg . . . and subsequent quotations, interview with Allen Ginsberg, December 22, 1971.

page

265 "He seemed in his own . . ." Trilling, *Gathering of Fugitives*, p. 50.

268 "the buildings looked . . ." Langston Hughes, *The Big Sea* (New York: Alfred A. Knopf, 1940) , p. 83.

"a high, horrible apartment-house . . ." Mizener, *The Far Side of Paradise,* p. 86.

IX.   Harlem   (pages 269–311)

271 "one of the most . . ." James Weldon Johnson, *Black Manhattan* (New York: Alfred A. Knopf, 1930) , p. 146.

274 "It was a period when . . ." Langston Hughes, *The Big Sea* (New York: Alfred A. Knopf, 1940) , pp. 227–28.

"Jessie Fauset at the *Crisis* . . ." Hughes, *The Big Sea,* p. 218.

275 "He wrote me . . ." Zora Neale Hurston, *Dust Tracks on a Road* (New York: Arno Press and the *New York Times,* 1969) , p. 176.

"Mr. Johnson, I believe . . ." Hughes, *The Big Sea,* p. 218.

276 "there was always quite . . ." Hughes, *The Big Sea,* p. 247.

277 "Mr. Johnson's appearance . . ." Blanche E. Ferguson, *Countee Cullen and the Negro Renaissance* (New York: Dodd, Mead & Co., 1966) , p. 86.

"We often speak . . ." Wayne Cooper, "Claude McKay and the New Negro of the 1920's," *Phylon, The Atlanta University Review of Race and Culture,* Vol. 25, No. 3, Fall 1964, p. 305.

278 "Nigger Heaven! That's . . ." Carl Van Vechten, *Nigger Heaven* (New York: Alfred A. Knopf, 1926) , p. 149.

279 "Like a flock . . ." Claude McKay, *Harlem: Negro Metropolis* (New York: E. P. Dutton & Co., 1940) , p. 16.

283 "$1.50, no job . . ." Hurston, *Dust Tracks on a Road,* p. 176.

"she went about Harlem . . ." Hughes, *The Big Sea,* p. 236.

284 ". . . 99 and 99/100 per cent . . ." Wallace Thurman, *Infants of the Spring* (New York: Macaulay Co., 1932) , p. 140.

"the only Negro reader . . ." Hughes, *The Big Sea,* p. 234.

285 "I know of only one . . ." Thurman, *Infants of the Spring,* p. 221.

286 "shortly left his . . ." Hughes, *The Big Sea,* p. 242.

"My family is from . . ." Jean Toomer, *Cane,* with an introduction by Arna Bontemps (New York: Harper & Row, Perennial Classic edition, 1969) , pp. viii–ix.

page

286 ". . . I have not lived . . ." Harper & Row press release, 1969.

287 "Harlem's Broadway . . ." Rudolph Fisher, *The Walls of Jericho* (New York: Alfred A. Knopf, 1928), p. 189.

"They say . . . that if . . ." Nella Larsen, *Quicksand* (New York: Collier Books, 1971), p. 169.

288 "big-hearted, night-dark . . ." Hughes, *The Big Sea*, p. 244.

"a one-woman foundation" Interview with Ted Poston, January 1971.

"She saw a real need . . ." Roi Ottley and William J. Weatherby, editors, *The Negro in New York: An Informal Social History* (New York: The New York Public Library, 1967), pp. 257-58.

289 "the Negro intelligentsia . . ." Ottley and Weatherby, *The Negro in New York*, p. 259.

291 "Everybody dropped in . . ." Interview with Arna Bontemps, November 25, 1970.

292 "Ride back! . . ." Claude McKay, *A Long Way from Home* (New York: Arno Press and the *New York Times*, 1969), p. 132.

"the most galling thing . . ." Lena Horne and Richard Schickel, *Lena* (New York: Doubleday & Co., 1965), p. 55.

293 "I care for nothing . . ." quoted in Larry Neal, "Eatonville's Zora Neale Hurston: A Profile," *Black Review No. 2* (New York: William Morrow & Co., 1972), pp. 23-24.

294 "You know white folks . . ." Milton Meltzer, *Langston Hughes, A Biography* (New York: Thomas Y. Crowell Co., 1968), p. 241.

"More than Paris . . ." Nathan Irvin Huggins, *Harlem Renaissance* (New York: Oxford University Press, 1971), p. 24.

295 "Had I been a rich . . ." Langston Hughes, "My Early Days in Harlem," in *Harlem: A Community in Transition*, edited by John Henrik Clarke (New York: Citadel Press, 1964), p. 62.

296 "It's a nice place . . ." The Schomburg Collection, vertical file on Langston Hughes.

"What happens . . ." Langston Hughes, *Montage of a Dream Deferred* (New York: Henry Holt & Co., 1951), p. 71.

297 "Layers and layers . . ." Ann Petry, *The Street* (New York: Pyramid, 1971), p. 17.

298 "[He] had just come . . ." Ralph Ellison, *Shadow and Act* (New York: Random House, 1964), p. 14.

" 'You must learn how . . .' " Ellison, *Shadow and Act*, p. 15.

page
299   "I did *not* come . . ." "A Very Stern Discipline, An Interview with Ralph Ellison," *Harper's Magazine,* Vol. 234, No. 1402, March 1967, p. 84.

"who shared, night after . . ." Ellison, *Shadow and Act,* p. 199.

"Harlem is a ruin . . ." Ellison, *Shadow and Act,* pp. 295–96.

300   "In my novel . . ." Ellison, *Shadow and Act,* p. 173.

"Here," he writes . . . Ellison, *Shadow and Act,* pp. 296–97.

301   "he and other children . . ." James Baldwin, *Another Country* (New York: Dell, 1963), p. 20.

"These streets hadn't . . ." James Baldwin, *Going to Meet the Man* (New York: Dial Press, 1965), p. 112.

"cloudy, and far away . . ." James Baldwin, *Go Tell It on the Mountain* (New York: New American Library, Signet, 1963), p. 30.

302   "since I was not stupid . . ." Fern Marja Eckman, *The Furious Passage of James Baldwin* (New York: M. Evans & Co., 1966), p. 113.

"the only human part . . ." Eckman, *The Furious Passage,* p. 39.

"where people know . . ." Interview with James Baldwin by John Hall, *Transatlantic Review,* Nos. 37 and 38, Autumn–Winter 1970–71, London, New York, p. 14.

304   "The strip is practically . . ." Tom Wolfe, "A Harlem Writer Who Makes James Baldwin Look Like A Tourist, *New York Herald Tribune, New York,* July 18, 1965, p. 4.

305   "perhaps the first . . ." Interview with Larry Neal, Fall 1972.

"hip, bourgeois . . ." Interview with Larry Neal.

"Folks are trying . . ." Interview with Larry Neal.

"in and around . . ." Interview with Larry Neal.

X.   The Bronx, Queens and Staten Island   (pages 312–327)

The Bronx

312   "I am living . . ." Edgar Allan Poe, *The Letters of Edgar Allan Poe,* edited by John Ward Ostrom (New York: Gordian Press, 1966), Vol. 2, p. 325.

314   "We drifted from room . . ." Albert Bigelow Paine, *Mark Twain, A Biography* (New York: Harper & Brothers, 1912), pp. 1141–42.

"Please tell him . . ." Marie Waife-Goldberg, *My Father, Sholom Aleichem* (New York: Simon & Schuster, 1968), p. 187.

page

314 "We rented an apartment . . ." Leon Trotsky, *My Life: An Attempt at an Autobiography* (New York: Charles Scribner's Sons, 1930), p. 271.

315 "a brick cliff . . ." Herman Wouk, *The City Boy: The Adventures of Herbie Bookbinder* (New York: Doubleday & Co., 1952), p. 16.

"The Bronx? No thonx . . ." Ogden Nash, *The Bronx County Historical Society Journal*, Vol. 1, No. 2, July 1964, pp. 67–68.

Queens

316 "This is a valley . . ." F. Scott Fitzgerald, *The Great Gatsby* (New York: Charles Scribner's Sons, 1953), p. 23.

"Over the great bridge . . ." Fitzgerald, *The Great Gatsby*, p. 69.

Staten Island

317 "nearly blinded me . . ." Robert L. Gale, *Francis Parkman* (New York: Twayne Publishers, 1973), p. 57.

"I have to say . . ." Max Cosman, "Thoreau and Staten Island," *Staten Island Historian*, January–March 1943, p. 2.

319 "The cedar seems . . ." Cosman, "Thoreau," p. 2.

"I want a whole continent . . ." Henry G. Steinmeyer, *Staten Island 1524–1898* (Staten Island: Staten Island Historical Society, 1950), p. 48.

"he has naturalized and . . ." Walter Harding, *The Days of Henry Thoreau* (New York: Alfred A. Knopf, 1965), p. 150.

320 "I seem more or less . . ." Henry James, *A Small Boy and Others* (New York: Charles Scribner's Sons, 1913), p. 28.

"to childish retrospect . . ." James, *A Small Boy*, p. 28.

"God might have made . . ." Vernon B. Hampton, *Staten Island's Claim to Fame, "The Garden Spot of New York Harbor"* (Staten Island: Richmond Borough Publishing & Printing Co., n.d.), p. 69.

321 "It was evident . . ." Virgil Markham, "Literary Tradition on Staten Island," *Staten Island Historian*, January–March 1957, p. 3.

"When we had guests . . ." Markham, "Literary Tradition," p. 3.

XI.   Brooklyn and Brooklyn Heights (pages 328–366)

Brooklyn

328 "From 1824–'28 our family . . ." Walt Whitman, *The Viking Portable Library Walt Whitman*, selected and with notes by Mark Van Doren (New York: Viking Press, 1960), pp. 486–87.

page

329 "We were both walkers . . ." Gay Wilson Allen, *Walt Whitman* (Detroit: Wayne State University Press, 1969), p. 85.

330 "Living in Brooklyn . . ." Van Doren, *The Viking Whitman,* pp. 489–90.

331 "In my dreams . . ." Henry Miller, *Black Spring* (New York: Grove Press, 1963), p. 5.

"Soon the street . . ." Henry Miller, *Tropic of Capricorn* (New York: Grove Press, 1961), p. 216.

332 "the street of early sorrows," Henry Miller, *My Life and Times,* abridged from the original edition (Chicago: Playboy Press, 1973), p. 110.

"I recall some wonderful . . ." Miller, *My Life and Times,* p. 111.

"It had pointed leaves . . ." Betty Smith, *A Tree Grows in Brooklyn* (New York: Harper & Brothers, 1947), p. 3.

333 "Every time I go . . ." Alfred Kazin, *A Walker in the City* (New York: Harcourt, Brace & Co., 1951), pp. 5–6.

"On the block itself . . ." Kazin, *A Walker in the City,* p. 84.

"One of the longest . . ." Norman Podhoretz, *Making It* (New York: Bantam Books, 1969), p. 3.

"am on right . . ." and "Piles of books . . ." George Plimpton, "The World Series with Marianne Moore," *Harper's Magazine,* October 1964, p. 51.

336 "My turf is mostly . . ." John Oliver Killens, *New York Times,* October 3, 1971.

337 "the version ten years later . . ." Interview with Arthur Miller, Spring 1970.

"My mother didn't . . ." Interview with Arthur Miller.

"gives a sense of hierarchy . . ." Interview with Arthur Miller.

338 "Once one gets off . . ." L. J. Davis, *New York Times,* September 26, 1971.

Brooklyn Heights

339 "a beautiful growth . . ." Henry R. Stiles, *The History of the City of Brooklyn,* published by subscription, Brooklyn, 1867–70, Vol. 2, p. 35.

340 "Families who . . ." Christopher Tunnard and Henry Hope Reed, *American Skyline* (Boston: Houghton Mifflin Co., 1955), p. 70.

"in a quiet . . ." James H. Callender, *Yesterdays on Brooklyn Heights* (New York: Dorland Press, 1927), p. 60.

page

342 "In a bare shed . . ." David McCullough, *The Great Bridge* (New York: Simon & Schuster, 1972), p. 302.

"A stunning act . . ." Lewis Mumford, *The Brown Decades* (New York: Dover Publications, 1931), pp. 96–97.

344 "Everytime one looks . . ." John Unterecker, *Voyager, A Life of Hart Crane* (New York: Farrar, Straus & Giroux, 1969), p. 364.

"O harp and altar . . ." Hart Crane, *The Bridge, A Poem* (New York: Liveright, 1970), p. 2.

345 "Brooklyn Bridge . . ." Marianne Moore, "The Plums of Curiosity," *Vogue*, August 1, 1960, p. 83.

346 "It was so esthetically . . ." Interview with Arthur Miller, Spring 1970.

"The place may seem . . . " Thomas Wolfe, *You Can't Go Home Again* (New York: Dell, 1934), p. 369.

"an entire floor . . ." Thomas Wolfe, *Thomas Wolfe's Letters to His Mother Julia Elizabeth Wolfe*, edited by John Skally Terry (New York: Charles Scribner's Sons, 1943), p. 217.

"very nice rooms . . ." Wolfe, *Letters*, pp. 233–34.

348 "The chief piece . . ." Wolfe, *Letters*, p. ix.

350 "as George Davis was . . ." Letter from W. H. Auden, April 20, 1970.
"Then there were those . . ." Letter from W. H. Auden.

"When he . . ." Anaïs Nin, *The Diary of Anaïs Nin, 1939–1944*, edited and with a preface by Gunther Stuhlmann (New York: Harcourt, Brace & World, 1969), p. 281.

"This is not . . ." Constance Webb, *Richard Wright: A Biography* (New York: G. P. Putnam's, 1968), p. 195.

"An amazing house . . ." Nin, *Diary*, p. 270.

351 "The street where . . ." Carson McCullers, "Brooklyn Is My Neighborhood," *Vogue*, March 1941, p. 62.

"At three o'clock . . ." McCullers, "Brooklyn," p. 138.

352 "It was just a nice . . ." Letter from Paul Bowles, May 19, 1970.

"Something from the lobby . . ." Letter from Paul Bowles.

"I remember having measles . . ." Letter from Paul Bowles.

"Benjamin Britten . . ." Letter from Paul Bowles.

353 "We lived there . . ." Interview with Arthur Miller.

"I used to sit . . ." Arthur Miller, "A Boy Grew In Brooklyn," *Holiday*, March 1955, p. 54.

page
354 "the rooms were . . ." Interview with Arthur Miller.

"We couldn't have . . ." *Brooklyn Heights Press,* March 6, 1958.

"never gravitated . . ." Interview with Arthur Miller.

355 "Everybody tried . . ." Interview with Norman Rosten, May 15, 1970.

"where I refused to . . ." Henry Miller, *Henry Miller Letters to Anaïs Nin,* edited by Gunther Stuhlmann (New York: G. P. Putnam's, 1965), p. 104.

"At No. 27 . . ." Moore, "The Plums of Curiosity," p. 140.

356 "I was most impressed . . ." Truman Capote, "Brooklyn Heights: A Personal Memoir," *Holiday,* February 1959, p. 66.

357 "In aggravated moments . . ." Capote, "Brooklyn Heights," p. 113.

"silent miles . . ." Capote, "Brooklyn Heights," p. 114.

"Every kind of sailor . . ." Capote, "Brooklyn Heights," p. 114.

359 "Writing about FBI . . ." *Writers At Work: The Paris Review Interviews,* Third Series, introduced by Alfred Kazin (New York: Viking Press, 1967), p. 268.

"lofty, tenting . . ." Brock Brower, "Always the Challenge," *Life,* September 24, 1965, p. 105.

"is tucked away . . ." Brower, "Always the Challenger," p. 105.

361 "Comparing the Brooklyn . . ." McCullers, "Brooklyn," p. 63.

Index

Numbers in boldface denote tour references,
those in italics refer to illustrations